Essential Trusts Law for SQE1

Essential Trusts Law for SQE1 explains the key principles of Trusts Law in a clear, concise and easy-to-understand style. Written specifically for SQE study, this book covers all of the topics contained in the syllabus for the contract law subject area in SQE1 Functioning Legal Knowledge (FLK) assessments.

The book aims to break down the apprehension and fear that many students have when encountering Trusts Law for the first time by dividing the subject area into six sections, each covering a separate part of Trusts Law within the SQE syllabus. The book also uses several practical features to allow students to test their understanding throughout the chapter. These include:

- Chapter overviews;
- Revision points: each chapter concludes with a concise list of key revision points;
- Problem scenarios to ensure that the key principles are fully understood when applied in practical situations;
- Multiple-choice questions in the format used for the SQE1 (with answers in an appendix to enable you to test your knowledge).

Part of Routledge's Essential Law for SQE1 series, this concise and accessible text provides a clear understanding of the key principles of Trusts Law and will enable you to test your assessment skills. Without the assumption of any prior knowledge of Trusts Law, it is suitable for both undergraduates and non-law graduates.

Judith Bray is an Emeritus Professor of Law at the University of Buckingham. She is a qualified Barrister. With many years of experience teaching law at degree level and for professional examinations, she has published extensively on Property Law, Equity and Trusts and Family Law, and is the author of several textbooks.

Essential Law for SQE1
Series editor: Wendy Laws

Essential Law for SQE1 is a series of concise textbooks aligned to the latest SQE1 curriculum. Providing candidates with an accessible summary of the core principles in each area of law, the style of each book is precise, with bullet-point lists summarizing key information and revision points concluding each chapter. The books also feature multiple-choice questions with answers, example problem questions and a glossary of key cases.

For more information about this series, please visit: www.routledge.com/

Essential Tort Law for SQE1
Wendy Laws

Essential Dispute Resolution for SQE1
Ben Waters

Essential Business Law and Practice for SQE1
Bill Davies

Essential Land Law for SQE1
Mohammad Sabuj

Essential Legal System and Legal Services for SQE1
Ian Bowden and Zaman F. Kala

Essential Criminal Law and Criminal Practice for SQE1
James Thornton, Amanda Parker and Orla Slattery

Essential Constitutional and Administrative Law for SQE1
Zaman F. Kala and Ian Bowden

Essential Contract Law for SQE1
Fred Motson and Stephen Bunbury

Essential Property Law and Practice for SQE1
Eliza Hakes and Martin George

Essential Trusts Law for SQE1
Judith Bray

Essential Trusts Law for SQE1

Judith Bray

Routledge
Taylor & Francis Group
LONDON AND NEW YORK

Designed cover image: Shutterstock

First edition published 2026
by Routledge
4 Park Square, Milton Park, Abingdon, Oxon, OX14 4RN

and by Routledge
605 Third Avenue, New York, NY 10158

Routledge is an imprint of the Taylor & Francis Group, an informa business

British Library Cataloguing-in-Publication Data
A catalogue record for this book is available from the British Library

Library of Congress Cataloging-in-Publication Data
Names: Bray, Judith, 1954- author
Title: Essential trusts law for sqe1 / Judith Bray.
Description: Abingdon, Oxon [UK] ; New York, NY : Routledge, 2026. |
Series: Essential law for SQE1 | Includes bibliographical references and index. |
Summary: "Essential Trusts Law for SQE1 explains the key principles of Trusts Law in a clear, concise, and easy-to-understand style. Written specifically for SQE study, this book covers all of the topics contained in the syllabus for the contract law subject area in SQE1 Functioning Legal Knowledge (FLK) assessments. The book aims to break down the apprehension and fear that many students have when encountering Trusts Law for the first time, by dividing the subject area into six sections, each covering a separate part of Trusts law within the SQE syllabus. The book also uses several practical features to allow students to test their understanding throughout the chapter. These include: Chapter overviews Revision Points- each chapter concludes with a concise list of key revision points; Problem scenarios to ensure that the key principles are fully understood when applied in practical situations Multiple-Choice Questions in the format used for the SQE1 (with answers in an appendix to enable you to test your knowledge). Part of Routledge's Essential Law for SQE1 series, this concise and accessible text provides a clear understanding of the key principles of Trusts Law and will enable you to test your assessment skills. Without the assumption of any prior knowledge of Trusts Law, it is suitable for both undergraduates and non-law graduates– Provided by publisher.
Identifiers: LCCN 2025052773 | ISBN 9781032952062 hardback |
ISBN 9781032952048 paperback | ISBN 9781003583660 ebook
Subjects: LCSH: Trusts and trustees--Examinations, questions, etc. |
Solicitors Qualifying Examination | LCGFT: Study guides
Classification: LCC K795 .B73 2026
LC record available at https://lccn.loc.gov/2025052773

ISBN: 978-1-032-95206-2 (hbk)
ISBN: 978-1-032-95204-8 (pbk)
ISBN: 978-1-003-58366-0 (ebk)

DOI: 10.4324/9781003583660

Typeset in The Sans
by Deanta Global Publishing Services, Chennai, India

Contents

	Introduction	vii
Part 1: Express and implied trusts		**1**
1	The creation and requirements of an express trust	3
2	The constitution of an express trust	21
3	Formalities of transfer of property from the settlor to the trustee and transfer from the beneficiaries to a third party	35
4	Vested and contingent gifts and the perpetuities rules	41
5	Five non-charitable purpose trusts: Charitable trusts	49
6	Implied trusts: Resulting trusts	59
7	The constructive trust in general: Trusts of the family home; proprietary estoppel	73
Part 2: Fiduciary relationships		**91**
8	The fiduciary relationship	93
9	Liability of strangers to the trust	109
Part 3: Trustees appointment, retirement, removal: The duties and powers of trusties, breach of trust and the liability of trustees		**125**
10	Trustees appointment, retirement and removal	127
11	The duties of trustees	135
12	Breach of trust	151

Part 4: Equitable tracing: Equitable remedies 169

13 Equitable tracing 171

14 Equitable remedies 185

15 Selected key cases in equity and trusts 197

Answers to multiple-choice questions 223

Index 239

Introduction

This book provides a clear, concise explanation of key principles of the Law of Equity and Trusts. Its main focus is on those areas which fall within the assessment specification for the *Solicitors Qualifying Examination Part 1 Functioning Legal Knowledge* (SQE1).[1]

In so doing it also covers the areas of the Law of Equity and Trusts central to most undergraduate Trusts modules. It covers some peripheral areas of law not necessarily required for the Solicitors Qualifying Examination (SQE) in order to increase understanding of some of the subject areas. For example, the book considers charities, which is an area of public law, but provides an important and helpful contrast to private purpose trusts which do form part of the SQE.

The style of the book reflects the SQE1 assessment specification:

- The SQE1 assessment requires knowledge and understanding of fundamental legal principles and the ability to apply them;
- Candidates are not required to recall specific case names or cite statutory or regulatory authorities (except where they are normally used in practice to describe a legal principle);
- Candidates will be tested on the current law and will not be tested on the historical development of law.

In order to reflect these requirements, the book explains the current legal principles of Equity and Trusts law in a clear and concise style using factual scenarios wherever possible to illustrate principles.

The book provides a fluent narrative account of key principles which is clear and accessible. This approach makes it easier for the reader to understand the principles, remember them and apply them in an assessment.

1 See SQE1 Functioning Legal Knowledge Assessment Specification, updated (August 2025).

References to some of the key cases and statutes are provided where deemed important, but discussion of case law is reserved for the final section of the book. This section follows a structured format which enables the reader to examine the application of key principles of Equity and Trusts in the context of decided cases.

Solicitors Qualifying Examination – SQE1

This book covers the following areas of Equity and Trusts law in the *SQE1* assessment specification:

- *Express and implied trusts*
- *The fiduciary relationship*
- *Trustees' duties, powers and liability*
- *Equitable remedies*

In addition, as mentioned above, the book does briefly consider the *law on charities* because this deepens understanding of the principles of private purpose trusts and also forms part of an undergraduate trusts module.

At all times, the book seeks to address the key assessment objectives of the SQE and to prepare the reader to meet the level of competence as stated by the Solicitors Regulation Authority (SRA), which is for candidates to apply relevant core legal principles and rules appropriately and effectively at the level of a competent newly qualified solicitor in practice.

The book is split into four parts as required for the SQE. The parts are split into chapters and, wherever possible, links are created between areas of law which link together.

Key features in the book to assist learning

Revision points: each chapter concludes with a concise list of key revision points.

Multiple-choice questions: the SQE assessment uses multiple-choice questions to test understanding of key principles. Multiple-choice questions, following the SQE format, are provided at the end of each section of the book (with answers at the end of the book). In addition, there are multiple-choice questions at the end of some chapters throughout the book.

Client analysis skills: this book considers key principles of trusts law in the context of client analysis skills. An essential skill for anyone sitting the SQE is the ability to take a clear, concise, structured approach to analysing the facts of a client's case and applying relevant principles of trusts law. It also provides a useful approach to answering questions in an undergraduate examination. This skill is introduced early in the book so that clear case analysis structures can be kept in mind as readers go on to develop their understanding of key principles. The final part of the book then develops those skills further by presenting a number of key decided cases within a structured framework which incorporates focused questions to enable readers to undertake a clear, structured analysis of legal principles arising in each case.

The law is stated as of October 2025.

PART I

Express and implied trusts

1 The creation and requirements of an express trust

1.1 Chapter overview

At the heart of this subject is the trust. In this chapter, we will be looking at the various aspects of the creation of a trust and also the reasons why the trust has become important in so many areas of law. So, this chapter provides an introductory overview of the creation and requirements of an express trust and its background. The chapter begins by looking at the essential features of a trust and also some of the terminology used in trusts. It also looks at the concept of a trust, comparing it to other types of rights such as those which arise under a contract. It considers the different types of trust, for example, fixed and discretionary trusts. The chapter then considers the first of a series of key features of a trust. They are referred to as the three certainties: certainty of intention, subject matter and object. Without these three features, a trust cannot exist. Each is examined in detail.

1.2 Essential features of a trust

The trust has long been considered to be an extremely useful way of holding property. It was used extensively many centuries ago to allow property to be held by a third party on behalf of vulnerable people such as children. In fact, it has its origins in the time of the Crusades when landowners who went off to fight in wars overseas would ask someone they trusted to look after their property on behalf of their families while these crusaders were away. This feature remains the same in many family trusts but today its use is far more extensive.

Today it is used in much wider ways such as pension funds, investments, unincorporated associations, charities and often as a tax-saving device. In reality, trusts occur often in everyday life, but most people do not realise that they are interacting with transactions involving trusts.

The mechanics of a trust are such that property is transferred by a donor called the *settlor* to a third party called a *trustee* who holds the property on behalf of a *beneficiary*.

DOI: 10.4324/9781003583660-2

The *beneficiary* receives the benefit of the property and also has the right to enforce the trust against the *trustee*.

How a trust works in practice

DONOR (SETTLOR) ————————————————> TRUSTEE

|

V

BENEFICIARY

Once the trust has been fully set up (fully constituted), the *settlor* loses any right to claim the property and use it for their own use. This is important as sometimes *settlors* may try to claim that they still retain rights over the property that they have transferred into the trust. A key feature of a trust is that once it is fully constituted and therefore enforceable, the legal owner of the property is now the *trustee*. The *trustee* will have no right of enjoyment but will carry the responsibility of caring for the property for the benefit of the *beneficiary*. These responsibilities will include investing the trust assets and also distributing them to the various beneficiaries and may even extend to making a choice amongst the beneficiaries as to who will benefit under the trust.

Consider this example:

Sam is seriously ill. He is concerned about how his wife, Beema, and his two young children, Ciara and Colm, will manage after his death. He is aware that Beema is not experienced in handling large sums of money and investments, so he decides to appoint his brother, Tom, and a friend, Tariq, to act as trustees on their behalf. He transfers a large sum of money which he has in a savings account to Tom and Tariq, having asked them to act as his trustees on behalf of Beema, Ciara and Colm.

In the example, the *settlor* is Sam; the *trustees* are Tom and Tariq; and the *beneficiaries* are Beema, Ciara and Colm.

If Sam recovers and wishes to then claim the property back, he will be prevented from doing so because, in the eyes of the law, Tom and Tariq own the property on behalf of the three beneficiaries: Beema, Ciara and Colm

1.2.1 The trust contrasts in a number of ways with other property rights

The following table sets out some of the ways property can be held and looks at key differences and similarities with a trust. You may already be familiar with a number of other property rights such as contracts and gifts. See how a trust overlaps with many other property concepts but has several key features which often make a trust more valuable as a property right.

Comparison of a Trust with other Property Rights

Type of right	Holder of the property	Enjoyment of the property	Key difference from a trust
A gift	The donor of the property of the gift.	Held by the donee.	The beneficiary under a trust can enforce against the trustee whereas the donee of a gift is a volunteer and cannot enforce against the donor if the donor chooses not to transfer the promised gift.
A debt	The creditor loans the property on specific terms.	The debtor receives the property.	The relationship between the creditor and debtor is based in contract. If the debtor fails to repay then the creditor will sue in contract. The creditor may not be able to recover all the money transferred whereas in a trust the beneficiary ranks above other creditors.
Bailment	The bailee receives possession of the property from the bailor.	The bailee possesses the property but does not hold legal title to the property.	The bailee cannot deal in the property as if it were their own because the bailee does not receive the title to the goods. The bailee will have certain duties in relation to the property bailed which is similar to the trustee. The bailee does not have rights of enjoyment over the property which is similar to a trustee. Unlike a trust the bailor retains ownership of the property throughout the bailment.

Type of right	Holder of the property	Enjoyment of the property	Key difference from a trust
Agency	The agent holds the property on behalf of the principal on the terms of the agency agreement.	The agent holds the property.	The relationship of agent and principal lies in contract but unlike bailment and contract the agent is authorised to act on behalf of the principal.
Interests under a will or intestacy	The property of a deceased person passes to a personal representative either an executor under a valid will or an administrator.	The personal representative can deal in the property as absolute owner.	The claimant under the will has no proprietary right to the property merely a personal right against the personal representative if he fails to transfer the assets. A beneficiary under a trust can claim the property itself.
A company	A company or corporation owns assets because it has legal personality. These assets are owned by the company. The shareholders do not own property but instead they own shares in the company.	The company can own and deal in the property.	A company has its own legal personality whereas a trust does not. It is the trustees who own the assets and they can be sued if they fail to carry out their duties. The company owns its assets in its own name whereas assets of the trust are owned by the trustees.

1.2.2 Capacity to create a trust

Anyone has the capacity to create a trust with *two provisos*.

Firstly, the owner of the property must have *mental capacity*. There is no strict rule as to when a settlor has mental capacity. Medical evidence can be adduced to ascertain whether a person has the mental capacity to create a trust. If there is evidence raising the presumption that mental capacity was lacking, then the trust will be ineffective unless there is other evidence in rebuttal.

Secondly, a person must be *over the age of 18* in order to create a trust. Where a person attempts to create a trust under the age of 18, it is voidable, which means it can be repudiated by the minor once they reach their majority. If it is not repudiated on their 18th birthday, then it becomes enforceable. This only relates to *personal property* and not land. Personal property includes items such as a car or jewellery or a painting. The rules are different for land because land cannot be held legally by a minor, so there would be no question that someone under the age of 18 could create a trust.

1.3 Different types of trust

Trusts come in a number of different forms, and we will be exploring these throughout the book. This chapter concentrates almost exclusively on the *express trust*, which, as explained below, arises because of the express intention of the settlor. They make a conscious decision to create a trust and carry that out.

Later in the book we will also consider the *implied trust* which contrasts with the *express trust*. It comes into operation in the absence of any express intention from the settlor to create a trust.

There are two types of *implied trust*: the *resulting* trust and the *constructive* trust, and these will be discussed in Chapters 6 and 7.

We discussed the mechanics of a trust earlier. A trust is created once a *settlor* transfers property to a *trustee* to be held for a *beneficiary*. It is the number and extent of decisions that can be taken by the trustees that will determine the type of trust.

The choice of *express trust* depends on whether the settlor wants to reserve for the *trustee* some of the future choices in relation to the trust such as who is to benefit and how much each beneficiary is to be given.

The two main types of trust are the *fixed trust* and the *discretionary trust*.

- If the *settlor* has a clear idea as to whom they wish the property to pass and also the size of the share, then the settlor will create a *fixed trust*. The *trustee* has a duty then to transfer the property allocated to each of the *beneficiaries*. They cannot impose their own ideas as to who should benefit and also the size of the share;
- Where the *settlor* wishes to delay the choice of *beneficiary* and the size of share each will get, then the *settlor* will create a *discretionary trust*. In a discretionary

trust, the *settlor* chooses a group whom they wish to benefit but leaves it to the *trustee* to choose a *beneficiary* or *beneficiaries* amongst the group. No one has an absolute right to be chosen, but all the group has a right to be considered.

1.4 Client advice

If a client asks for your advice as to whether or not to choose a *fixed* or *discretionary* trust, the key factor is how much control the *settlor* wishes to transfer to the *trustee*. If your client has a clear idea as to who should benefit and how much each share should be, then a fixed trust is preferable. If there are lots of possible variables, such as in the example above where there are young children, for example Ciara and Colm, both of whom may have different needs in the future, then a settlor may wish to leave the final decision-making to the trustees. In such a case, a *discretionary trust* should be chosen.

Revision Points

- A *trust* differs from other types of property holding because the trustee owns property but without any enjoyment;
- An *express trust* comes into operation because of the express wish of the settlor;
- The settlor has a choice whether to create a fixed trust or a discretionary trustee-beneficiary;
- The settlor will choose a *fixed trust* if they wish to make all the decisions with regard to the trust property for themselves;
- The settlor will choose a *discretionary trust* if they wish to leave some decisions with regard to the trust property to the trustees.

1.5 The three certainties

A key requirement of all express trusts is satisfaction of the three certainties. Every valid trust must comply with the *three certainties*: certainty of intention, certainty of subject matter and certainty of object.

A trust that fails to comply with any of these three certainties will not come into operation as a trust and usually the property will remain as part of the settlor's estate.

The basis behind these requirements is to ensure that the *intention to create a trust* is clear on the face of the instructions and also the *trust property* must be clearly defined and the *beneficiaries of the trust* must be clear[1] so the trustees can carry out

1 See *Knight v Knight* (1840) 3 Beav 148, which sets out the law on the three certainties.

the terms of the trust. In this way, the settlor limits the control over the property held by the trustees and ensures that his wishes are carried out.

1.5.1 Certainty of intention

It must be shown that the settlor intended to create a trust. This means that when the property is transferred the recipient or transferee is aware that they hold the property as a trustee and not as an absolute gift.

Often someone intends to create a trust but uses words that do not mention the word trust.

The law is pragmatic and looks behind the words to see what the settlor really intended to do.

Consider these examples:

If Frankie transfers property to Gary and says, 'I want you to hold this ring for Haima', then the intention seems clear that Gary is not to enjoy the property for themselves.

If the words were slightly different, for example, Frankie says, 'I am transferring this ring to you, and I feel confident that you will give it to Haima', then the intent is not clear.[2]

Can Haima claim the ring if at a later date it is not transferred to her? Can Frankie say the ring was given to me with an indication of a secondary purpose but there was no absolute obligation for me to transfer the ring? Haima will want to know here if she can confidently claim the ring for herself from Gary.

1.5.1.1 Does the law require the use of the word 'trust'?

People will rarely use legal terms such as the word 'trust' but a trust can still arise if the intention to create a trust can be shown. So the use of words such as 'I want you to hold this ring for Haima' can still be sufficient so long as there is no doubt that the transferee is not to keep the property for themselves. If the intent cannot be shown then the words are considered to be '*precatory*' and the transferee can keep any property transferred. When looking at the words used, the important point to consider is whether there was an obligation on the transferee to hold the property for someone else. In many cases, there may be other relevant facts that may assist in understanding what has been meant by the settlor in making the transfer.

2 Consider the facts of *re Adams and Kensington Vestry* (1884) LR 27 Ch D 394, where the words used by the settlor who transferred property to his wife were, 'in full confidence that she would do what is right'. The court held that no trust arose in this case.

1.5.1.2 Examples of precatory words

- Confidence
- Belief
- Desire
- Hope
- Wish

Consider this example:

If a bank account has been registered in the sole name of P but over the years there have been many statements made by P that suggest that the money is held in that account on behalf of two people, P and Q, then on P's death, it may be possible for Q to claim the money in the account. This is important if, for instance, P has been married to M and never divorced but has, over the past ten years, been living with Q. M, as a wife, will have a claim on P's property. Q has no claim to the money unless Q can prove that the money in the account is held on trust for them both.

For instance, P may have said, 'This money is as much yours as mine', and although P does not use the word trust, it shows an intention of joint ownership. The courts would look at who P and Q are and consider whether they were inexperienced in financial matters and so would not be aware of the importance of using a word such as trust.[3]

1.5.1.3 Certainty of intention in commercial cases

It is particularly important to decide whether there has been an intention to create a trust in commercial cases. The reason for this is that if a trader is insolvent, all purchasers before the insolvency will simply rank as a *creditor* if goods have already been paid for but have not been supplied. The claim will be in *contract*. It is unlikely that there will be enough money or goods to pay back all the purchasers in full.

If the purchaser can show the goods were held *on trust*, then all the property or the whole value must be transferred to the purchaser. This is because under a trust, title or ownership of the property will have already transferred to the purchaser. In these circumstances, it is advantageous to claim that a trust has arisen, but it must first be shown that there was an *intention* at the start of the transaction for a trust to arise rather than a simple sale under contract. Most important would be an intention that the property should be held separately from the other assets of the company for the purchaser. This could be shown even if payment for the goods from the purchaser was held in an account with other monies.

3 In *Paul v Constance* [1977] 1 WLR 527, these words were used, and the court held that a trust had been created over the bank account.

1.5.2 Certainty of subject matter

Where the words used by the transferor show a *clear intention that they wish a trust to arise*, the trust may still fail if the property to be transferred is not clearly identified.

There are two ways in which the *subject matter of a trust* may be uncertain.

Firstly, the trust property itself may be uncertain. If the settlor does not specify a particular item or type of property, then the trust will fail. The words used by the transferor may be very general.

Consider this example:

I am transferring 'the bulk of my estate' or 'most of my estate' to you to be held on trust for Rose. There is no certainty in a word like 'bulk' or 'most'. In these circumstances, the trust will fail.

Secondly, there will be uncertainty in cases where the transferor specifies the property to be held on trust clearly but there is no certainty about how much of the property is to be held for each beneficiary.

Consider these examples:

'I am transferring my jewellery box to you. Please choose two of my favourite pieces for Haima'. In this case, it is unclear which pieces can be claimed by Haima. Alternatively, if the transferor says, 'I want you to hold "most of my jewellery" for Haima', then it is clear that the subject matter is the jewellery, but how much is to be held on trust is unclear.

If the transferor makes it clear which property is to be held for the transferee, then the trust will be upheld. If the settlor says to the recipient, 'I am giving you my diamond ring, but please transfer it to Haima', then the subject matter is clear.

1.5.2.1 Homogenous groups of items of property

Some trusts have succeeded where the transferor names a clear portion of a homogeneous group to be held for another.

For example, if the transferor is a wine merchant and they sell part of their stock to a purchaser [40 bottles of red wine], and the purchaser pays immediately on the day of purchase, can that purchaser claim the 40 bottles of red wine if the wine merchant goes bankrupt the following day?[4]

In this example, based on the case discussed below, the law will only allow the purchaser to claim them if the bottles have been separated from the rest. The reason for this is that the value of the bottles of wine may vary. In such a case, the trust may fail for uncertainty of subject matter unless the bottles have already been separated from the whole.

A trust will not be enforceable where there is any doubt as to what property is held on trust for the beneficiary.

The law distinguishes between *tangible property* and *intangible property*.

- *Tangible property* is objects that can be physically seen such as the bottles of wine mentioned above, grain, jewellery, cars or tanks of oil;
- *Intangible property* cannot be seen physically but is often very valuable. It includes shares in a company and money in a bank account. Share certificates and paper money represent the value of what the owner holds.

Where the property is *intangible*, the law on certainty of subject matter applies differently. A trust will have arisen over part of the property even if the property has not been set aside, as in the example of the bottles of wine. The reason the law treats intangible property in this way is because, in most cases, there is no clear difference between the various items. So we would describe all the money in a bank account as exactly the same. There will be certainty of subject matter where a settlor gives an instruction to the transferor to hold, for example, 'half of the money in my current bank account to be held for Kaye'. Assuming the settlor has only one bank account, then the subject matter of the trust is clear. The law does not expect the settlor to set up a new account in order for the subject matter to be certain.

There may be uncertainty with some types of *intangible property* such as shares because, unlike money in a bank account, the shares may vary in nature. For example, some shares may carry rights not enjoyed by others, but the law still holds that this will not make the subject matter uncertain.[5]

4 In *Re London Wine Co (Shippers) Ltd* [1975] PCC 121, large quantities of wine were held by a wine merchant in his warehouses. Whenever a customer purchased a consignment of wine, it was earmarked for that customer and they were then held for them, but they were never separated from the whole. When the wine merchant became insolvent, the customers could not claim that they were held on trust because of a failure of subject matter. You could not walk into the warehouse and identify the bottles that belonged to each customer. Therefore, they only ranked as ordinary creditors rather than recovering the wine or the value of the wine.

5 In *Hunter v Moss* [1994] 1 WLR 452, it was held that trusts of intangible objects, in this case shares, are different from trusts of tangible objects such as bottles of wine.

So with regard to the *certainty of subject matter*, the first question to ask is whether the type of property is clear rather than generic, and secondly, has the property to be held on trust been clearly identified and, in commercial situations, kept separate from the rest of the property.

Consider this example:

B runs a business supplying expensive garden ornaments. Their business runs into financial problems. 30 customers have already paid in advance for ornaments to be delivered. Before delivery, B's business collapses and they become insolvent.

Can the customers claim delivery of the goods that they have ordered?

A key fact will be how B dealt with the payments. If they paid them into his ordinary account that they use for utility bills and paying their staff, then it is unlikely that the customers can claim a trust has arisen, particularly if they have not separated their orders from the rest of his stock. The situation will be different if they have already put the ornaments of the customers in a different part of the warehouse and kept their money in a separate account or made it clear that they are treating the money of the customers in the account as separate from the rest of their money.

1.5.3 Certainty of objects

The last of the three certainties relates to the *object or beneficiary of the trust*. If a trust has been properly set up it becomes enforceable by the beneficiaries as each beneficiary immediately has an interest in the property. This is referred to as an *equitable interest* and such an interest has a value and can be transferred by the beneficiary to another person or sold. Remember it is the trustee who holds the *legal interest*. In trusts we always have to think about property being separated into two distinct legal parts once a trust has been created.

As the beneficiary has the right to claim an *equitable interest*, it must be absolutely clear who is to benefit from the trust and who can enforce their rights against the settlor.

Usually it is quite clear who the beneficiaries of a trust are because the settlor will often refer to them by name or to a group of people who are recognisable.

Consider this example:

'£400 to my niece Gail; my house, "Chestnut Cottage", to my grandson Hector; £500 to MacMillan Nurses'. Each person or persons in this group is clear.

Problems can arise where the settlor uses a description which is unclear. These are some examples.

'£500 to my friends; "Chestnut Cottage" to the nicest person I know. £600 to the Saturday walking group on Hampstead Heath'.

There are rules to help decide whether the settlor has been sufficiently clear as to who is the object of the trust where there is any doubt. In most cases where there is doubt about the objects of a trust, the gift will fail and the property will revert back to the settlor.

1.5.3.1 Certainty of object in fixed and discretionary trusts

The rules on *certainty of object* will depend on the type of trust that has been created.

As discussed earlier, there are two types of express trust: the *fixed trust* and the *discretionary trust*, and each type of express trust uses different rules:

- The *fixed trust* where the settlor has set out the terms of the trust and the trustee has no discretion about the way the property is allocated, e.g. 'I leave my estate to T to hold on trust in equal shares for my two children Ada and Ben'. The trustee has no discretion in this case. The trustee cannot transfer the property to Connie even if they are one of the settlor's children;
- The *discretionary trust* where the settlor has set out the terms but has left some discretion to the trustees, e.g. 'I leave the whole of my estate to Trev and Theo to be distributed among my grandchildren at their discretion'.

1.5.3.2 The test for certainty of objects in a fixed trust

Under a *fixed trust*, as soon as the trust is complete or 'constituted', Ada and Ben will be able to claim that they own an *equitable interest* under the trust and will be able to enforce their interests against the trustee T. The trustee has no discretion as to whom to choose among the beneficiaries and no discretion as to the size of the share for Ada and Ben.

The law requires a higher degree of certainty in a *fixed trust* than in a discretionary trust or other types of transfer. The test for certainty of objects in a fixed trust is the *'complete list' test.*[6]

The question to ask is whether the trustees can draw up with certainty a complete list of all the beneficiaries. This test is simple to apply. If the trustees cannot draw up a complete list, then the trust will fail for lack of certainty of objects.

6 This test comes from *IRC v Broadway Cottages Trust* [1955] Ch 20.

1.5.3.3 The test for certainty of objects in a discretionary trust

Under the *discretionary trust* described above the trustees must choose amongst the group e.g. the grandchildren named as beneficiaries. They must decide the size of the share or shares to be received if more than one is to benefit. None of the grandchildren has an *equitable interest* until they are chosen but they have sufficient interest to be able to bring an action against the trustees if they mishandle the funds or keep the estate for themselves. The description of the group is clear as the law is quite clear who is a grandchild. Each grandchild must wait and see if the trustees choose them over the others or perhaps decide to benefit them all as a group.

1.5.3.4 Conceptual certainty

The 'concept' of the beneficiary must be clear. It would be fairly straightforward to draw up a list of the settlor's grandchildren because the concept or definition of who is a grandchild is already clear. This is also referred to as *conceptual certainty*.

Sometimes a beneficiary or group of beneficiaries chosen by the settlor will be unclear. What if the settlor chooses a group like my 'favourite grandchildren' or my 'kindest grandchildren'? Then it is impossible for the trustee to make a choice because terms such as 'favourite' or 'kindest' are unclear.

A term like grandchild has conceptual certainty whereas a 'favourite' or 'kind' grandchild is conceptually uncertain. There is no clear definition in law of who would come within the group of a 'favourite' or a 'kind' grandchild.

Consider the words used by a settlor in the examples below and decide whether they have conceptual certainty or not.

I leave £5,000 to:

- My oldest friend
- All the librarians at my local library
- All the members of my book group
- All my cousins in Australia

'My oldest friend' is not conceptually clear. It could be a friend you have personally known for the longest, or it could be the oldest person amongst a group you call your friends. Even if that was clear, the term 'friend' is not conceptually clear. The other groups 'librarians', 'members of my book group' and 'cousins' are all conceptually clear. The law applies a different test for certainty of objects in discretionary trusts from that in fixed trusts.

The test in law for certainty of objects in a *discretionary trust* is not the 'complete list' test but the *'individual ascertainability test'*. This test is also called the *'is or is not test'* or the *'any given postulant test'*.[7]

The test sounds rather complicated apart from the *'is or is not'* test, but in practice, it is fairly straightforward.

This test works as follows: imagine a long queue of people in front of the trustees; it must be possible to decide whether any person in the queue *is or is not* within the definition of the settlor e.g. 'a relative' of the settlor; 'a grandchild'; 'a kind person'.

In this group, relatives are clear, and they have been defined in case law; grandchildren are clear, but there is no legal definition of what a 'kind person' might be, and it is not possible to decide whether a person comes within this group, so such a gift will fail.

The difference in applying the *'individual ascertainability test'* is that it is not required to draw up a *complete list* of all the potential beneficiaries in the group but instead to consider whether a person or persons chosen fall within the group. Even with this less stringent test, as we see above, some terms used by a settlor may still be regarded as uncertain.

Although there may be some people who are clearly within the group and some clearly outside the group, there may also be some who are neither clearly within nor without the group, and for this reason, the trust would fail.

1.5.3.5 Evidential certainty

A second test for certainty of objects must also be applied and again the rules differ between *fixed* and *discretionary* trusts. The second test is *evidential certainty*. It involves proving that a beneficiary comes within a named group. Even where the test for conceptual certainty has been satisfied, it may be difficult to prove who is within the group.

Consider this example:

'£100,000 for all the employees working for Vegan Foods between 2021 and 2025'. This is a fixed trust as it suggests that the fund is to be split equally between all the employees within the group. The law has fairly clear parameters as to who is or is not

7 This second test was introduced in the case of *McPhail v Doulton (also known as Re Baden)* [1971] AC 424. In this case, the trustees had to distribute the fund for the benefit of any officers and employees or ex-officers and ex-employees of the company or to relatives or dependants of any such persons...'

an employee, so the group is conceptually certain, but there may be problems proving who is within the group.

Suppose record keeping was very poor at Vegan Foods; then it will be very difficult to prove who was actually working there between the dates given.

1.6 Evidential certainty in fixed and discretionary trusts

1.6.1 Fixed trusts

In this example, the trust is a *fixed trust* and the trust would fail as it cannot be upheld unless everyone within the group can be named, as everyone has an interest in the £100,000. Without a record of everyone who worked in the factory between 2021 and 2025, the trustees cannot draw up a proper list of beneficiaries. A *fixed trust* will always fail if there is no *evidential certainty.*

1.6.2 Discretionary trusts

Consider if the wording was different e.g. '£100,000 for any of the employees at the trustee's discretion who were working for Vegan Foods between 2021 and 2025':

This is a *discretionary trust*, and it will never fail if not all the group can be named because it is not necessary for the trustees to draw up a *complete list* of all the beneficiaries. An employee has conceptual certainty so it satisfies this test and it does not need to satisfy the test for evidential certainty.

In a *discretionary trust*, the trustees have a duty to 'survey the range' of beneficiaries rather than consider each and everyone. In the example above, even if the record keeping had been poor, there will still be other means of checking who had been working for the company and this would be sufficient. So long as the trustees can identify a group of potential beneficiaries, then the test for certainty will be satisfied. It may mean that some employees will not be considered but this will not cause the trust to fail.

Chapter 1 Revision Points

If you are trying to decide if a trust has satisfied the three certainties or not, consider the following questions:

- Has the transferor shown an *intention to create a trust* by the words used or other evidence to make a gift or an intention to transfer property to be held on trust?

- If there is an intention to create a trust, then consider, *what is the subject matter of the trust*? Is it clear what property of the settlor is to be held under the trust? Are the terms used ambiguous?
- If the subject matter of the trust is clear, then you need to consider *whether or not the objects or the beneficiaries of the trust are clear*;
- Decide whether it is a *fixed* or a *discretionary trust*;
- If it is a fixed trust, then the objects must satisfy both *conceptual and evidential certainty*;
- If it is a discretionary trust, then only *conceptual certainty must be satisfied for the objects*.

If all these questions are answered positively, the property is now held on trust, and a settlor can no longer seek to recover the property for themselves, even if they have changed their minds about transferring the property to the beneficiaries.[8]

1.7 Multiple-Choice Questions

Question One

Conrad is a collector of art. He wishes to leave some of his estate to his two grandchildren, Dee and Eva, in particular his paintings. He contacts his two brothers, Ted and Tex, and asks them to act as trustees. He does not consult a solicitor. One of the terms of his trust is as follows: 'I give all my paintings to Ted and Tex. I am confident that they will decide which of my grandchildren should benefit most from them'.

Consider the following statements and decide which of them *best* explains whether this is a valid trust in favour of the grandchildren:

A. The trust will not fail because the settlor made it clear that he wanted to transfer his property on trust for the benefit of his grandchildren.
B. The trust will not fail because Conrad has clearly identified the beneficiaries and the subject matter of the trust.
C. The trust will fail because Conrad uses precatory words in setting up the trust.

8 In *re Bowden [1936]* Ch 71, the settlor wanted to become a nun, and before doing so, she transferred her property to a number of beneficiaries. Later, she changed her mind and left the convent. She tried to recover her property from the trust, but the court held that it was a valid trust and she could not recover the property back. The beneficiaries now owned the property.

D. The trust will fail because Conrad does not use the word trust in his instructions.

E. The trust will fail because Conrad does not clearly identify the shares of each of the beneficiaries.

Question Two

T1 was a childless widower. He had a huge number of colleagues at the Further Education College where he worked between 2010 and 2019 as a lecturer. He wanted to benefit as many of his colleagues as he could but could not decide whom to benefit. He died last month and the following instructions have been found in his will.

'I leave £100,000 to be shared between my colleagues in the English Department at my trustees' complete discretion'.

It has been discovered that the records of some of the employees at the college between 2015 and 2019 have disappeared as there was a cyber-attack in 2021 and most of the employment details were lost and could not be recovered.

Consider the following statements and decide which of them *best* explains whether this is a valid trust:

A. The trust will not fail because evidential certainty is not required for a discretionary trust.

B. The trust will fail because T1 has not made his intentions clear.

C. The trust will fail because the objects of the trust have not been clearly identified by T1.

D. The trust will fail because the trustees cannot draw up a complete list of all the potential beneficiaries.

E. The trust will fail because evidential certainty is required in all trusts.

2 The constitution of an express trust

2.1 Chapter overview

This chapter looks at the second stage of creating a valid trust. Once the three certainties have been satisfied, the trust can only come into effect if it is fully constituted. Even if the settlor has told the beneficiaries that they are to benefit under the trust, they cannot compel the settlor to carry out their promise. The beneficiaries are volunteers and will not have given valuable consideration. The rights of the beneficiaries will only arise when the trust is fully constituted. A trust will be fully constituted if all the formalities of the transfer of property to the trustees have been undertaken and the property is now in the hands of the trustees. The chapter starts by looking at the various ways that a trust can be fully constituted. It then considers some of the formalities of transfer of property. Sometimes the trustee is the settlor, so the rules for transfer are usually simpler because the property is already in the ownership of the settlor. Some of the rules of transfer are the same for a gift from one person to another, so many of the examples come from cases of gifts, but they are also applicable to trusts. The chapter ends by considering two exceptions to the rules on constitution: gifts made in contemplation of death and the application of the rule in *Strong v Bird*.

2.2 The constitution of an express trust

Even where a trust satisfies the three certainties it will not be enforceable until it is *fully constituted*. Constituting a trust means to take steps to transfer the property to the trustee. In law this is referred to as *vesting*. It is only when all the trust property has been vested in the trustees that it can be called a *fully constituted trust*. For some types of property such as land and shares there are several formal steps to take. Sometimes a settlor may decide to hold property they own for others. In these cases the settlor becomes the trustee and there is no need for a transfer of title of the trust property but there may be a need for other formalities to show that the settlor is now holding property for others. This may involve steps like putting their intentions into writing for some types of property such as land but for personalty an oral intention can be sufficient. If the settlor says from tomorrow, I hold my mother's

DOI: 10.4324/9781003583660-3

diamond necklace for Chloe it is important that the intention is clearly stated and others are present to hear it. In those cases where the settlor has failed to vest the property in the trustees the trust will be seen as *incompletely constituted.*

Once a trust is *fully constituted*, a settlor cannot go back on the trust and attempt to recover the property for themselves. This means that the settlor has taken all the further steps necessary to ensure that the property is in the hands of the trustee. Once this can be shown, the beneficiaries can enforce the trust against the trustee, who from that moment forward is under a duty to act on their behalf.

So, until the trust is *fully constituted* the settlor has a right to change their mind and the beneficiaries are viewed as volunteers. One of the maxims or informal rules of equity is that 'equity will not assist a volunteer'.[1] In practice this means that where a promise to make a gift or a transfer of property into a trust has been made but not carried out the court will not intervene.

Consider this example:

A promises to give B a car as a present for B's 17th birthday. As B is only 16, A tells B that he will transfer the car to trustees T1 and T2 to hold until he is 17. Suppose A fails to transfer the car to the trustees; B will want to know if he can enforce the promise that A made to him. In these circumstances, B cannot enforce A's promise. The reason why he cannot enforce the promise is that B is receiving a gratuitous gift.

The law will not step in and enforce just as the law will not enforce a contract where consideration has not been exchanged. A can change his mind and decide that B should not have the car.

There is a second maxim of equity, 'Equity will not perfect an imperfect gift', which would apply to these facts. This means that courts will never intervene where a promise has been made to make a gift or to transfer property into a trust but has not been carried out.

By way of contrast, where B gives A something in exchange for the car, the promise would be enforceable. Likewise, if after promising the car, A follows it up and transfers the car to the trustees, it is a fully constituted trust and A cannot change his mind the next day and ask for the car back; it now belongs to B in equity, and when he is 17, he will receive the car.

1 This rule can be traced back to *Milroy v Lord* (1862) 4 De G F & J 264.

2.2.1 Reasons for the strict enforcement of the rules for the constitution of a trust

There are several reasons why the constitution of a trust has been so strictly enforced:

- Firstly, in practical terms, it *protects a person from making a disposition by a simple promise*. In the example above, if A, in a generous mood, says to B, 'from tomorrow you can have my car', then there is a possibility that B can claim the car on the basis of a mere conversation when perhaps A had no intention of actually transferring it.
- Secondly, in making sure that only properly constituted trusts can be enforced, it *protects the donee from becoming a trustee*.

Imagine if you were given a present such as the car in the example above. If you found later that you were a trustee for someone else, then you would become responsible for the car and could possibly be sued by the beneficiary if the car is damaged in any way.

If you knew before the transfer that it was not for you, and you were becoming a trustee, you may have refused the transfer.

There is also an argument that the creation of trusts should be monitored more closely because they tie up property rather than allow it to be freely transferable. The need to ensure that the trust is fully constituted ensures that only those trusts which are genuinely intended will take effect.

2.2.2 Ways for a trust to become fully constituted

There are a number of ways that a trust can become *fully constituted*. The rules differ as to whether the trust was set up as part of a gift in a will or as a transfer during the settlor's lifetime.

Different ways that a trust can become fully constituted:

- If the settlor makes a *valid will*, then if under the terms of the will he has created a trust, it will be automatically *constituted* on his death under that will;
- Where a trust is to take effect during the life of the settlor, then it can be constituted if the *settlor declares himself as trustee*. This means that the settlor no longer enjoys rights over the property even though it is still registered in their name;
- The law also recognises a *valid transfer from the settlor to a third party* to act as trustee so long as it complies with the relevant formalities of transfer.

In each of these cases, the property becomes trust property, and from the moment the trust is said to be fully constituted, it can be enforced by the beneficiary.

Revision Point

It is important to remember that a *settlor can become a trustee of their own property* to be held in the future for another person. They may decide that they would like to hold the property for the time being for that person. Once they declare themselves as trustee and undertake any formal requirements, they will be trustee of that property for the named beneficiary, and they will lose any right to enjoy the property for themselves.

2.2.3 Equity will not assist a volunteer

In the section above we considered how the law treats trusts and gifts and will not enforce unless there is a delivery of the property. This is because the law does not allow volunteers to claim any rights. The law regards anyone who has been promised property but has not in exchange transferred valuable consideration as a volunteer.

Consider these facts:

Your friend has been promised a new car if she passes a certain set of examinations. She passes the examinations and receives excellent marks. She sends her marks to her father and waits for the delivery of her new car. He told her last week that he is sorry but he has less money than he thought at the moment and cannot now give her the car.

She asks you for your advice. Can she enforce the promise?

The problem for your friend is that she has not given valuable consideration. Passing the exams is unlikely to be regarded as consideration in this scenario and so the father is free to change his mind. The law regards your friend as a *volunteer.*

The rule that 'equity will not assist a volunteer' was first introduced in a nineteenth-century case *Milroy v Lord* and initially it was strictly enforced.

2.2.4 A more lenient approach to the rule: the transferor has done everything in his power

A new flexibility has been brought in more recent times which allows a trust to become *fully constituted* if it can be shown that the settlor has done everything in their power to transfer the property.

If the settlor had formally transferred property to trustees, such as shares, but there was a further stage, such as registration of the shares in the names of the trustees, then strictly the trustees would not own the property at that stage.

However, the settlor could not reclaim the property as the final steps are out of the settlor's hands but are waiting for the trustees to act. In these circumstances, the law is pragmatic and accepts that the trust is *fully constituted*.

Consider this example:

Fred transfers 10,000 shares to his wife. The correct form had been completed by Fred on March 30th and forwarded to the company. The transfer was registered by the company on June 30th. Fred died three years later. In order to avoid estate duty (the tax which preceded inheritance tax), the shares had to have passed to his wife before April 10th Had the title to the shares passed to her or did it remain with Fred's estate? The law held that the shares had passed to his wife. Fred had carried out all the necessary steps to transfer the shares. The registration was the responsibility of the company.[2]

This flexibility has developed further and the courts have shown a willingness in some circumstances to uphold a transfer even though there are remaining steps to be taken by the transferor. An example of this would be where the trust has been created for charitable purposes.[3]

This can, however, lead to uncertainty. The law always prefers certainty, especially where property is involved. When it comes to property, there should not be any doubt about ownership. If you are given a gift of a car, then it either belongs to you or it does not. If you are stopped in the street for speeding, you cannot say to the police officer, 'I think it belongs to me', and if you wish to sell it, you have to have clear proof that you own it.

Nevertheless, the system of equity believes in the principle of 'fairness', so it remains flexible at times. This can lead occasionally to uncertainty. We will discuss when this might arise later.

2.3 Rules for transfer of different types of property

The rules of transfer vary according to the *different types of property*. These rules must be followed in order for the title to pass to the trustees and ensure that the

2 These facts are based on the case of *Re Rose (Deceased)* [1952] Ch 499.

3 In the case of *T Choithram International SA v Pagarani* [2000] UKPC 46, a businessman who was terminally ill with cancer had attempted to create a charitable trust when he had days to live. He signed a deed transferring a number of interests that he owned into the new charitable trust. Although he was a trustee, the legal title to the interests had not been transferred to the other trustees, so the law was incompletely constituted. In spite of this, the court applied the rule in *Re Rose* and held that he had done everything in his power to transfer the property to the trustees. The trust was upheld. It was a charitable trust which must have persuaded the court to take a generous approach.

trust is properly constituted. These rules will also apply to a transfer of a gift. As mentioned earlier, we can apply the rules and decided cases to both types of transfer.

We have already considered one of the maxims of equity 'equity will not assist a volunteer' and seen how that has influenced the way the law on trusts has developed. We have also briefly considered a second maxim which is very relevant here 'equity will not perfect an imperfect gift'.

In practice this means that the transferor must have taken *all the steps necessary* to transfer the property to a transferee before it can take effect. There are always stricter rules for the transfer of *land* than for other types of property.

Where the settlor declares themselves as trustee, then no transfer is necessary, as the settlor already owns the property. Of course, there must first be a *self-declaration* by the settlor that the property is now held in trust and no longer for the settlor's benefit.

Consider this example:

A owns a Jaguar motor car. If A declares that, 'From today, I hold my Jaguar car for B', then a trust has been declared and will be constituted because no documents of transfer are necessary.

Suppose the following week A gets an offer from C for the car; he cannot sell the car as it is now in trust for B. Although he still has the car in his possession, he is holding the car as trustee, so the car is not his to sell. The important point here is A's declaration of trust, which is regarded in law as binding. As this is personalty, it is not required to be in writing. Writing is necessary for some types of property.

We will now look at various types of property and consider the steps necessary for effective transfer of the property to a trustee or a transfer by way of gift.

2.3.1 Land

Unlike the creation of a trust of personalty such as shares or jewellery, a trust of land must be evidenced in writing and signed by the settlor.[4] What is needed is written proof that the settlor intended to create a trust of land. It does not matter if the written proof is made at a date later than the declaration of trust.

4 The need for a written declaration of a trust of land is set out in s.53(1)(b) Law of Property Act 1925. The main requirement is to include the terms and also for the settlor to sign it.

The next stage is the transfer of the property to the trustees. If the settlor is to hold the property as a trustee, then no transfer of the property is needed, as it is already in the hands of the settlor.

The transfer involves the execution of a formal document called a deed, which transfers title to the trustees. Finally, the trustees seek to be registered as legal owners of the property.

Consider this example and advise Owen:

Owen owns Greenacres, a holiday house by the sea. Owen now wants Greenacres to be held in trust for his two daughters, Bea and Cam. They are both still at school, so they cannot own the land until they are 18. He intends to appoint his two good friends, Tessa and Tex, to act as trustees.

Step one

The trust property is land, so you should advise Owen that the creation of this trust requires evidence in writing, and this must be signed by Owen. If the trust property were shares or personal property, he would not need a written document.

Step two

The next step will be the transfer of the title to Greenacres by Owen to Tessa and Tex. This needs a legal document called a *deed*. Land is often the most valuable asset anyone owns, and for this reason, it is important that ownership is clear. So, evidence of ownership, particularly written documentation, has always been preferred. Today, a *deed* is used. This is a formal document which requires a signature, a witness, and must be delivered by the transferor to the transferee.[5] In this case, the settlor Owen is the transferor, and the transferees will be the trustees, Tessa and Tex. They will become the new owners of the property and will now hold Greenacres for the beneficiaries, Bea and Cam.

Step three

Legal ownership of land only passes when the title to land is registered in the new owner's name (Tessa and Tex), so there is a further step to be taken after the deed is delivered. The property must be registered in the name of the trustees. However, once the trustee has the documentation necessary to register the property, the settlor (Owen) can no longer recover the land, and so under the rule of *re Rose* at that stage, the trust will be fully constituted.[6]

5 The requirements for a deed were changed by the 1989 Law of Property (Miscellaneous Provisions) Act. Today it is necessary for the document to be signed, and there must be one witness.

6 See *Mascall v Mascall* (1984) 50 P & CR 42, where a father wanted to give his house to his son. He handed him the land certificate and executed a transfer document. The son needed to get the transfer

Revision of stages in the transfer of land to be held on trust:

i) The settlor, Owen, declares that his house, Greenacres, is to be held on trust by trustees Tessa and Tex for his daughters, Bea and Cam;
ii) The declaration of trust is made in writing by Owen and he signs it. It is then signed by a neighbour, Ned, as a witness and handed to Tessa and Tex;
iii) The land is transferred by Owen to Tessa and Tex by deed and they register themselves as legal owners of Greenacres.

Remember if Owen has a row with his daughters after the property has been transferred to Tessa and Tex he cannot recover the property. He is no longer regarded as the owner of Greenacres.

2.3.2 Shares

If a settlor wishes to transfer shares in a private company either by way of gift or on trust for the benefit of named beneficiaries, they must execute a *stock transfer form* in favour of the trustees. This form must be delivered to the trustees with the share certificates. Once this is done, the transfer is binding, but the shares do not belong to the trustees until they are registered in their name.

The settlor now cannot give or sell the shares to anyone else as they have transferred the *stock transfer form* to the trustees. Once it has been transferred, they have done all that is in their power to transfer ownership to the trustees.

Consider these facts and advise Owen:

Owen wishes to create a trust of shares that he owns in a private company in favour of his daughters, Bea and Cam. He appoints his friends, Tessa and Tex, to be trustees.

Owen must execute a stock transfer form in favour of Tessa and Tex and send it to them. The trustees must approach the company and ask for registration of their names as the new owners. The company will have to take the final step of adding their names to the register.

Consider these alternative facts

Suppose Owen does not give the transfer form to the trustees Tessa and Tex but instead gives it to Ned, a neighbour, for safekeeping. In this case, there is uncertainty. The stock transfer form must be transferred to the trustees. It is only at that stage

documents stamped and then register his title at the Land Registry, but before he could do this, the father and son had an argument and the father demanded the house back. It was held that this was a valid gift. The transferor had done everything in his power to transfer the house to the transferee.

that he loses the right to take back the shares. If he hands the form to someone other than the trustees, he has not done all in his power to transfer ownership as the form is not held by the trustees, Tessa and Tex.

Who now owns the shares? The settlor or the trustees? It is uncertain because technically the settlor Owen can go to Ned and demand the form back as it has not been handed to the trustee.[7]

2.3.3 Chattels

The rules for the transfer of personal property such as jewellery, cars, furniture and animals are simpler. The property must be physically transferred to the trustee or the donee, and the settlor or donor must indicate that it is now to be held on trust[8] unless it is an outright gift. The declaration of trust can be made orally and does not have to be made in writing. The transfer of property as a gift, for instance on a birthday, is usually accompanied by some declaration such as, 'I bought this for you'. The delivery of the property and these words would be sufficient to perfect the gift.

Consider this example:

Owen hands a piece of jewellery to his friend, Dee, and says, 'This is for you'. The physical transfer and the words used are enough for the title to the jewellery to pass. Owen cannot go back a week later having had a change of mind and say I want my jewellery back as it now belongs to Dee.

Compare this situation:

Owen hands over the piece of jewellery to Dee but says, 'I want you to keep this for Bea while she is at university'. In this case, the property neither belongs to Dee nor to Owen but is held in trust for Bea. The three certainties are satisfied, and there is delivery of the property to the trustee. In this case, Dee becomes a trustee of the jewellery. Bea has the right to claim it later if Dee does not transfer the jewellery when Bea leaves university. The transfer to Dee is complete, and the trust is fully constituted, so Owen cannot then go back to claim the jewellery if he changes his mind.

7 In *Pennington v Waine* [2002] 1 WLR 2075, the owner of shares had told P that she intended to transfer shares to her nephew as a gift. She made a number of oral declarations to that effect, including telling her nephew that she was transferring the shares to him as he needed the shares to become director of the company, but she did not hand the STF to him. She died, and her nephew claimed the shares. Although technically the steps needed to constitute the gifts had not been taken, the Court of Appeal upheld the transfer on the basis that it would be unconscionable for her to go back on her intention. This has been criticised for bringing uncertainty into this area of law.

8 In *Paul v Constance* [1977] 1 WLR 527, a man opened a bank account in his sole name but declared on a number of occasions it was for his partner as well. After his death, his partner, Mrs P, could claim the contents of the account for herself.

Occasionally there will be symbolic transfer even where there has not been delivery. Suppose a document was handed to the trustee, such as the history of various sales of a valuable painting, and this was handed to the trustee by the settlor; then this could be sufficient transfer.

It would be evidence of ownership, especially if the settlor said something to signify ownership. 'As you are now the owner of the painting, I am giving you this document recording the first and all subsequent sales of this picture'.

Symbolic transfer is most likely to be acceptable where the property transferred is very large or heavy and difficult to move from one person to another.

2.4 Exceptions to the rules for the need for a completely constituted trusts or gift

In one or two limited situations the law will uphold an incompletely constituted trust or an imperfect gift. In these cases, the law is being pragmatic and allowing the transfer because of the circumstances at the time. These are very limited and only arise in two sets of circumstances.

2.4.1 Gifts made in contemplation of death

The law allows gifts made in *contemplation of death* to be regarded as fully constituted gifts or trusts. These gifts are also referred to as a *donatio mortis causa*. If the settlor or donor intends to transfer property to the trustee or to a donee but, for specific reasons, cannot fulfil the key formalities, then the transfer will be upheld. The reasons that have been accepted include being a member of the armed forces about to go to a war zone, or that the settlor has recently become seriously ill and is in hospital or a hospice, so it is difficult to carry out formal requirements. In such circumstances, the rules are relaxed with regard to the formalities of transfer.

There are *three requirements* in order for such a gift to take effect:

- The donor should contemplate their impending death;
- The gift must be made in such a way as to take effect only on their death; until then the donor has the right to take the gift back. It will lapse if the donor recovers or survives the life-threatening event;
- The donor must transfer the gift in such a way that the donee has control over the property. This could either be a physical transfer or a symbolic transfer.

It is important to note that not all property is capable of passing under this rule. An example would be a cheque because it is regarded as a mandate to the donor's bank and it will automatically be terminated on the death of the donor. In the case of a car, delivery of keys to the car would be enough. Land is also regarded as being incapable of passing under this rule because it would be difficult for there to be a symbolic transfer.

Handing over the keys to a property is unlikely to be enough since keys are often held by different people at the same time and holding the keys does not always suggest symbolic transfer; if it were so, there would be a reluctance to give a set of keys to a neighbour![9]

2.4.2 Exceptions to the rules of completely constituted trusts: gifts made under the rule in Strong v Bird[10]

The law allows some gifts to take effect even though the formalities have not been complied with because fortuitously the property falls into the hands of the donee. The rule allows someone who has been promised a gift but the transfer has not complied with the legal requirements to enforce the gift if they have acquired the property in the capacity of executor of the will.

In practice, the rule relies on the done showing that they have been *appointed executor.*

An *executor* is the person or persons appointed by a person in their will to deal with their property on death. The law regards the *executor* as stepping into the shoes of the deceased on their death.

If someone dies without making a valid will (intestate), then their estate is dealt with by a *personal administrator.* This will be someone close to the deceased who will also step into their shoes and deal with the deceased's estate. During the period immediately after the death of the deceased, the *executor* and the *personal administrator* will deal with the estate of the deceased as if they were the owner.

Consider this example:

A donor, X, says to the donee, Y, 'You are now released from paying me a debt that you owe me'.

This could be significant for Y if Y owed a large sum of money to X. If X had failed to record this conversation in writing before death, then according to the law, the release could not take effect, as a release from a debt has to be put into writing.

9 There was one case which allowed the transfer of land to the donee. The donor handed the keys to a strong box to the claimant who was visiting him in hospital. The strongbox contained documentation relating to ownership of the house. The claimant was able to claim the house after the owner died in spite of the lack of compliance with the formalities necessary for the transfer of land. (*Sen v Headley* [1991] 2 WLR 1308).

10 (1874) LR 18 Eq 315.

The special rule in *Strong v Bird* could assist Y. Under the rule, if Y had been named as executor to X in their will, Y would then escape from the debt.

The reason for this is that having been named as *executor*, Y takes control of all of X's property, including all debts owed to the estate. Y can argue that X had told him during his lifetime that he need not pay back the money, and such a promise stayed enforceable after X's death because of Y's position as executor. It is as if it were a promise made by Y to Y.

There are *four requirements* in order for the rule in Strong v Bird to take effect:

- The donor must show that they intend to make a gift to the donee during their lifetime;
- The intention must carry on until the donor's death;
- The donee must be appointed either as executor of the donor's estate if they died testate (i.e. having made a valid will). If the donor dies intestate (without a valid will), then if the donee is appointed as administrator of the donor's estate, the rule will still apply;
- The property must be capable of passing after the death of the donor.

Consider this example:

Jaz borrows £5,000 from his Auntie Kerry in March. He wants to put it towards buying a new car.

In July, Auntie Kerry says to Jaz, 'I have had some luck this month; I have won some money on the lottery. You do not have to pay me back the money I lent you. Please keep it for yourself'.

That statement should be put into writing in order to be enforceable; otherwise, Jaz will still have to pay back the money if Auntie Kerry died suddenly. If Auntie Kerry does die sometime later but Jaz has been named as her executor in the will, the rule in *Strong v Bird* will apply and the debt need not be repaid.

The rule will equally apply if Auntie Kerry died without making a will but Jaz acts as her administrator and deals with her affairs because he is her closest relative.

Summary of rules for the constitution of a trust and perfection of a gift:

- No trust can be enforced unless it is fully constituted;
- A trust is fully constituted once the settlor has taken all the necessary steps to transfer the property into the hands of the trustee;

- The law regards a transfer as effective if a third party rather than the transferor takes steps such as registration;
- Land, shares and chattels have specific rules of transfer;
- A beneficiary cannot enforce an incompletely constituted trust because they are volunteers;
- Gifts made in contemplation of death and gifts made under the rule in *Strong v Bird* can be enforced even where the trust is not fully constituted.

2.5 Multiple-Choice Questions

Question One

Konrad has suffered from failing kidneys all his life. He was recently offered a kidney transplant. He has been told that because he is in poor health, there will be a risk if he agrees to the operation, but he is likely to recover. The day before the operation, he asks his daughter Leila to come to visit him in hospital. He says to Leila, 'I am very worried about the operation tomorrow and I want you to have Mum's jewellery stored in the loft if anything happens to me; it is very valuable'. He gives her a key to the jewellery box.

Konrad died three days after the operation. Under the terms of his will, all his property passes to a charity.

Which of the following statements best describes who is entitled to claim the jewellery?

A. The charity can claim the jewellery because under the terms of the will, it is to inherit all of Konrad's estate.
B. Leila cannot claim the jewellery because Konrad may recover from the operation.
C. Leila cannot claim the jewellery because it was not delivered to her during Konrad's lifetime.
D. Leila cannot claim the jewellery because Konrad did not put his intentions into writing.
E. Leila can claim the jewellery because this would be deemed a valid gift made in contemplation of death.

Question Two

Maddie is a very successful businesswoman. She owns several flats in Manchester and decides to give one, Flat Two Chestnut Drive, to her sister, Nina, who she knows has recently lost her job and is in a difficult financial situation. She telephones Nina on July 10th and tells her that she wants to help her, and she is giving her Flat Two Chestnut Drive. 'It will be yours to enjoy for yourself from now on'.

Maddie unexpectedly dies in August. In her will, she appoints Nina as her executor. Under her will, all her estate goes to her only son, Oz.

Which of the following statements best describes who is entitled to claim the flat?

- **A.** Oz can claim the flat because Oz is entitled under the will to all Maddie's estate.
- **B.** Oz can claim the flat because he is Maddie's only son and therefore will inherit her estate on her death.
- **C.** Oz can claim the flat because the formalities of transfer of the flat to Maddie were not carried out correctly.
- **D.** Nina can claim the flat because she was appointed executor under Maddie's will.
- **E.** Nina can claim the flat because Maddie showed a clear intention that she was to have the flat immediately before she died.

3 Formalities of transfer of property from the settlor to the trustee and transfer from the beneficiaries to a third party

3.1 Chapter overview

You will recall from Chapter 1 that when a trust is created, the property separates into two parts: the *legal estate* and the *equitable estate*. The trustee controls the legal estate and can deal in the property; for example, they can sell the property if needed. The beneficiary has rights in the other part of the property called the equitable estate. They too have an interest that they can deal in. A beneficiary has the chance to deal in that interest; for example, they can give their interest away or sell it. This chapter looks at the formalities involved in both setting up a trust and also where the beneficiary deals in their equitable interest. Some of this will be familiar as we touched on a number of the rules in Chapter 2 about the formalities of transfer.

3.2 The importance of formalities in trusts

Formalities play a significant part in the creation of a trust as well as a later transfer of the equitable interest by a beneficiary. The formalities have developed because they promote certainty and also reduce the possibility of fraud. If all trusts or dealings in trust property simply relied on oral promises, they would be far more open to uncertainty and possibilities of misunderstandings.

3.2.1 Who has capacity to create a trust

You will recall that anyone can create a trust with the exception of anyone under the age of 18 and those who lack the capacity through a mental health condition.

3.2.2 The different ways that an express trust can be created

Revision Points

By way of revision, take a moment to remind yourself of the different ways that a trust can be created.

i) **The settlor can declare themselves to be a trustee.** Remember in this case, the settlor continues to own the legal title to the trust property, but now it is held on behalf of the beneficiaries. It is for that reason that it is important

DOI: 10.4324/9781003583660-4

to recognise the exact moment rights in equity pass to the beneficiaries. You should recall here that when a settlor declares a trust over land, that should be evidenced in writing, whereas a trust of other types of property does not need written evidence;

Consider this example:

Ben owns an electric bike, and he wishes to transfer it to his nephew Arif, who is 16, but only when he has reached the age of 17. He decides to create a trust over the bike and declares that he now intends to hold it for Arif.

Revision Checklist

- **Have the three certainties been satisfied?**

The three certainties have been satisfied. Most importantly, Ben has shown the intention to create a trust.

- **What formalities are necessary for this trust?**

As the bike is a chattel, there are no extra formalities to be satisfied. At this point, the trust has been created and is enforceable by the beneficiary, Arif, who can claim the bike as soon as he reaches 17. Even if Ben and Arif argue the following day, the trust cannot be revoked. Ben cannot change his mind.

ii) **A trust can be created by transferring the property from the settlor to the trustees.** Ownership passes to the trustees, not for themselves to enjoy but for the enjoyment of the beneficiaries on the terms of the trust. In this situation, there may be formalities to be complied with;

iii) **a trust can be created under the terms of a will;**

a trust can come into operation on the death of a settlor as a term of a will. The need for any formalities for the creation of a trust is addressed because the will is a written document and will cover any formalities needed where land is incorporated into the trust property.

3.3 Formalities necessary for the creation of a trust?

In general, the creation of *a trust does not require specific formalities*. The key requirement is for there to be clear evidence that the settlor *intended to create a trust*. This is particularly important where the settlor declares that they are now to hold their own property on trust for someone else. This can be confusing as many people think a trust must be put into writing. It would be possible to create a trust of a considerable sum of money or very valuable chattels such as jewellery or paintings without written evidence.

3.3.1 Land

Land is treated as an exception when a trust is created. This is because it is often the most valuable asset that someone owns and the law is concerned about fraudulent claims to property.

Under *s.53(1)(b) Law of Property Act 1925*, written evidence is needed in order for a trust to become effective. The trust itself does not need to be in writing; all that is necessary is for there to be a piece of written evidence that is signed by the settlor, showing the intention to create the trust and incorporating key information such as:

- The terms of the trust
- The beneficiaries of the trust and
- Also what property is now to be subject to the trust

Here is an example of how s.53(1)(b) works in practice.

Cora owns Timber Farm but decides that eventually Devi should own it; but until then, Cora wants to hold it on trust for Devi. Devi is currently working abroad and is not coming back to the UK for two years. Cora tells Devi about this one day in February, and three weeks later, Cora makes a declaration as follows:

> 'I now hold Timber Farm as trustee for Devi'.

The declaration is signed by Cora, and she hands it to a solicitor for safekeeping. The farm is now held for Devi by Cora. Even if Cora died leaving the farm to someone else in her will, Devi can claim it for himself. That is because it is a lifetime declaration of trust over property, and Cora no longer owns it for herself to deal with on her death. The declaration satisfies the formal requirements.

3.4 Formalities necessary for the transfer of an equitable interest

A beneficiary of a trust owns an equitable or beneficial interest in the trust property. This is something that can be transferred to another person either by gift or by sale.

Revisit the facts of the example above of the trust for Devi. Cora owns the *legal interest* in the farm, but Devi now owns the *equitable interest*. Devi may decide to stay working abroad and transfer his *equitable interest* to Edi, who is his son. If he decides to do so, he must follow the formalities of an equitable interest.

There are strict rules for the *disposition or transfer of any equitable interest*. It does not matter what property is being held on trust. The rules are the same whether the trust property is land, shares or a car. It is still regarded as an *equitable interest*, and if there is a *'disposition'*, then it must comply with *Law of Property Act s.53(1)(c)*. This section requires any disposition of an equitable interest to be put into writing and signed by the transferor. Unlike *s.53(1)(b)* in connection with the creation of a trust of land, the disposition of the equitable interest must be in writing at the time of the disposition itself and not evidenced in writing at a later date.

There are *exceptions* where writing will not be needed for what appears to be a disposition, which are discussed later in the chapter.

Consider this example:

Lou is the beneficiary under a trust created by her father, Sam. She has decided to transfer her interest to Mel, her daughter. If Lou meets Mel for coffee and tells her, 'I am assigning my interest under Grandfather Sam's estate to you', there is no effective transfer to Mel. In order for Lou to effectively transfer her interest, she must put the assignment into writing.

3.4.1 The equitable interest can be disposed of in a number of different ways

i) Assigning the interest to a third party (s.53(1((c) needed for the transfer)
ii) Asking the trustees to hold the property for a third party (s.53(1((c) needed for the transfer)
iii) Declaration by the beneficiary that the equitable interest will be held on trust for another (no writing needed for the transfer)

i) **Assigning an equitable interest to a third party**

This is regarded as a *disposition*, and this must be in writing in order to be effective. If the assignment is not put into writing, the transfer will be void and the interest remains with the original beneficiary.

In the example discussed above of Lou, who wishes to assign her interest under Sam's estate to her daughter, Mel, she has to comply with *s.53(1)(c)*, and the assignment itself must be in writing and signed by her.

ii) **Asking the trustees to hold their equitable interest for a third party**

In this case, the beneficiary is asking the trustees to hold their equitable interest for someone else.

Consider this example:

T1 and T2 hold shares on trust for Bea. Bea would like those shares to be held from now on for her niece Carrie. T1 and T2 hold the legal interest and Bea holds the equitable interest. Bea does not own the shares but instead an *equitable interest* in the trust property, which happens to be shares.

Bea messages T1 and T2 and instructs them to now hold the shares for Carrie. This telephone instruction is ineffective.

Bea must now write to the trustees if it is to take effect. If she does not do this, the interest remains with her, even though she telephoned the trustees. Without the phone call, if anything happened to her, the equitable interest would pass with Bea's estate on her death.

iii) **Declaration by a beneficiary that the equitable interest should be held in trust by the beneficiary for someone else**

This differs from (i) and (ii) because the original beneficiary still holds the equitable interest in their name but is *now trustee for another.* The law treats this situation differently. In this case, no written declaration need be made by the original beneficiary in order for the new trust to take effect. This is because there has been no transfer of the equitable interest, so although the original beneficiary is no longer able to enjoy the benefit of the equitable interest, there has not been a disposition within *s.53(1)(c)*.[1]

Consider this example:

T1 and T2 hold shares in a trust for Bea. T1 and T2 hold the legal interest and Bea has the equitable interest. She decides that from now on she wants any dividends from the shares to go to her niece Carrie. She makes a formal declaration of this but does not put it into writing.

Is it effective?

In this case, Bea becomes the trustee for Carrie, not T1 and T2. She has created what is regarded in law as a *sub-trust*. The law does not regard this as a *disposition*. Bea

1 An example of how this works can be found in the case of *Grey v IRC* [1960] AC 1. The facts are rather complicated. Mr H wanted to benefit his grandchildren, so he created six trusts in each of their favour at first of nominal value. In an attempt to avoid tax, he created a trust in his own favour of 18,000 shares, and then in a second transaction, he asked his trustees to transfer part of his interest in the shares (his equitable interest) to each of the six trusts for his grandchildren. He then put this instruction into writing. It was held that the oral direction would not transfer the interests (applying s.53(1)(c)); his interest would only be transferred by the written document, which attracted tax.

remains the owner of the equitable interest, namely the interest in the shares, but remember that the legal interest still rests with T1 and T2.

When Bea receives a dividend, she must hand that to Carrie. Carrie can enforce the promise by Bea that she holds the dividends for her. The key point to look for is whether or not Bea has any active duties, and here she has a duty to hand over the dividends from the trust to Carrie.

A sub-trust:

Trustees T1 and T2 (Legal estate) ——————> Bea/Beneficiary (Equitable estate)

(Trustee) (Now holding the
equitable
Estate for Carrie)

|

V

Carrie (beneficiary of the sub-trust)

Chapter 3 Revision Points

- Anyone has the capacity to create a trust except for those under 18 and those lacking mental capacity;
- There are no formalities necessary to create a trust of personalty;
- The creation of a trust of land requires evidence in writing;
- Some types of property require strict formalities when transferred to trustees, e.g. land;
- The disposition of an equitable interest must be in writing whether the trust property is personalty or land;
- The creation of a sub-trust of the equitable interest by the beneficiary does not require writing; it is not a disposition.

4 Vested and contingent gifts and the perpetuities rules

4.1 Chapter overview

This chapter looks at the different types of interest that a beneficiary holds under an express trust. The interests can be either *vested or contingent* and the two vary according to whether the settlor has imposed any specific conditions on the gifts under the trust. So firstly, we consider those trusts where the beneficiary has a *vested interest*. In these types of trust, a beneficiary has an immediate right to the gift. We next consider *contingent interests* where a claim might be delayed because conditions have been imposed by the settlor. We examine what sort of conditions a settlor might impose as a term of the trust. These can vary from an age contingency, i.e. reaching a certain age before benefiting under the trust, or imposing a condition that the beneficiary must choose a certain career path before benefiting. We then consider when the beneficiaries as a group can accelerate the receipt of their property. This can happen under the rule in *Saunders v Vautier*, but it only takes effect if the conditions are met. The chapter concludes with a brief consideration of the perpetuity rules. The law lays down some time limitations which are referred to as the 'perpetuity period'. These rules are explained and applied to practical scenarios.

4.2 Vested gifts

Rights under a trust can be described as being either *vested or contingent*. This is important for the beneficiaries as it can affect their rights to claim property under the trust, especially the timing of when they can claim their property.

In a traditional family trust set up by a settlor, the rights of the beneficiaries are often immediate in the sense that their rights are immediately enforceable.

Consider this example of a vested interest:

Stuart (the settlor) creates a trust on these terms:

> 'To my wife, Dee, for her life, and on her death, to our daughters, Emmy and Fran, in equal shares'.

DOI: 10.4324/9781003583660-5

The terms are that Dee, Emmy and Fran are named as members of the settlor's family. Once this trust is fully constituted, the rights of Dee, Emmy and Fran are said to be *vested*. It is known immediately that they are entitled to their shares under the trust. There are no conditions to be fulfilled. However, although Emmy and Fran have *vested gifts*, there will be some delay because they are only enforceable when Dee has died. We refer to Dee's interest as a *life interest* and Emmy and Fran's interests as *remainder interests*. Their interests are *future interests*.

The law divides vested gifts into two groups: those *vested in possession* and those *vested in remainder*.

4.2.1 Vested interests can be vested in possession or in remainder

In the example above, Dee has a vested interest *in possession* because she has a right to any income immediately the trust becomes fully constituted, but Emmy and Fran each have an *interest in remainder*.

The reason for this is that Emmy and Fran have to wait until Dee has died before they can claim their interests in the trust. We will see later in the chapter that they may be able to accelerate their interests under the trust so they can receive them earlier.

It is also important to note that as Emmy and Dee have *vested interests*, they now each own an equitable interest which would form part of their assets. Although they are *future interests*, if anything happened to Emmy and Fran, their rights under the trust would pass with their estates.

4.3 Contingent gifts

The settlor Stuart in the example above could have laid down some specific conditions before Emmy and Fran could become entitled, e.g. to Dee for her life and to Emmy if she qualifies as an accountant and Fran if she becomes a solicitor.

Stuart could also have imposed an age contingency such as to Dee for life and then to the first of my children to reach the age of 30.

These are *contingent gifts*. When the trust is drawn up, if Emmy and Fran are still at school, there is no certainty that either Emmy will qualify as an accountant or Fran will qualify as a solicitor, in which case the shares are not *vested* but *contingent*. Likewise, you could argue that either Fran or Emmy may qualify for the interest by reaching the age specified.

Once Emmy qualifies as an accountant or Fran qualifies as a solicitor, then the interests become *vested*. If either of them decides that she wants to be an actress and not an accountant or a solicitor, then the gift will never become vested. The interests will be lost. If either of them dies before meeting the contingency, then the interest under Stuart's trust will be lost.

4.3.1 Types of contingency

The contingency will only be upheld if it is legal. A trust will be declared void if the condition is illegal. A term will be illegal if it breaks the law, such as a gift being denied if the recipient marries someone from a certain faith.

4.3.2 Failed contingent gifts

Where the settlor creates a *contingent gift*, there is a potential problem as to who can claim the property if the named beneficiary does not fulfil the criteria. Suppose the settlor had specified that the beneficiaries could only enjoy the gift if they had met the condition of becoming an accountant and none of them had satisfied it because no one amongst the group of beneficiaries wanted to become an accountant, then the fund would revert back to the settlor. This is a very unsatisfactory situation, and it is far better if a settlor has made alternative provision. So usually, contingent gifts will include a *gift over in default* in case the condition is not met.

The *gift over in default* will be enforceable if the contingency has not been fulfilled; so rather than the property going back to the settlor's estate, it will pass to another named beneficiary. Stuart may have named another beneficiary, Fergus, who is to benefit if Emmy fails to satisfy the contingency of becoming an accountant. Fergus will only benefit in these circumstances.

Stuart(settlor)____________________ Dee (for life)

Fran (if she becomes a solicitor)

Emmy (if she becomes an accountant)

------Fergus

(gift over in default)

4.3.3 Client advice

If you were advising a client who wished to attach a contingency to a gift under a trust fund such as reaching a certain age or fulfilling a certain condition, then you should always discuss what the settlor would like to happen if no beneficiary satisfies the condition. You would need to discuss the problem that if the contingency is not satisfied, the property will automatically revert back to your client's estate and advise that a second beneficiary (to receive the gift in default) should ideally be chosen in these circumstances.

4.4 The rule in *Saunders v Vautier*

You will have seen that a beneficiary with a *vested or contingent gift* is often faced with a long delay before any property passes to them. If you are advising clients who themselves have a *contingent or vested gift* under a trust, you can raise the possibility of bringing forward their entitlement under the rule in *Saunders v Vautier.* If this applies, then the beneficiaries can accelerate their gifts so they receive them much earlier than envisaged by the settlor.

In the scenario above, Fran and Emmy must wait until Dee has died to receive anything from the trust set up by Stuart. They may have real needs now, and so they may want to try to receive their shares before the death of Dee. However, there are strict rules before the rule can apply.

4.4.1 The mechanics of the rule in *Saunders v Vautier*

The rule allows beneficiaries to claim their share under the trust immediately and deal in the property in a particular way *or* bring the trust to an end if the following conditions are satisfied:

i) All the beneficiaries are of *full age*

ii) All the beneficiaries are of *sound mind*

iii) Together the beneficiaries are *absolutely entitled to the trust property*

iv) All the beneficiaries are in *full agreement*

In other words, the beneficiaries can collectively rewrite the terms of the trust and deal with it immediately as if it were their own.

Consider these facts:

A settlor, Pete, creates a trust of a share portfolio in favour of his wife, Queenie, for her life and then in equal shares to his three children, Rozz, Sam and Tariq. All the children are over 18. They want their shares now as they need the money for various projects and do not want to wait until after Queenie's death. Queenie is in agreement with them.

Your client Rozz comes to you to see whether it is possible to bring forward the date of her entitlement.

All four are of age and we presume are of sound mind and, when combined together, are absolutely entitled to the property, and the four are in full agreement. In this case, you can advise Rozz that all the beneficiaries combined can bring the trust to an end under the rule in *Saunders v Vautier*, and each can claim a share. If the rule applies, then the property will be divided equally between all the parties,

Compare the following facts:

Pete creates a trust of a share portfolio in favour of his wife Queenie and his three children Rozz, Sam and Tariq. Rozz wishes to set up a business and would like their share immediately. Sam and Tariq are both under the age of 18, and Queenie does not wish to bring the trust to an end.

Advise your client Rozz.

In this case, conditions (i) and (iv) are not satisfied. Not all the beneficiaries are of full age, and the life tenant, Queenie, does not agree with bringing the trust to an end. In this case, the rule in *Saunders v Vautier* will not apply. There is nothing Rozz can do at the moment to bring forward her enjoyment of her share in the trust.

She will have to wait until Sam and Tariq reach the age of 18 and whether or not Queenie changes her mind.

4.5 The rule against perpetuities

The law does not allow property to be tied up for long periods of time. This is because it is seen as making that property unavailable for transfer from one person to another. Lawyers refer to this as making property *inalienable*, meaning that during that time it cannot be transferred from one person to another.

In order to address that the law has laid down certain periods of time called *perpetuity periods* in which a gift must take effect. These vary according to the type of trust that has been created.

Consider this example:

Franz has inherited a large estate, and he wants to set up a trust of the estate for future generations of his family. Suppose he specified in the trust that he would like his estate to be held for the first of his great-grandchildren to reach 21. This would tie up the land for several generations. Franz may have children late in life, and so it could be many years before he has a great-grandchild.

4.5.1 The perpetuity period in law

The law has laid down a specific period in which a gift must *'vest'*. If the gift vests outside this period, it will fail.

The rule requires any gift to vest within a period specified at 21 years after the *life-time of a human being* alive at the creation of the trust.

The rule, therefore, is based on determining who is the *life in being* at the time the trust is created.

If the trust has named beneficiaries, then the *perpetuity period* is *'a life in being'* plus 21 years. The *'life in being'* can be named or can be implied from the context of the trust. Usually, the *'lives in being'* will be the named parties to the trust

4.5.2 The perpetuity period in practice

Consider this example:

Frederic leaves his estate to his wife, Gaynor, for her life and then to their son, Hal, with remainder to any of Hal's children who reach 21 years of age. This appears to tie up the property for a long period of time, but it is likely to be valid and it will not contravene the perpetuity period.

The law will consider all the parties. Gaynor and Hal will be assumed to be the *lives in being* as they are the two main parties to the trust:

- Firstly, on Frederic's death, the property will vest in Gaynor and she will have an immediate *right of possession* to enjoy the property;
- Secondly, on her death, Hal's interest will *vest in possession* and he will enjoy the property until his death; then
- Thirdly, the property will pass to any child of Hal who has reached 21. When Hal dies, there is no chance for further children, so it is only those children of Hal that can finally benefit.

In this case, each gift will comply with the perpetuity period. As Gaynor and Hal are the lives in being, the 21 years will not start until Hal's death, and any child of his alive at his death will reach 21 within the specified period.

Compare these facts:

Frederic has two children, Hal and Ira. He decides to set up a trust on the following terms:

> 'My entire estate to any grandchild who reaches the age of 21'.

The law will consider all the parties. Frederic, Hal and Ira will be assumed to be the lives in being at the time the trust was set up. The perpetuity period will be 21 years after the death of the last survivor of the 'lives in being'. The problem here is Frederic may go on to have a further child, Jude, who would not be 'a life in being' as he is not alive at the time the trust was created. If Frederic, Hal and Ira all die before Jude and Jude goes on to have children, the gift is going to vest 21 years after the death of the last survivor of the *'lives in being'*. The gift will fail.

Chapter 4 Revision Points

- A vested interest is one that gives the beneficiary a right to claim the interest without having to fulfil any conditions;
- A vested interest can be either in possession or in remainder;
- A contingent interest is one where a beneficiary must first satisfy a condition laid down by the settlor before being able to claim an interest;
- A contingent interest does not give the beneficiary any rights until the contingency is met;
- A gift must vest within the perpetuity period;
- The perpetuity period for most gifts is a 'life in being' plus 21 years;
- The rule in *Saunders v Vautier* allows the beneficiaries to claim property under a trust early if they satisfy the conditions.

5 Five non-charitable purpose trusts

Charitable trusts

5.1 Chapter overview

The last areas to consider under express trusts are two categories of trusts: the purpose trust, which will usually fail for lack of named beneficiaries, and charitable trusts. Although most purpose trusts fail, the law has occasionally allowed exceptions, and some trusts have been upheld for purposes rather than people. We will return again to the perpetuity period and apply that to purpose trusts. Charitable trusts are treated rather differently from all other trusts, including purpose trusts. We will discuss in the chapter the reasons why the law is so lenient with charitable trusts and also look at the various categories of charitable trusts.

5.2 Introduction to private purpose trusts

One of the main rules of an express trust is the need to satisfy the *three certainties* which we considered in detail in Chapter 1. You will recall that the three certainties are:

The intention to create a trust
Certainty of subject matter and
Certainty of object; in other words, who is entitled under the trust as a beneficiary

The law will not uphold trusts without *identifiable human beneficiaries*. A trust for private purposes will not be upheld because it has *no identifiable beneficiaries*. These are trusts that are created for a 'purpose'. One of the main reasons for the rule is to prevent the creation of trusts which cannot be enforced by an individual. If there are no beneficiaries, then there is no one to enforce the trust and to ensure that the trustees act properly. There are no safeguards in place in case the trustees act improperly or simply do nothing to carry out the terms of the trust.

Consider the following facts:

Two trusts have been set up by Hector, who has appointed Iris and Jude as trustees:

'£50,000 to be divided between my children'.

DOI: 10.4324/9781003583660-6

'£50,000 to promote happiness in the world'.

If the trustees fail to transfer the money to the children, then it is the children who can enforce the trust against the two trustees.

By contrast, there is no one obvious who will ensure that the trust promoting happiness is carried out by the trustees. You could also argue that the purpose of such a trust is uncertain.

How could you measure whether happiness is being promoted?

The second part of the trust will fail and the money will return back to the testator's estate.

Although this is a rule that has been enforced strictly, there are some very limited *exceptions*.

5.3 Exceptions to the principle preventing private purpose trusts

Trusts will be upheld for the following:[1]

- Trusts for named animals;
- The erection of a tomb or monument;
- A trust leaving money for saying masses in a church. The last exception has very rarely been applied, and where the mass is held in public, it will usually be upheld as a charitable trust.

Although these trusts will be upheld on principle, there is a further restriction on them.

5.3.1 The perpetuity rule for purpose trusts

The trusts still need to satisfy the *perpetuity rule*. This was discussed in the previous chapter.

As you will recall, it is a rule that tries to limit how long a trust can last. The *perpetuity rule* varies according to the type of trust. In Chapter 4, we looked at the perpetuity rule for express trusts with named beneficiaries; in this chapter, we are looking at purpose trusts coming within the exceptions mentioned above.

1 These were categories of non-charitable trusts upheld in the case of *re Endacott* [1960] Ch 232.

For all purpose trusts, the *perpetuity rule* is as follows: a purpose trust will be upheld if it lasts 21 years or less. Where it is uncertain whether the trust will last beyond 21 years, the courts can either take a pragmatic approach that the trust can last for 21 years and then it will fail if the named animal is still alive, or it will be void from the start.[2]

For purpose trusts there will not be a life in being so the perpetuity period is simply 21 years. So where money is left to a named animal the testator must think about the length of life that the animal may enjoy. Most domestic pets have a limited life expectancy, but there are exceptions such as parrots and tortoises, so the testator must be made aware of this. Either the trust will be upheld for the perpetuity period and then the money will cease to be held for the named animal or it will fail from the start. These are important rules because it is surprising how many people wish to leave property to a pet in their will, but normally they are domestic animals with a shorter lifespan!

Sometimes the testator uses words such as 'as far as the law will allow it' and that will save the gift.

5.3.2 Purpose trusts in practice

Consider the following facts:

Your client Janet Brown wants to make a will. She has no close family and wishes to include the following terms:

i) '£5,000 to my cat, Pickles';
ii) '£5,000 for the erection and maintenance of a gravestone in my memory after my death';
iii) '£5,000 to promote peace'.

Although the law is strict about ensuring that the object of a trust is certain, there are some unusual cases where the law has upheld a trust without a human beneficiary. Trusts for single named animals can be upheld under the law. This is an unusual exception to the rule about the need for every trust to have a human beneficiary.[3] One obvious point is that these trusts will be difficult to enforce since the beneficiary is an animal and cannot take action to enforce it. One can only assume that members of the judiciary have been animal lovers!

2 In *Re Haines* (1952) The Times 7 November, the court took judicial notice of the life expectancy of a cat, accepting that cats do not live beyond 21 years.
3 In *re Dean* (1889) 41 Ch D 552, a testator set up a trust of £750 to be paid annually for the maintenance of his horse and hounds.

i) In the above scenario, you can advise your client, Janet Brown, that she can leave money to Pickles. The law allows this even though Pickles is a cat and cannot enforce a trust. In practical terms, there is usually someone associated with Janet Brown who can ensure that the cat will be cared for. The only requirement is that it must satisfy the *perpetuity rule*. The law accepts the fact that cats do not generally live beyond 21 years;
ii) It is also possible to leave money to erect a gravestone in one's memory or in memory of another. Again, the *perpetuity rule* must be upheld. So, if the money left by Janet was just for the erection of the gravestone, the gift would succeed, but if it was for the erection and maintenance of a gravestone, then it would be likely to fail as it would last for many years and again would breach the *perpetuity rule*. Again, it can be saved if Janet uses words to ensure that the maintenance is only for 21 years.[4] Alternatively, it could be saved if the two gifts could be severed. This would mean that the gift to build the monument can go ahead, but the gift to maintain it would fail;
iii) The third gift is likely to fail because it is both uncertain and does not satisfy the rules of certainty of objects. It is not clear what is meant by the promotion of peace. We will consider later whether this gift could be upheld as a charitable gift, but it will *fail as a private purpose trust*. There are no obvious beneficiaries to enforce the trust.

On your client's death, any money left over once the gifts have been carried out will pass under what is known as the *residue* (any property not specifically left under the terms of the will).

5.3.3 Client advice

When meeting your client, you should explain the potential problems with the first and the third gift. Your client must specify what should happen to the money once Pickles dies. Should it pass with the residue, or is there someone who your client would like to benefit? You should point out the likelihood of the third gift failing and passing into the residue. It would be far better if she made provision now for the money in a way that will be upheld by law. You should also discuss with her what provision she may want to make for the *residue* should any other gift fail.

5.4 Charitable trusts

Charitable trusts are not in the SQE syllabus as they are public trusts, *but* they need to be understood as they provide an important comparison with purpose trusts, and

4 In *Musset v Bingle* [1876] WN 170, a testator had left a sum of money for the erection of a monument and a further gift for the maintenance of the monument, which could last well beyond the perpetuity period. The courts were prepared here to sever the two gifts. The gift to erect the monument was upheld, and the gift for its maintenance was declared invalid.

so this part needs to be understood and studied in conjunction with the previous section on private purpose trusts.

Charitable trusts are considered to be public trusts and are treated differently from *private trusts*. They are exempt from many of the rules of trusts, in particular, rules about their creation and the way that they operate. The reason they are exempt is because they are seen as being for members of the public in general, and so are trusts that provide a benefit for everyone.

In order to come within the definition, they do need to comply with certain key criteria.

i) They must be *exclusively charitable*. This means that their funds must only go to charitable objects;
ii) The purposes must be for the *public benefit*. This means for the public as a whole or for a sufficiently large section of the public.

5.4.1 Advantages of charitable status

- The objects of a charitable trusts do not have to be *certain*. The only requirement is that the settlor has specified that the funds must be used solely for charitable purposes. Unlike private trusts, charitable trusts are enforced by the Attorney-General;
- Charitable trusts do not have to comply with the *perpetuity rule*. It means that a charitable trust can last indefinitely;
- Charitable trusts have a number of *tax advantages* such as relief from income tax and capital gains tax;
- If a private trust fails, the funds go back to the settlor's estate. If a charitable trust fails, for example, because the charity has closed down, the funds can be applied for another similar charitable purpose. This is called the *cy-pres doctrine*.

5.4.2 The main categories or 'heads' of charitable purposes

For centuries, there was no definition of a charitable purpose, but now there is a statutory list of what purposes are charitable.

There are 12 'heads' of charity laid down in the Charities Act 2011 and one residual category:

- **The prevention or relief of poverty.** The law recognises that there are degrees of poverty. Case law suggests that people who have to 'go short' in the ordinary meaning of that term can be regarded as 'poor'.[5] The important point is that the trustees can choose only to benefit those who are 'poor';

5 This term was used in *re Coulthurst* p1951] 1 WLR 910.

- **The advancement of education.** This has always been a wide category, but it must include an element of teaching or education rather than just the increase of knowledge.[6] This group includes providing funds for buildings and also providing scholarships;
- **The advancement of religion.** This covers a wide range of religions where followers believe in a supreme being or entity. Advancement includes pastoral and missionary work as well as practical contributions towards buildings.
- **The advancement of health** (this head includes the prevention or relief of sickness, disease or human suffering);
- **The advancement of citizenship or community development.** This head includes rural or urban regeneration and volunteering;
- **The advancement of arts, culture, heritage or science;**
- **The advancement of amateur sport** (games which promote health by involving physical or mental skill or exertion);
- **The advancement of human rights, conflict resolution or reconciliation or the promotion of religious or racial harmony, equality or diversity.** This is a relatively new head of charity. The key problem is that charitable purposes must not pursue political objectives;
- **The advancement of environmental protection or improvement;**
- **The relief of those in need because of youth, age, ill-health, disability, financial hardship or other disadvantage.** This head is quite separate from the relief of poverty. It is looking at a special need arising through the specified heads such as 'age'. So subsidised housing for elderly people would be upheld even if the beneficiaries had to make a substantial financial contribution;
- **The advancement of animal welfare.** Under this head, it is important to differentiate between trusts for single named animals or groups of animals which would not be charitable and trusts under this head which will be upheld so long as there is an element of public benefit. This does not necessarily mean the public should be allowed access. The care of the animals should be sufficient;
- **The promotion of the efficiency of the police, fire and rescue services or ambulance services;**
- **Any other existing charitable purposes or analogous purposes.**

Consider the following:

Your client, Clive, has a number of varied interests and wishes to set up a trust in support of some of them. He would like your opinion as to whether the following purposes would be considered to be charitable.

i) A trust to set up unemployed people in a trade or business;
ii) A trust for the publication of law reports;

6 *Re Shaw* [1957] 1 WLR 729 failed as a trust to advance education. The writer George Bernard Shaw had attempted to set up a charitable trust to replace the 26-letter alphabet with a 40-letter alphabet.

iii) A trust to set up gyms in order to promote health and well-being. A monthly fee of £75 is to be charged to each member;
iv) A trust to promote general awareness of human rights and to assist members in putting pressure on the Government to change its policies;
v) A trust to provide sheltered and safe homes for stray cats. The public will not be allowed access.

5.4.2.1 Client advice

i) The law would uphold any trust which seeks to find jobs for the unemployed as charitable. They would be regarded as someone 'in need', so this would be charitable.[7] *Charitable*;
ii) It was held in the *Incorporated Council of Law Reporting for England and Wales* [1972] Ch 73 that the publication of law reports advanced education and would therefore be charitable. *Charitable*;
iii) Normally a trust to set up gyms would be upheld as it would advance health. In fact, these gyms are specifically set up for that purpose, but the high monthly charge, which does not appear to allow discounts for poorer people, would prevent this from being charitable.[8] *Not charitable*;
iv) A trust to promote understanding of human rights would usually be charitable, but this trust has an ancillary political purpose, so it would not be charitable.[9] *Not charitable*;
v) This trust appears to advance animal welfare. Care of stray animals comes within the head of charity. The fact that the public is not granted access will not prevent it from being charitable because it promotes humanity and morality to care for animals in this way.[10] *Charitable*.

5.4.3 Public benefit

Public benefit is not defined in the statute. It has developed through case law. It has been applied more leniently under some heads, e.g. the relief of poverty, than others.

5.4.3.1 Public

The trust must benefit either the public in general or a sufficiently large section of the public. It is important that, even where the group is large, it is not connected to the settlor personally except in the case of the relief of poverty.

7 *IRC v Oldham Training and Enterprise Council* [1996] STC 1218. This case decided that such a purpose was charitable.
8 See *Nuffield Health v London Borough of Merton* [2021]EWCA Civ 826.
9 See *R v Radio Authority ex p Bull* [1998] QB 294.
10 See *Re Moss* [1949] 1 All ER 495.

5.4.3.2 Benefit

The benefit must be tangible and measurable, and the benefit must outweigh any detriment suffered at the same time.

With the exception of charitable trusts that aim to reduce poverty, the law does not allow a personal nexus between the settlor and the charitable objects.

Compare these facts based on two well-known cases and decide if they will be charitable or not:

i) A settlor created a trust to provide for the education of all employees and ex-employees of a company or any of its subsidiary companies. The number of employees who could qualify exceeded 110,000.[11]

Could this be a charitable trust? Will it pass the public benefit test?

A trust to provide education will be a charitable trust. It comes under the advancement of education. However, it fails the public benefit test because there is a personal nexus between the employees and their employer, and this prevents it from benefiting the public as a whole or a section of it. *Not charitable*.

ii) A settlor created a trust for his 'poor and needy' relatives provided that they were born within 21 years following his death. There are currently 26 persons within the category.[12]

Could this be a charitable trust? Will it pass the public benefit test?

The public benefit test for any trust addressing the poverty exception will be treated more leniently than trusts in the other heads of charitable purposes. A trust for the advancement of education, as mentioned above, would fail where there is a personal nexus between the settlor and the potential beneficiaries. If the trust is for 'poor and needy' relatives, it will be upheld even where the potential group of beneficiaries is quite small. *This can be upheld as a charitable trust*.

11 The facts are based on *Oppenheim v Tobacco Securities Trust* [1951]AC 297.

12 The facts are based on the case of *Re Segelman* [1996] 2 WLR 173. In this case, the potential group of beneficiaries was 26.

Chapter 5 Revision Points

- Purpose trusts will not generally be upheld because they do not have human beneficiaries;
- There are some limited exceptions allowing purpose trusts, namely single animals and the erection and maintenance of a memorial;
- Purpose trusts within the exception will only be upheld if they comply with the perpetuity period;
- Charitable trusts are public trusts. They are treated more generously in law than private trusts;
- A charitable trust will only be upheld if it is exclusively charitable and for the public benefit;
- The different heads of charity are now defined within statute.

5.5 Multiple-Choice Questions

Question One

Ezra is a wealthy businessman, and he has approached you as he wishes to set up a trust. He asks for your advice on the validity of one of the terms in the trust, which is set out as follows.

'£2 million for the provision of temporary housing for my impoverished family members'. Ezra tells you that he has a large family and he regards at least 20 as being impoverished.

Which of the following statements best represents the advice that you should give to Ezra?

A. This is an invalid purpose trust because the beneficiaries are not clear.
B. This is an invalid charitable trust because the beneficiaries have a personal nexus to the settlor.
C. This is an invalid charitable purpose trust because it is providing housing for family members of the settlor.
D. This is an invalid charitable trust because it fails the public benefit test for charitable trusts.
E. This is a valid charitable trust because the public benefit test is relaxed in trusts for the relief of poverty.

Question Two

Eddie asks you for your advice on the following matter. His uncle, Alan, has recently died, and Eddie is the residuary beneficiary. There is a term within the will which reads as follows:

'£50,000 to the Beamshire Parish Council for the installation of a statue in the park in my memory. £10,000 for the maintenance of the statue thereafter'.

As residuary beneficiary, he wishes to know if this gift is valid.

Which of the following statements best represents the advice that you should give to Eddie?

- **A.** This is an invalid purpose trust because it infringes the perpetuity period.
- **B.** This is an invalid purpose trust because the erection of a statue in the park does not come within any of the exceptions upheld by law.
- **C.** This is a valid purpose trust because it is possible to sever the erection of the statue from its maintenance.
- **D.** This is a valid purpose trust as it comes within one of the named exceptions for purpose trusts
- **E.** This is a valid purpose trust because the amount set aside for maintenance will run out before the end of the perpetuity period.

6 Implied trusts

Resulting trusts

6.1 Chapter overview

So far, this book has been concentrating on the *express trust* so it has examined what a settlor has to do in order to create an express trust. It has been looking at the situation when the settlor takes the active decision to create a trust. You will recall also that an express trust must satisfy certain key requirements: the three certainties; it must be fully constituted, and all the formalities of transfer must be satisfied. These are all strictly enforced. This chapter focuses on the second type of trust, namely an *implied trust*. This type of trust comes into effect in a different way to an express trust. *Implied trusts* can come into effect even where the settlor does not necessarily want a trust. It may be that the settlor never thought about the possibility of a trust. The key thing to note in this chapter is that implied trusts arise through the *operation of law*, which means the law is responding to a set of circumstances. Implied trusts often arise in informal circumstances, so there is no need to satisfy strict formalities such as the need to show that there is written evidence of the intention to create a trust. Indeed, these trusts do not require proof of intention to create a trust. The chapter examines the first type of *implied trust*: the *resulting trust* and explores the various circumstances in which it can arise.

6.2 Different types of resulting trusts: general overview

There are two types of *resulting trust*: the *automatic resulting trust* and the *presumed resulting trust*. In this chapter, we shall be looking at the definition of both types of resulting trust and then look at each in more detail.

A *resulting trust* literally means that the trust property 'results' or 'springs back' to the settlor. It often comes into operation when a settlor attempts to create an express trust but it fails because the requirements have not been satisfied. In these circumstances, the trust property returns to the estate of the settlor. *Resulting trusts* are divided into two groups which arise in different circumstances.

DOI: 10.4324/9781003583660-7

6.2.1 Failure of an express trust

A resulting trust will occur where an *express trust fails*. The law has to be clear about ownership of property. We discussed in Chapter 1 that once an express trust has been created, the property immediately belongs to the trustees on behalf of the beneficiary. If the trust fails, the most obvious owner of the property will be the original settlor. The settlor may not have thought about what should happen to their property if the trust fails for any reason, so the law steps in and offers a solution. The property is still held by the trustees, who now hold as trustees for the settlor rather than the beneficiaries. This type of resulting trust is referred to as an *automatic resulting trust*. We will discuss this in more detail later.

Consider these facts:

Suppose a fund is set up for the building of a brand-new hospital in Norfolk. Collections are made amongst local people, and local businesses have agreed to match fund the amount. The fund gathers momentum, and contributions come from a number of donors. It later becomes impossible to build the hospital because the chosen site is declared unsuitable.

This poses the question of what should be done with the funds raised?

If the original purpose was charitable, then the funds can be applied to another charitable purpose. But suppose the purpose doesn't come within the definition of a charity; what should happen to the funds?

The obvious choice is to return the money to the original donors as they had contributed their money for a specific purpose and that cannot now be fulfilled. In those circumstances, the law declares that the money should go back to the donors on an *automatic resulting trust*.

6.2.2 Purchase of land or property in the name of another

Secondly, a resulting trust occurs where money is provided for the purchase of land but it is purchased in the name of another. This is a different situation from the one described above, but the outcome will be the same as the property will remain with or return to the settlor. This type of resulting trust is often referred to as a *'purchase money resulting trust'* or a *'presumed resulting trust'*.

6.2.2.1 Why do we have this rule?

It is based on the idea that no one willingly gives away their property. This is referred to in law as a *presumed intention*. If you give someone money to buy a house, then surely you would expect to have a share in the property. Of course, it will turn on the reason why you gave the money and whether you made it clear that the money was a gift and you did not wish to have a share.

This rule is not just restricted to the purchase of land; it can also apply to personal property. In cases of a lottery syndicate, anyone who purchases lottery tickets in the name/s of others will hold any winnings as resulting trustee for them.[1]

E.g. your friend suggests that you buy five lottery tickets together every week. You hold the money and make the purchase, but you hold it on resulting trust for your friend, so any winnings must be handed over to your friend according to how much they paid towards the tickets.

6.3 Automatic resulting trusts

An automatic resulting trust arises where there is a *surplus of trust money* because the purpose of a trust has failed for some reason or the purpose has been satisfied. In those circumstances, the law imposes a resulting trust. This means that any surplus property goes back to the original settlor. *Automatic resulting trusts* do not necessarily reflect the intentions of the original settlor. We looked at an example above in relation to the building of a hospital. The donors had probably not thought about what should happen to their money if for any reason the hospital was not built, but if they had done so, they would probably have said, 'I would like my money returned to me'.

The law has to distinguish between whether there has been a *failure of the trust* or whether the transfer can be regarded as an *absolute gift*. Where a trust fails because the wording does not show a clear intention to impose a trust, then the property might pass as a gift.

Below are a series of examples: A, B, C and D; some of the examples are based on well-known cases. Look at the wording used in each example and then look at the way each case would be decided and the reasons for the decision.

A. Trust failing for uncertainty of object

Consider the following facts:

Gemma declares a trust on the following terms: 'I give £50,000 to be distributed between my closest friends'. This gift satisfies certainty of intention and subject matter, but as we noted in Chapter 1, making a gift to 'closest friends' will not satisfy the test for *certainty of object*.

1 In *Abrahams v Trustee in Bankruptcy of Abrahams* [2000] WTLR 593, a wife separated from her husband continued to make payments into a lottery syndicate. The syndicate won, and the trustee in bankruptcy who had taken over her husband's estate claimed the winnings. This was rejected by the court on the basis that Mrs Abrahams had made a voluntary payment on his behalf, and the syndicate therefore held any winnings on resulting trust for her.

The whole trust will therefore fail.

The key question here is if the trust fails for uncertainty of object, who then owns the property?

The logical conclusion is that the property should return to the settlor, Gemma. If the gift fails because the objects named by Gemma are too uncertain, then the property should go back into Gemma's estate.

There have been arguments that the property should go to the state in these circumstances, but this is difficult to justify.

B. Trust failing for uncertainty of intention

Compare these facts:

'I leave £50,000 to my wife, Kati, in full confidence that she will benefit our three children'.[2] The law would not regard the words 'in full confidence' as incorporating a clear intention to impose an obligation on Kati. Without such an obligation, there is no intention to create a trust.

So, can Kati now claim the money for herself or would it return to the settlor's estate?

The direction is clear: 'I leave £50,000 to my wife, Kati'. In these circumstances, Kati can enjoy the property.

C. Surplus funds left after the purpose of a trust has been carried out: no gift intended

Compare the following facts:

A collection was made amongst the residents of a small town for the care and maintenance of two elderly ladies in need.

The money was transferred to the two ladies and was used for their care and maintenance, but on their death, there was a surplus. (These facts are based on a well-known case on automatic resulting trusts.)

What do you think should be done with the surplus monies?

2 Consider the facts of *Adams and Kensington Vestry* (1884) 27 Ch D, where similar wording was used. It was held that no trust was imposed on the wife.

Should it return or 'result back' to the people who gave the money, or should it pass to the relatives of the two ladies?

In this case, compared to the previous example, there is no indication that the money was to be enjoyed by the old ladies for anything other than their care. If there is no evidence of an outright gift, then the money should go back to the original contributors.[3]

The outcome would be different if there were anything in the way the gift was worded by the settlor to suggest that it could be an absolute gift. It could also be different if, for instance, the beneficiaries were still alive. If a gift was made to a child for their education and there was money left over after they left further education, it is possible to argue that that money was for them absolutely after using it for the primary purpose of their education, and so they could keep any surplus for themselves. We discuss this in the following section.

D. Surplus funds left after the purpose of a trust has been carried out: gift intended

Compare the following facts.

Look at these facts and decide who can keep the money after Y finishes her university education.

X makes a gift to his widow 'for her maintenance and... to my daughter, Y, for her training... up to university grade...'.[4] The daughter completes her university education. Y's mother dies, and on her death, there is surplus money from the original gift. There is a residuary beneficiary of X.

Who has the right to claim the money?

The settlor's estate or the child, Y?

These facts are based on a true case. The surplus money could be kept by the daughter. The reason was that the settlor had not been specific about the use of the money.

3 These facts are similar to those of *Re Trusts of the Abbott Fund* [1900] 2 Ch 326. The money given to the two ladies was returned to the donors. It did not pass to the family on the death of the ladies.

4 These facts are based on the case of *Re Osaba* [1979] 2 AER 393. The actual facts in this case were as follows: a testator set up a trust 'for the training of my daughter, Abiola, up to university grade and for the maintenance of my aged mother'. The mother died and Abiola had finished her university education leaving a surplus in the fund. In this case, the claimants were the daughter, Abiola, and the testator's second wife and daughter who had been left the residuary estate by the testator. The Court of Appeal decided that the wording of the gift indicated that the settlor intended an absolute gift.

It could be considered to be merely an expression of hope or wish. It could be held that X had merely indicated a general use for the money.

6.3.1 Client advice

If you are advising a client who wants to leave money to a named individual to be used by the donee for a specific purpose, then it is important to explain the consequences if there is a surplus of money once the purpose has been carried out. You need to explain that a decision must be made as to what should be done with that surplus. The client will need to understand the difference between an outright gift with an indication of use of the money or a gift only for use for the purposes specified.

6.3.2 Quistclose trusts: money transferred for a specific purpose which cannot be carried out

Another example of an *automatic resulting trust* occurs when money is transferred for a specific purpose but cannot be carried out because there are specific obstacles in the way.

If that purpose cannot be carried out, who can claim the sum of money that has been transferred for the specific purpose?

We considered these circumstances at the start of the chapter when looking at money left over after fundraising for the building of a hospital. In that case, we assumed that the money would result back to the contributors, although there are practical reasons why that would be difficult to achieve.

It becomes even more complicated in a commercial situation where the transferee of the money goes bankrupt. The transferor will want to recover their money in full and try to argue that their claim is ahead of general creditors.

6.3.3 Quistclose trusts

This situation arose in an important case called *Barclays Bank v Quistclose*.[5] The case has given rise to a type of trust called a *'Quistclose trust'*. The case concerned a loan made by a company called Quistclose to a company called Rolls Razor. The purpose of the loan was to pay out dividends to investors to encourage investment. The problem was that Rolls Razor was in serious financial difficulties and before the dividends were paid out it went into liquidation. The liquidators, who were Barclays Bank, claimed the money as part of the assets of the company, but Quistclose argued that the purpose of the loan had failed and so the money should result back to it.

5 [1970] AC 567

This argument was successful and the money was returned in full to the lenders. It was important that in this case the money had been *assigned expressly for a purpose*, i.e. to pay a dividend to the shareholders. This has become very significant in the law on bankruptcy as it is a way for a creditor to recover the money loaned in full rather than simply to be relegated to the list of general creditors. Unless Quistclose was successful in arguing this, their claim for the money loaned would simply have been distributed amongst the general creditors.

6.3.4 How do we know if money has been assigned for a purpose?

Consider what circumstances would be key in this situation.

The case law shows us that:

- The purpose must be clear and not open to interpretation;
- Another important feature is keeping the money separate from general funds even if they are mixed in a bank account;
- If it is in the general funds of the borrower, the most important feature is whether the funds can be used for *general purposes* or is that money being kept for the one named purpose?

6.4 Presumed resulting trusts

Presumed resulting trusts that are imposed by law but appear to give general effect to the intentions of the settlor, although such intention is *presumed*.

These trusts do not give effect to an express intention.

The law is just drawing a conclusion based on the fact that most people do not mean to give away property or their rights in property.

Consider this example of the way a *presumed resulting trust* works in practice.

X provides the money to Y for Y to buy a house in their name.

We do not know any facts about who X is or who Y is, and we do not know the circumstances of the purchase. Without knowing any other facts, the law will draw certain conclusions and hold that Y now owns the property on resulting trust for X. So if Y later sold the house, the money would be held for X.

Why does the law presume this?

We presume that the main motive for X to provide the money is so that X will have an interest in the new house.

6.4.1 Rebutting the presumption of a resulting trust

Sometimes the transferor may intend to give away property by way of a gift, in which case no resulting trust will be imposed. If there was evidence in our example that X intended Y to own the property absolutely and X did not intend to keep any interest, then there would be no resulting trust. This is referred to as *rebutting the resulting trust*.

6.4.1.1 Evidence of an outright gift

Consider these facts:

Felix has paid part of the cost of the purchase of a semi-detached house at 21 Hill Road. The property is registered in the sole name of Begum. In these circumstances, although Felix is not named as owner at the Land Registry, the law will automatically imply that he has a share of the property. Felix has an equitable interest in the property and will remain part owner of the property, although he is not registered as a legal owner. Begum will hold the property as trustee for them both.

This arises automatically and does not depend on any discussion between Felix and Begum about who should own the property.

Of course, the principle would not apply if there are other facts that show Felix never intended to have a share in the property.

Perhaps Felix had written to Begum at the time of the purchase and said, 'I want you to have this property for yourself and I do not want any share in 21 Hill Road; this house is for you'.

6.4.2 Presumption of advancement

In some relationships within a family, the law will automatically presume that an outright gift was intended. No discussion about whether it is a gift or not is needed. This is called the *presumption of advancement*. The relationships where this arises are actually rather out of date and relate to a time when the ability to earn money and own property was restricted for certain groups.

6.4.2.1 Husband and wife

For instance, it arises where the man in a married relationship provides the money for the purchase of property in the name of his wife, but it does not arise where a wife provides the money for the purchase of property in the name of her husband. It also does not apply where a mother gives money to a child for the purpose of purchasing property.

6.4.2.2 Father and child

The presumption also arises between father and child, but it is limited to fathers, so property purchased by a mother for a child will not attract the presumption. It will apply where the transferor is in *loco parentis* to the child. This means that the man is acting as if he were the child's father, so evidence would be needed to show that the person was acting as if he were a parent.

There have been cases which have challenged the limits of these presumptions, but they still stand today.

Consider the following two examples:

i) Eli is the father of Arif. He says to him, 'I have some spare cash, and I am going to give you £40,000 towards the purchase of a house'. Arif finds a one-bedroom flat, and Eli contributes the £40,000 towards it as agreed. Arif completed on the sale last week.

Under the rules of a *presumed resulting trust*, Eli would have a share in the property as he contributed towards the purchase.

Under the *presumption of advancement*, as he is Arif's father, the law presumes it was a gift. So the presumed resulting trust is rebutted by the presumption of advancement.

The presumption of advancement could also be rebutted. This could happen if Eli had said to Arif, 'I want you to have this money now to buy the flat, but it is not an outright gift for you'.

ii) Ezra is married to Begum, and she sees a beautiful house by the sea whilst they are on holiday. She says, 'I really want this house so I can build a yoga centre for me and for my friends. This site is perfect for it'. Ezra has some spare cash because he has had a lucky win on the lottery, and he gives her the money to buy the house.

Under a *presumed resulting trust*, Ezra will have a share in the property.

Under the *presumption of advancement* because Ezra is Begum's husband, the presumption of a resulting trust is rebutted, and Begum could argue that the house is hers absolutely.

The presumption of advancement could also be rebutted. This could be rebutted by evidence that he never intended her to have absolute ownership. For example, he could have said at the time of the purchase, 'I want you to have this house but I want a share in it as well'. Then the *presumption of advancement* is rebutted.[6]

In both these examples, there is *firstly* a presumed resulting trust in Ezra's favour, and then *secondly*, a presumption of advancement would apply. Because of the relationship between Ezra and Arif and Ezra and Begum, it then means the resulting trust will not apply. As discussed above, the presumption of advancement can also be rebutted, so that would allow Ezra to retain a share in both the house purchased by Arif and the house purchased by Begum.

Presumed resulting trusts and the presumption of advancement

ELI (£40,000) <———————————————— ARIF (SON)
(FATHER) (presumed resulting trust. House owned at law by Arif. Eli owns in equity)

|

(Presumption of advancement applies)
ELI (FATHER) ————————————————> ARIF (SON)
(House owned at law and in equity by ARIF)

Before we leave the topic of the *presumption of advancement*, we need to briefly mention *s.199 of the Equality Act 2010*. This section appears to abolish the presumption of advancement so you would assume it would no longer apply, **but** the section has not been brought into force so this old-fashioned presumption remains.

6.4.3 Client advice

If you are approached by a father wishing to help a child purchase property, it is important to discuss whether or not they wish to retain a share in the property. The law will assume that the contribution is a gift, but any evidence indicating that they wish to retain an interest in the child's property will rebut that, as the presumption of advancement is a presumption that is easy to rebut.

6 A good example of this happening in practice can be found in the case of *McGrath v Wallis* [1995] 2 FLR 114, where a family home was purchased in the name of a son. At the time, a declaration of trust had been drawn up, but it had not been signed. This would not have been a valid declaration of a trust of land, but this was accepted as evidence that the father had not intended an outright gift to the son. It served to rebut the presumption of advancement.

6.4.4 A transfer for illegal purposes

In some circumstances, property may be transferred from X to Y for an illegal purpose. The most obvious example would be where someone is in financial difficulties and thinks they may be about to be declared bankrupt.

The natural reaction is to try to transfer as much of your property as possible to family members before the declaration to minimise the amount that will fall into the hands of the trustee in bankruptcy. In most cases, such transfers cannot take effect as the trustee in bankruptcy will look at transfers made immediately before the declaration of bankruptcy. But supposing one transfer did take effect, how will the law view such a transfer?

Consider this example:

Amos transfers 500 shares in a listed company to his wife, Bea. This was done with the intention of hiding the shares from his creditors. He then tried to claim the shares back from his wife, arguing they were never intended for her as a gift.

Will the transfer of the shares from Amos to Bea be upheld as a *gift*?

Or will the shares be held on *resulting trust* by Bea for the transferor?

The answer will depend on whether or not the court will be prepared to admit evidence from Amos that he did not intend to make a gift to Bea and the only reason he transferred the shares to her was because he was trying to defeat his creditors.

Today it may be possible to admit the evidence of Amos in support of his claim to the shares.

Before 2016 and the decision of the Supreme Court in *Patel v Mirza*,[7] the court would not have been prepared to accept this evidence. The reason given was that it would have involved pleading an *illegal purpose*. The previous law depended on whether or not the claimant needed to rely on the illegal purpose. The law did not want to be

7 [2016] UKSC 467. *Patel v Mirza* concerned an illegal agreement between the claimant and the defendant. The claimant transferred £620,000 to the defendant intending the defendant to place a bet on share movements using insider information. This would constitute a criminal offence. The plan was never carried out and the defendant refused to return the money. The claimant sued for breach of contract. The defendant argued that he could retain the money as its recovery depended on relying on evidence of an illegal agreement. The Supreme Court held that the money should be returned. The claimant could recover his money because the illegal purpose had never been carried out but it may still have been possible for him to recover the money as the defendant would have been unjustly enriched had he been able to keep it. The court laid down the circumstances in which a claimant can rely on evidence of an illegal purpose.

seen as condoning illegal motives and contracts. Today the approach of the court is more pragmatic as shown below.

NB For the SQE you need to know whether or not evidence of an illegal purpose will be admissible in a civil case to support a claim based on the principles of *Patel v Mirza*.

The case of *Patel v Mirza* changed the rules on the admission of an illegal plan as evidence to support a claim. The court now has *discretion* whether or not to admit it. The case laid down circumstances which should be considered in deciding whether or not to admit evidence. The court concentrated on balancing the need to allow some claims which depended on evidence which in itself displayed an illegal purpose and the need to ensure that the integrity of the legal system as a whole was not harmed.

The circumstances laid down by the Supreme Court are outlined below. You should use these as guidance where you are presented with a problem which will need to rely on evidence of an illegal transaction for proof.

6.4.5 Circumstances when a claimant can rely on an illegal purpose as evidence in support of a claim

The court thought that the overriding concern should be to *uphold the legal system*, so would allowing the evidence challenge that?

- What was the underlying purpose of the prohibition of the conduct?
- The impact on other public policy considerations in denying the claim;
- Whether or not the denial of the claim would be a proportionate response to the illegal purpose of the parties (this involves looking at issues such as the seriousness of an unlawful transaction, the extent to which it is central to the contract and whether it is intentional conduct).

Consider these facts:

Mrs Conn is purchasing a large piece of land on which she wishes to build some houses. She asks a firm of solicitors, Bradders and Co, to represent her. She is relying on a mortgage to make the purchase. Unknown to the solicitors, she has made a number of false representations to the lenders, so the money she receives has been received fraudulently. Bradders and Co represent her during the purchase, but they fail, through their own negligence, to register the title to the land in Mrs Conn's name. The failure to register results in a significant loss to Mrs Conn. She sues the solicitors to recover her loss. Bradders and Co argue that they should not be liable and that Mrs Conn's claim should be barred through illegality.

On the basis of the reasoning discussed above, do you think a court would uphold Mrs Conn's rights?

- Consider the underlying *prohibition of the conduct* (Mrs Conn's false information given to the lenders);
- The impact on *public policy considerations* if the claim is refused (the general public rely on solicitors to give advice on legal matters and there should be sanctions if they give the wrong advice or act negligently);
- Would the refusal of Mrs Conn's evidence in support of her claim be *proportionate to her illegal purpose?* (Here you need to consider the seriousness of the unlawful transaction i.e. the fact that Mrs Conn lied to the lenders.) Was this central to the contract for the purchase of the land? Was it intentional conduct?

These facts are based on the case of *Grondona v Stoffel and Co* [2020] UKSC AC 540, and in that case, the Supreme Court was prepared to uphold the claim of the purchaser. On the facts, although she had given false information to the lenders, her claim was based on the negligence of the defendant solicitors. On the facts above, Bradders and Co could not rely on the defence of illegality.

Chapter 6 Revision Points

- There are two types of implied trust: the resulting trust and the constructive trust;
- Resulting trusts are divided into two types: presumed resulting trusts and automatic resulting trusts;
- Presumed resulting trusts arise when property is purchased in the name of one person, but the purchase price is provided by another;
- The presumed resulting trust is based on the presumption that a transferor does not voluntarily transfer money without expecting a share in the property;
- The presumption of a resulting trust can be rebutted by evidence such as proving the money was intended as a gift or by the presumption of advancement;
- The presumption of advancement arises when the transferor and the transferee are limited to certain relationships: father and child, husband and wife;
- S.199 Equality Act 2010 abolished the presumption of advancement, but the section is not in force, so the presumption remains;
- The presumption of advancement can be rebutted by evidence that no gift was intended;
- Where the claimant needs to rely on conduct that is illegal, the illegality is not a bar to its admission;
- A court considers a number of factors before deciding whether illegality can be relied on as a defence by defendants to an action.

6.5 Multiple-Choice Questions

Question One

Winston sells luxury cars. Earlier this year, his friend Basil transferred £200,000 to Winston on the understanding that he would use the money to modernise his showroom. He only used a small amount of the money for this purpose and put the rest of the money, which amounted to £150,000, into his bank account. Winston was declared bankrupt last week. Basil wants to claim the £150,000.

Which of the following statements best describes the entitlement to the £150,000?

A. Winston holds the money on presumed resulting trust for Basil.
B. Winston holds the money as it was a transfer for his own use with merely an indication of what it should be used for.
C. Basil can claim a share of the money in the account but only as a creditor.
D. Winston holds the money on automatic resulting trust for Basil.
E. Basil can claim an interest in the showroom on presumed resulting trust, but he has no claim over the £150,000 in the bank.

Question Two

Timmy paid for the purchase of a flat which was registered in his girlfriend Suzi's name. He said he would pay because Suzi was a student at the time and did not have any money, whereas he had just inherited some money from his grandmother. They moved in together, but after three years, Timmy moved out, saying he did not think their relationship was going to work. Suzi sold the flat last week. Timmy wants the proceeds from the sale back from Suzi, but she is saying that the flat belongs to her as she is registered as the owner at the Land Registry.

Which of the following statements best describes the entitlement to the flat?

A. Suzi is entitled to claim all the proceeds from the sale of the flat because she is the registered owner at the Land Registry.
B. Timmy is entitled to claim the proceeds of sale from the flat because he paid for it.
C. Timmy and Suzi should share the proceeds of sale because they lived there together for three years.
D. Suzi and Timmy should share the proceeds of sale, but Timmy should receive more because he paid for it in the first place.
E. Suzi can claim the proceeds of sale for herself because the law will apply the presumption of advancement.

7 The constructive trust in general

Trusts of the family home; proprietary estoppel

7.1 Chapter overview

This chapter examines the *constructive trust*. This is the second type of *implied trust*. A constructive trust arises by operation of law in the sense that it is not usually based on the express intention of the settlor. Indeed, a constructive trust may sometimes be imposed in such a way that it is contrary to the wishes of the constructive trustee. In this chapter, we will be looking at some of the circumstances when a constructive trust comes into operation. It is used in a variety of situations, but one of the most significant is in relation to the family home. We will note here that, unlike a resulting trust, it is difficult to categorise all the circumstances when a constructive trust is imposed. There is no specific list in law, but in general, it is used to prevent *unconscionability*, in particular to prevent a recipient of property from retaining property for themselves personally when it would be *unconscionable* for them to do so.

The second part of the chapter will be spent looking at ownership of the family home. The constructive trust plays a very significant part in this, and it is rare today that the courts apply resulting trusts to the family home.

The chapter ends by looking briefly at the doctrine of proprietary estoppel, which can also be applied in deciding ownership of the family home.

7.2 Introduction to the constructive trust

The constructive trust is the second type of *implied trust*. It is similar to a resulting trust in that it also arises from the operation of law and not from an express or deliberate act of the parties. However, it arises in a number of different circumstances from a resulting trust, and it covers a much wider variety of situations. This makes it difficult to find a definition for it. However, underlying all the situations is one key feature, which is that the constructive trust arises when the *conscience* of the recipient of the property is affected.

In practice, it means that where appropriate, the law will regard property held by someone to be now held by them as a constructive trustee on behalf of someone

DOI: 10.4324/9781003583660-8

else. This applies where it would be *unconscionable* for the owner of the property to deny the rights of the other party.

7.3 Examples of when a constructive trust may arise

The role of what is meant by 'good conscience' needs to be examined so we understand when it may apply. Look at the following situations. They are all examples of how a constructive trust might apply because the behaviour of one of the parties can be seen as unconscionable.

Consider this example:

T1 is the trustee of a family trust. There are some valuable paintings amongst the assets of the trust. All the trustees wish to sell them to raise money for the trust. T1 decides to buy one of them named 'The Seagull' and offers £3,000. He thinks he is helping the trust but also knows it is a valuable painting and likely to be much sought after.

Later T1 finds out that the painting could be worth well over £7,000 if it had been sold at auction.

T1 has profited by being a trustee and the beneficiaries of the trust have lost £4,000.

Suppose T1 sold the painting for £7,000 the following week.

Can T1 keep the profit on the painting, or should that money be given to the trust?

In this case, T1 has used his position as trustee to make a personal profit when that profit should rightly be owned by the beneficiaries. T1 cannot keep the profit made; it will be held on *constructive trust* for the beneficiaries and should be transferred to them. In this case, T1's conscience has been affected. T1 must know that he has made a profit out of his position as trustee, and it would be wrong for him to retain that profit. In these circumstances, even if he had no knowledge of the value of the painting but still made a profit, he would be liable to pay this to the trust unless there had been full disclosure and an independent valuation of the trust property.

The role of the trustee and in particular the duties owed to the beneficiaries will be discussed in more detail in later chapters.

Consider this example:

A purchases property from B. The purchase is expressly subject to the rights of C to continue living in the property for as long as C wishes. Suppose B has personally granted rights to C. Is A subject to that right, particularly if it is a right that is not recognised as a right in the land but merely a right against B, such as a licence?

Suppose A, having agreed to C's rights within a year, tries to evict C, preventing C from enjoying the right. Can we argue that A's conscience has been affected? Perhaps A has had a reduction in purchase price and has signed an agreement promising to uphold C's rights during C's lifetime. Should A hold the property on constructive trust for C?[1]

The key feature here would be the advantage that A has obtained in negotiating a lower price for the property. This would affect A's conscience and make A's behaviour unconscionable. Simply knowing that C was living there will not affect A's conscience.

Constructive trust imposed where formalities have failed.

Another circumstance when a constructive trust may be imposed is where formalities have failed in a sale. We have already seen that certain transactions require specific formalities, e.g. land must be conveyed by a written document, so what happens if the formalities are not complied with? Sometimes the law will impose a constructive trust where the purchaser has taken advantage of the seller knowing that formalities are required but not telling the seller.

These are just three examples of when a constructive trust may be used. The list is not closed, and the court can always impose a constructive trust in any situation where, in good conscience, the receiver of property could not retain it. We will consider the constructive trust further when we look more closely at the duties of a trustee.

7.4 Trusts of the family home: informal trusts of the family home

This is a very important *category of constructive trusts* and should be considered in connection with the cases on a presumed resulting trust or purchase money resulting trust. Today rights in the family home where the parties are cohabiting but are neither married nor in a civil partnership will usually be decided on the basis of a constructive trust. It is rare today that a presumed resulting trust is used to decide rights in the family home although it may be used in other cases for the purchase of property. If a constructive trust is proved, then a resulting trust will no longer apply.

1 This situation arose in an old case called *Binions v Evans* [1972] Ch 359, and the court upheld the rights of C and found that they were binding on A. A held the property as constructive trustee. It would be unconscionable to deny C's rights as A had had a reduction in the purchase price and had agreed to honour C's rights as part of the purchase agreement.

7.4.1 Background to the law on trusts of the family home

In English law, where two adults live together in the family home and are not married or in a civil partnership, there is no presumption of 'community of ownership' of land; in other words, the law does not presume that both adults will receive a share of the property.

It is irrelevant how long the two adults have lived together or whether or not they have children. The law looks only at ownership of the land in law and also in equity.

The best solution to any disagreement about rights in the family home would be if the parties expressly stated how they wish the property to be shared between them; but where they fail to agree, then the law of trusts will apply.

7.4.2 Where the parties are married or in a civil partnership

If the parties are married or in a civil partnership, then different laws may apply to ownership of the family home. The law will allow a party who does not own at law or in equity the right to claim a share in the family home on the basis of their relationship rather than just looking at contributions or agreements.

Rights arise for married spouses under the *Matrimonial Causes Acts*[2] and for civil partners rights arise under the *Civil Partnership Act*.[3]

These Acts look at a wide range of practical aspects of the relationship when assessing rights in a family home; these include:

- How long has the relationship lasted
- Whether there are children of the relationship
- The standard of living enjoyed by the parties before the breakdown of the relationship
- If either party suffers from a disability

7.4.3 Ownership of the family home where the parties are cohabitants

If the parties are cohabitants, then ownership will be decided according to the *rules of property law*. This is because, there, law does not recognise cohabitation as a relationship giving rise to rights in the family home although there may be some rights arising in other contexts.

2 Matrimonial Causes Act 1973.
3 Civil Partnership Act 2004.

Many more people today choose to cohabit rather than enter into a legally recognised relationship, so if their relationship breaks down, the law has to fall back on the general rules of equity and trusts to decide who owns the family home.

7.4.3.1 Establishing an interest in the family home where there is no express agreement as to ownership

Where the parties are cohabitants and they have not expressly stated how they wish the land to be held the issue of ownership is resolved by asking a number of questions

Firstly, is the family home jointly owned at law? This means that both parties will have been registered as legal owners at the Land Registry.

If so, then the law automatically presumes *joint ownership in equity* so both parties can claim a share in the property and the presumption is in favour of *equal shares*. The size of contributions at this stage will not be relevant. This was decided in the key case of *Stack v Dowden*.[4] This case also established how one party may be able to claim a larger share in the value of the property.

The case shows that if there are factors that suggest the parties had *no intention to own the property equally*, such as where the parties *did not pool their assets* but instead kept their financial affairs separate, there would be a presumption against equality.

The courts will then consider all the facts and decide on how much each party can claim.

Secondly, if the family home is registered *at law in one name alone*, then other rules will apply. In these cases, the only way the claimant party can establish rights is if they can show they have rights under an express or implied trust.[5]

It is rare that the parties expressly agreed their interests under an *express trust*. Even if they did expressly agree their rights, you will remember that they would need to follow certain formalities, such as putting their intentions into writing.[6] If you think

4 [2007] UKHL 17. In this case, the parties were not married; they had four children and had been together for almost twenty years. They had contributed towards the purchase of the property in unequal shares, but both parties were paying towards the mortgage. The House of Lords decided that the shares should be 65% in favour of Ms Dowden and 35% in favour of Mr Stack.

5 These requirements were laid down in a case called *Lloyds Bank v Rosset* [1991] 1 AC 107. In an important judgement given by Lord Bridge, he held that rights will only arise if the claimant can show a common intention to share the property. In order to prove this, there must be evidence of an agreement or an understanding between the parties, or it can be inferred from financial contributions towards the purchase price.

6 The parties would need to show written evidence of their intentions to comply with s.53(1)(b).

about this situation, ordinary people will not look at the purchase of the property in the way lawyers might.

Imagine a young couple buying their first home together; it is unlikely that, firstly, they will discuss shares in the house they are buying and, secondly, that they will sit down and put their agreement into writing. The law of trusts is a complex area of law, and for most people, it is unlikely that they have enough knowledge of the requirements of a trust to satisfy the law.

There is another route that the claimant can take in order to prove rights in the family home which does not require a formal agreement in writing. The law will sometimes recognise an *informal agreement* between the parties to share the property or alternatively evidence that the other party has made a financial contribution towards the purchase of the property.

7.4.3.2 An informal agreement: a common intention constructive trust (1)

Case law shows us that there has been flexibility in what the court will accept as an informal agreement. What the courts are looking for is evidence of a *common intention to share the property.*

The law is looking to see if the parties actually discussed ownership of the property either on purchase or at a later date.

Examples of a common intention constructive trust

In one case, the legal owner of a property told his new partner that he would have put her name on the title, but he thought that she was too young to own property. This was, in fact, untrue as she was 18 and able to own property at the time because the law had recently changed, but the court accepted this as evidence of an agreement or an understanding.[7]

Another example of evidence to prove a common intention constructive trust was where the owner at law told the claimant that he had not added her name to the title because at the time she was divorcing her husband and he believed that she would get more if she did not own a share of his property.[8]

Compare the following facts which show that the law has not been consistent in what it views as sufficient evidence to prove an agreement.

7 These were the facts of two cases *Eves v Eves* [1975] 1 WLR 1338. The couple had not properly discussed ownership of the property.

8 *Grant v Edwards* [1986] Ch 638.

An owner of property said to the other party, 'you will be well provided for' and 'this will benefit us both'; neither statement was held to show evidence of an understanding.[9]

So it is important to see that in this area of law, there is still uncertainty as to which words will be sufficient to give rise to rights.

A cohabitant can only claim a share in property owned at law by the other party if they can show some evidence that satisfies the courts that the property is to be shared. The position would be different if cohabitants had rights in the same way as married couples and civil partners, but currently, it is unlikely that the rights of cohabitants will be recognised in the near future.

7.4.3.3 Client advice

If you were advising clients in a relationship embarking on the purchase of a home together, it is important to discuss how they wish to hold the property. It is important to record their wishes formally in the event of their relationship breaking down. They need to be advised whether they wish their shares to be equal or perhaps reflecting the size of their contributions. This is particularly important where a couple are cohabiting.

7.4.3.4 Detrimental reliance

Once a common intention to share has been established, a second requirement must be proved.

The claimant must prove acts of detriment in reliance of the common intention. This is also known as *detrimental reliance*.

So, what sort of acts will be considered *detriment*? The best proof of detrimental reliance is to show that there has been a financial contribution towards the property by the claimant. This could be payments towards the purchase price or the mortgage but will include paying for improvements to the property. Various acts have been acceptable; for instance, in *Eves v Eves* (mentioned above), the claimant could prove that she had carried out heavy building work on the property in which she had made a claim. Childcare was sufficient as proof of detriment in *Grant v Edwards*.

Note that informal acts can be regarded as *detriment*, but they can never be regarded as sufficient to give rise to *rights*; so remember, the first step always will be to look for evidence of a *common intention constructive trust*.

9 These were the words used in *James v Thomas* [2007] EWCA 1212.

7.4.3.5 Financial contributions towards the purchase price (2)

An easier and clearer way to establish rights is to show that a financial contribution has been made towards the purchase. Any direct financial contribution will give rise to rights in the property.

This will include an initial payment including costs of purchase such as the legal costs or surveyor's fees as well as contributions towards the deposit, purchase price or the mortgage.

Can *indirect contributions* towards the property count as financial contributions?

NB Payments towards living expenses, child care, domestic chores and maintenance of the property *will never count* towards the acquisition of rights in the property.[10] This is contentious as they may count in law where a couple are married or civil partners and increase the share, and these payments may also be counted as detrimental reliance.

Consider this example:

Owen owns a house and when he meets Nadia she quickly moves in with him. Nadia is a poet and earns little from her work. They have three children and she stays at home looking after them and also writing and publishing her poetry and performing her work. Everything she earns she puts towards the family expenses and pays for all the children's clothes and holidays in their caravan. After 15 years together, the relationship breaks down.

Nadia claims a share in the house which she says has been their family home for 15 years, and she argues that she has consistently spent all her money on the family expenses.

Will Nadia get a share?

Nadia will not get a share unless she can prove a common intention to share the property. Her indirect contributions will not be regarded as sufficient to infer that she was to get rights in the family home. They are not directly related to the property.

10 It was established in *Burns v Burns* [1984] Ch 317 that a cohabitant cannot rely on indirect contributions towards family life such as childcare and domestic duties even if carried out over a long period of time as giving rise to rights in the family home, even though it allowed the other party to work and earn money towards the payment of the mortgage.

Revision Points

How one party can claim rights in the family home under a common intention constructive trust:

- Are the parties in a relationship recognised in law as either *married* or *in a civil partnership*?
- If not, is there written evidence of an *express trust of the property*?
- If no express trust, is there evidence to establish a *common intention constructive trust*? Is there either evidence of an *express informal agreement*, or *could the court infer common intention from conduct*, i.e. *direct contributions towards the purchase price*?
- If there is evidence of a *common intention constructive trust* either through an informal agreement or financial contributions, is there evidence of *detrimental reliance*?

7.5 Quantifying the shares in the property: what size is the share for the claimant?

The court will have to decide the *size of shares* for each party once the claimant can show that

- They have an interest in the family home either under an *express trust* or an *implied trust*
- There is evidence of *detriment*

If the parties have *expressly agreed* how much each can claim in the property, then the agreement will be binding. As mentioned earlier, as it is unlikely that the parties will have agreed on whether a party will have a share, it is unlikely that they will have addressed the question of the size of each share.

If there is *no agreement*, then the court will have to decide the size of the share. Where property is *jointly owned*, the starting point will always be *equal shares*.

If there is evidence suggesting that the parties intended unequal shares, then the court has a fairly free hand in deciding this, and it may not be limited to the amount contributed to the purchase price.

Chapter 7 Revision Points – Constructive Trusts

- The constructive trust arises from the operation of law and not from an express or deliberate act of the parties;
- The constructive trust arises when the conscience of the recipient of property is affected by the receipt of the property;
- Ownership of the family home is often based on a common intention constructive trust of land;
- A common intention constructive trust depends on proof either of an informal agreement that the parties are to share ownership of the property or proof of a capital contribution towards the purchase, and there must also be proof of detriment;
- Indirect contributions cannot be proof of a contribution towards the purchase;
- The court assesses the shares under a common intention constructive trust unless the parties have already agreed the size of each share;
- Where property is jointly owned, the parties will usually have equal shares in the value unless one party brings evidence rebutting that.

7.6 Proprietary estoppel

7.6.1 Overview of proprietary estoppel

There is an alternative claim for rights in the family home under the *doctrine of proprietary estoppel*. This is also an informal basis of claim and does not require written proof.

In simple terms under the doctrine a landowner is prevented from denying rights in the family home to the claimant because a promise of rights in the property has been made to the claimant and the claimant has relied on that promise and acted to their detriment.

This is another informal way of acquiring rights in the family home and does not require strict formalities to be satisfied, but It is based on *four requirements*.

7.6.2 Four requirements for proprietary estoppel

i) A promise or assurance must be made by the legal owner A to the claimant B;
ii) The promise must be that B will be given rights in the land by the landowner;
iii) B must show that they have relied in some way on that promise or assurance;
iv) It would be detrimental to B if A now went back on the promise.

Consider this example:

Suppose Andrew, aged 80, said to his daughter Bea 'come and live in my house with your family; I cannot mange on my own anymore. If you do this I will transfer my house to you'.

Bea lives 100 miles away and has a good job as a head teacher. She has two children and a partner who has to give up their job and apply for a new job in the area.

Bea moves to the house and gives up her job as does her partner. If eight years later Andrew dies and under the terms of his will he leaves the house to a charity and not to her, Bea can make a claim based on the principle of *proprietary estoppel.*

Under the rules of land law, Andrew should have transferred the property to Bea by using formal documents, but the behaviour of Bea is such that the informal rules of proprietary estoppel will support Bea's claim. The promise was made orally, but because Bea resigned from her job, as did her partner, and moved to her father's house and changed her life in order to look after Andrew, the law will accept this behaviour as supporting Bea's claim.

7.6.3 Proprietary estoppel cannot be claimed

i) If an oral promise is made by A to B but B *does not act on it*
ii) If the promise does not involve *rights in land*

Consider this example:

A says to B, 'I will transfer my house if you move in with me'. B says she will do so but never acts on it. The promise cannot be enforced and B has no claim on the property.

Alternatively, if A says to B, 'If you move in with me, I will make sure you are financially secure'. This promise is unlikely to give B rights, as the promise does not involve rights in land.

In the example above, Bea will not be able to claim rights if Bea decides to move and come and look after her father, Andrew, because she is worried about him. The law on proprietary estoppel depends on a *promise of property rights.*

7.6.4 Client advice

It is important to advise clients in all dealings with property, particularly in relation to family members, to record their intentions in writing. In family relationships, promises are often made informally and actions taken in support without the party making the promise thinking about the full implications of the promise.

7.7 Remedies for the claimant in proprietary estoppel

The court has complete discretion in what remedy to award in proprietary estoppel to any claimant. This could include a monetary sum, the right to occupy the land or even the transfer of the legal estate.

7.7.1 Principles guiding the court in choice of remedy

i) Any remedy awarded must be proportional to the detriment suffered by the claimants;
ii) The remedy awarded must try to reflect the expectations of the claimant rather than compensate for the detriment suffered by the claimant.[11]

Chapter 7 Revision Points – Proprietary Estoppel

- Proprietary estoppel is an informal means of acquiring rights in property;
- It is based on the principle that it is unconscionable to go back on a promise of property rights if the claimant has acted to their detriment on that promise;
- Proprietary estoppel requires proof of a promise or assurance of property rights, reliance on that promise and detriment suffered;
- The court can grant a wide variety of remedies, but the remedy must be proportional to the detriment suffered and must reflect the expectations of the claimant.

7.8 Multiple-Choice Questions

Question One

Cassie and Dee live together. Five years ago, Dee purchased a property, 'Greenacres', in her name. At the time, she said to Cassie, 'This house belongs to us both'. Cassie pays for all the outgoings on the house and also all the day-to-day living expenses. Their relationship has broken down.

Cassie is claiming a share in the property, but Dee says, 'You paid nothing towards it; the house is mine'.

11 *Guest v Guest* [2022] UKSC 27. In this case, one child of a farmer had been promised rights in the family farm. The child had worked on the farm for 25 years in reliance on the promise of rights. Family relations broke down, and the farmer rewrote his will, cutting out the child who had been promised the farm. The court upheld the proprietary estoppel claim of the son.

Which of the following statements best explains ownership of the Greenacres?

A. Cassie has no rights in the property because she did not contribute to the purchase of Greenacres, and Dee owns the property absolutely.
B. Cassie has no rights in the property because she was cohabiting with Dee and the law does not recognise cohabitation as giving property rights.
C. Cassie has no rights in Greenacres because although she was promised rights by Dee, there is no evidence of detrimental reliance.
D. Cassie has a share in Greenacres under a common intention constructive trust because she has paid the outgoings of the house for five years.
E. Cassie has a share in Greenacres because she can prove a common intention constructive trust and she can prove detrimental reliance.

Question Two

Tex has two daughters, Una and Vera. For many years, they both lived some distance from Tex. He is retired and has been living on his own in his large house, Brambles, since his wife died three years ago. His health is failing, and he often says to each of his daughters, 'I need a lot more help. I do wish you lived closer'. Six years ago, Una decided to move in with Tex with her family. She said to him, 'I am going to come and look after you now', but she said, 'I hope I am going to get rights in the house from now on'. Tex has always thanked her for all her help, but he has never mentioned anything about ownership of Brambles. Last month, Tex died. Under the terms of his will, all his property, including the house, has been left to the RSPCA, a charity.

Which of the following statements best explains who has the best right to the house?

A. Both daughters have rights in the house because they are his daughters.
B. Both daughters have rights in the house because they are his daughters, but Una will receive more than Vera because she has looked after Tex for six years.
C. Neither daughter has any rights in the house because he has left the property to a charity and he did not transfer rights informally during his lifetime.
D. Una will get rights in the house because she made it clear she expected rights in the house if she moved into Brambles.
E. Only Una has any rights in the house because she has been looking after him for the last six years. Vera will not have any rights.

7.9 Multiple-Choice Questions – Part 1

Question One

Jeff Northgate has left a gift in his will on the following terms: '£50,000 to be divided at my trustee's discretion in such amounts and at such times as they think fit amongst the employees and ex-employees of Northgate Publishers Ltd'. Northgate Publishers were established in 1970, and there are no records of employees before 1980.

Which of the following statements best explains whether the trust can be upheld or not?

A. The trust will fail because the objects are uncertain.
B. The trust will fail because the intentions of the settlor are not clear.
C. The trust will fail because the trustees cannot draw up a complete list of beneficiaries.
D. The trust will not fail because the trustees do not need to draw up a complete list of all the beneficiaries.
E. The trust will fail because the instructions to the trustees are unclear.

Question Two

Earlier this year, Sami said to his daughter Tessa, 'I am going to give you the field next to my house'. At the time of the conversation, it was let to Ravi to graze his sheep. Ravi was a friend of Sami. The following day, Sami messaged their solicitors and asked them to draw up the paperwork necessary to transfer the field to Tessa. Last week, Sami died, and in his will, he appointed Tessa and his wife, Uma, as his trustees and executors. Under the will, all his property passes to Uma. She is refusing to transfer the field to Tessa. It appears that the documentation was never drawn up transferring the field to Tessa before Sami's death.

Which of the following statements best explains whether Tessa can claim the field or not?

A. The gift will fail because Sami did not intend an immediate gift to Tessa.
B. The gift will fail because Sami left all his property to Uma in his will.
C. The gift will not fail because Sami immediately telephoned his solicitors and asked them to draw up the necessary paperwork for the gift.
D. The gift will not fail because Tessa was appointed an executor.
E. The gift will fail because the paperwork for the transfer had not been completed before Sami's death.

Question Three

Jane Smith is the beneficiary of a trust which comprises a large shareholding in a publicly listed company. She won a large sum of money in the lottery last month, and she immediately telephoned her trustees, asking them to hold her interest under the trust for her friend, Katie. Jane then telephoned Katie and told her about the transfer, and Katie wrote back thanking her for the gift.

Jane and Katie had an argument last week, and Jane has changed her mind about transferring her interest.

Which of the following statements best explains whether Jane has transferred her interest to Katie?

A. Jane still holds her interest under the trust because any transfer of a beneficial interest must be made in writing.
B. Katie can claim the interest under the trust because Jane immediately telephoned her about the transfer.
C. Katie can claim the interest because Jane immediately telephoned the trustees about her intentions.
D. Katie can claim the interest because shares are personalty and do not require written evidence of transfer.
E. Jane can claim the interest because she has no right to transfer her beneficial interest to anyone without the settlor's consent.

Question Four

Liam Murphy has drawn up his will. He asks you whether the gifts under his will are valid. He has made the following gifts: '£40,000 for my cat, Lizzie, for the next 20 years; £10,000 to erect an appropriate gravestone in my memory; £10,000 to say a private mass in my local church after my death'. Liam is a devout Roman Catholic. Lizzie the cat is ten years old when he makes his will.

Which of the following statements best explains whether the gifts under Liam's will can be upheld after his death?

A. The gift to the cat will fail because you cannot leave money to an animal, but the rest are valid.
B. All the gifts will fail because the gift to the cat and the gift to erect a gravestone in Liam's memory do not comply with the perpetuity period.
C. The gift to erect a gravestone will fail because it does not comply with the perpetuity period, but the others will be upheld.

D. All the gifts will be upheld.

E. The gifts for the cat and the erection of a gravestone are valid, but the saying of the mass will fail because only masses said in public are upheld as a purpose trust.

Question Five

Janice is Kev's mother. Kev has a new job in Norwich, and Janice agrees to buy him a flat. Janice has been left some money by her grandparents, and she agrees to provide the money for the purchase. The flat is registered in Kev's name. She thinks it is simpler if it is in his name, but at the time of the purchase, she did not want to make a gift to him. Kev has been living in the flat for four years, but Janice hears that he sold the flat last week without telling her, and she wants the purchase money back. Kev is refusing to give it to her.

Which of the following statements best explains who can claim the proceeds of sale for the flat?

A. Kev can claim all the proceeds of sale because it was registered in his sole name.

B. Kev can claim the proceeds of sale because Janice is his mother and the presumption of advancement will apply.

C. Kev and Janice must share the proceeds of sale because Janice had the equitable interest and Kev had the legal interest.

D. Kev and Janice must share the proceeds of sale, but Janice will have a larger share because she provided all the purchase money.

E. Janice can claim all of the proceeds because she alone provided the purchase money.

Question Six

Jofra and Anise meet as students at the same university. Anise qualifies as a lawyer and earns a good salary after leaving university. Jofra was studying art and wants to be a sculptor. They decide to buy a house together using Anise's savings and her salary for the mortgage payments. Jofra has no money of his own, but when they move in, Anise says, 'This house is for us to share together'. Jofra does small improvement jobs in the house and decorates the bedrooms. He also uses any spare money to buy food and any furniture and plants for the garden. Last month, after three years together, they split up, and Jofra is claiming a half share in the house. Anise is refusing to give him any money, saying she was the one who paid for it.

Which of the following statements best explains whether Jofra can claim a share in the house?

A. Jofra can claim a share in the house because Jofra and Anise have been living together as a couple for over three years.
B. Jofra can claim a share because he has used his spare money to buy things for the house.
C. Jofra can claim a share because he has made contributions towards the improvements of the house, and these can be regarded as capital contributions towards the purchase.
D. Jofra can claim the value of any money he spent on improving the property.
E. Jofra can claim a half share because Anise said that the house was for them to share together.

PART II

Fiduciary relationships

8 The fiduciary relationship

8.1 Chapter overview

This part of the book explores relationships between parties that, by virtue of their duties and knowledge about each other, can carry extra responsibilities. We refer to these relationships as *'fiduciary'*. The first chapter explores the *nature of a fiduciary relationship*. It is a complex relationship and plays a very significant role in the law of trusts, so it is important to understand what is meant by *fiduciary*. Fiduciary duties play an important part in many relationships, particularly in Company Law, but it is the relationship between a *trustee* and a *beneficiary* that illustrates best what is at the core of the fiduciary relationship. In trusts, all trustees automatically become fiduciaries, and there are other similar situations where the nature of the relationship will always make it fiduciary, for example, a solicitor and client and partners in a partnership. The chapter also considers those relationships which are fiduciary in some situations. We examine how we can tell whether a relationship is fiduciary or not. Where there is a fiduciary relationship, then the law may impose a *constructive trust*, which we discussed earlier in Part 1. Note that this type of constructive trust is not the same as the *common intention constructive trust* imposed where two people own a piece of property. In these situations, trusteeship will be imposed because of the relationship between the parties and usually reflects the wishes of the parties. Property held by the fiduciary may, in some circumstances, be held on behalf of another, and the fiduciary may lose any rights over it. The *fiduciary* will hold the property under a constructive trust. This will be contrary to what they intended. Where property is held under a *constructive trust*, the rights of the claimant become *proprietary* in nature, which is valuable if the fiduciary becomes bankrupt, as these rights will take priority over the rights of general creditors.

8.2 Definition of a fiduciary relationship

There is no single definition of a fiduciary relationship. It includes several different obligations, but at the heart of it are *honesty and loyalty*. It usually arises when someone has agreed to act on behalf of another on a specific matter, and it gives rise to a relationship of *'trust and confidence'*. In these circumstances, you would expect the fiduciary to act with total *honesty* and also to be totally *loyal*, always putting the interests of the other party first.

DOI: 10.4324/9781003583660-10

Think about what happens when property passes from the settlor to the trustee. It could be tempting for the trustees to take advantage of holding the property in their names and to enjoy the property for themselves.

A trustee could also use information that they gain from the trust to make a personal profit, but the settlor has put their trust in the trustee, and so the law imposes a high standard on them. This duty is much higher than if someone were dealing with their own property.

Personal use of trust property or information gained would be *in breach of the special relationship between the trustee and the beneficiary*.

The law takes the fiduciary relationship very seriously and it is enforced strictly. Any profit made by the fiduciary is owed to the trust even if it is made innocently and even if the trustee makes a profit for the *benefit of the beneficiaries of the trust*.

8.2.1 Key features of a fiduciary relationship

i) Acting in good faith
ii) Loyalty
iii) Not to put oneself in a position of conflict with the trust
iv) Not to make a profit from the trust

8.3 Different types of fiduciary relationships

The problem when studying fiduciary relationships is that they have never been defined, so it is really the *key features* that define whether a relationship falls into the definition of fiduciary.

There are a number of *established fiduciary relationships*. These extend beyond trustee and beneficiary. Think of any relationships where *trust and confidence* are at the core of the relationship.

These will include the following: agent and principal; *banker and customer*; *solicitor and client*; *government employees and the Crown*; *company director and shareholder*; *partners in a partnership*.

Fiduciary relationships can also arise in situations where the relationship is not normally regarded as fiduciary, such as *employer and employee* (not in senior management). It will depend on the circumstances of the relationship. The key feature is whether or not there is a *'relationship of trust and confidence'*.[1]

1 See *Bristol and West BS v Mothew* [1998] 1 Ch 1, where it was stated 'a fiduciary is someone who has undertaken to act for or on behalf of another in a particular matter in circumstances which give rise to a relationship of trust and confidence'.

Compare these two situations:

i) An employee is employed in an ice cream factory to work on the factory floor. Their main duties are to check the conveyor belts while the machines fill the ice cream boxes. The relationship will not be regarded as fiduciary as there is no *'relationship of trust and confidence'*;

ii) Suppose another employee is employed in the same factory but their job is in a laboratory and they are employed to create a new flavour of ice cream. Here there is a relationship of *trust and confidence* as the employer trusts his employee to act only *in his best interests*. If that employee uses the information to make a profit for themselves by leaking the information to a competitor who pays him for it, then he will hold that profit on *constructive trust* for his employer as well. This can be seen as particularly onerous for the trustee.

In the next section, we will look at the *trustee/beneficiary relationship* and the expectations that are placed on the shoulders of the trustee when they are appointed. After that, we will move on to looking at other types of fiduciary relationship.

8.4 Different categories of fiduciaries

8.4.1 Trustees

When someone is appointed as a trustee, they immediately assume the role of a *fiduciary*, so any dealings with the trust must always be carried out with the needs of the beneficiaries at the forefront. The trustee must never put their own interest before those of the beneficiaries. This means that any purchase of trust property or any opportunity to profit from their position as trustee will need certain safeguards put in place in order to avoid an action for breach of fiduciary duty.

i) Purchase of trust property

Sometimes trust property will need to be sold to raise money for the trust. There may be costs to pay on other property or beneficiaries may have come into their rights to claim their share. Sales will usually be at the instigation of the trustees. Where trust property is being sold, the trustees themselves may wish to purchase that property from the trust.

If a trustee wishes to purchase trust property, it could be in the interests of the beneficiaries, especially where no other buyer comes forward to purchase the property. The problem here is that there is an obvious *conflict of interest*, as it is the trustee who owns the legal title to the property. The law has been very strict in this area. The rule is that trustees *must not sell any trust property to themselves*. There are exceptions, but the onus is always on the trustee to show that they did not take advantage of their position.

Two rules are applied to trustees purchasing trust property for themselves:

i) *'The self-dealing rule'* and
ii) *'The fair dealing rule'*.

8.4.1.1 'The self-dealing rule'

The *self-dealing rule* applies where the trustees sell trust property to one or more trustees. This is treated with suspicion. The sale is effectively to oneself as the trustee has the legal estate in the trust property. When trustees purchase trust property, the purchase will be regarded as *self-dealing*. This is because the trustees are *selling to themselves*.

Any sale by the trustees to a trustee can be rescinded (or undone) by the beneficiaries unless it was carried out with their *consent or authorised by the trust instrument or by the court*. Consent can only be given by beneficiaries who are over 18, all in agreement and it is freely given.

Consider these facts:

Elle and Farah are two trustees of a trust of a farm held on behalf of a widow, Gina, and her son, aged 18, Hari. The farm has 100 acres attached and has been farmed by a tenant farmer, Ivan. Elle wants the land because she is also a farmer. The trustees go ahead and have the land and farm valued by an independent valuer, but it is never put up for sale on the open market. Elle buys the farm. Gina and Hari are very upset when they find out about the sale. They believe it was worth far more than Elle paid for it.

Think about what Gina and Hari can do about the sale. Would it make any difference that Elle had the farm valued independently?

As Hari is of age, Elle should have approached him and Gina to discuss the sale of the farm, and together they could have given consent to the sale, which would then be binding and they could not ask for the transaction to be set aside.

It appears that this was not done, so they have the right to ask for the sale to be rescinded/set aside. It does not matter if the farm was valued for Elle independently or the amount paid by Elle was above market value.

It also does not matter if the sale was in the trust's interests because it was a quick sale or because there were no other buyers. Such a sale is still viewed suspiciously.

Consider this situation:

A family trust consists of a number of pieces of very valuable antique jewellery. The beneficiaries would like some of the pieces sold. One of the trustees, T3, is an antique dealer who specialises in jewellery and would like to purchase some of the pieces. In many ways, this is an ideal purchase – an instant buyer avoiding potential problems and delays, as well as the costs of taking the pieces to auction. Nevertheless, it is highly problematic for T3, as the law assumes that T3 could take advantage of their position and try to get a favourable deal for themselves.

Family Trust (Trust property = Jewellery)

(legal owner of the jewellery = T1+T2+T3) ————> PURCHASER (T3)

|

(Equitable owner of the jewellery = the beneficiaries)

This is a clear conflict of duty as the trustee *T3* has the advantage of fixing the price and could easily benefit from the sale. The law will presume against the trustee in this situation. The same rules will apply where the trustee sells their own property to the trust. It will be regarded with the same suspicion.

Where there has been a sale which is regarded as self-dealing, the sale is *voidable* at the instance of the beneficiaries. It does not matter if the sale was *fair, open or honest*. The use of an independent valuer or independent advice will not prevent the beneficiaries later being able to ask that the sale be rescinded.

A trustee would always be advised not to enter into a transaction which could be regarded as *self-dealing* unless it comes within any of the exceptions listed below.

Exceptions to the self-dealing rule:

- Authorisation under the trust instrument;
- Agreement from the beneficiaries if all agreed and all sui juris and fully informed; and
- Authorisation from the court either in advance or after the transaction has taken place.

Suppose the terms of the family trust of the jewellery discussed above contain a clause allowing the sale of the trust property to any or all of the trustees once it has been independently valued. T3 purchases some of the jewellery. The sale now would not be voidable at the instance of the beneficiaries. The sale has been authorised under the terms of the trust.

8.4.1.2 Client advice

If a trustee seeks your advice on a potential purchase of trust property, it must be made clear the difficulties involved. It is a potential breach of fiduciary duty, and this carries serious consequences. You should advise the client that steps should be taken to seek authorisation unless it is already contained in the terms of the trust.

Compare the rule below which is treated more generously.

8.4.1.3 The fair-dealing rule

This rule concerns any sale between the *trustees* and the *beneficiaries*. This would involve a sale of the *equitable interest* owned by the *beneficiary to a trustee.*

This is a different type of sale as the beneficiaries own the *equitable interest*, so unlike *self-dealing*, the trustee is not selling the property to themselves. Nevertheless, safeguards are still put in place to ensure that the trustee does not take advantage of what is regarded as a position of strength against the beneficiary.

8.4.1.4 Safeguards imposed in fair-dealing

In order to avoid having the transaction set aside, the trustee must carry out the following:

i) Show that he has not taken *advantage of his position*;
ii) Show that the land was *independently valued*;
iii) Show that the beneficiaries were *fully informed*;
iv) *Ensure that* the beneficiaries received full value for the property.

If we return to the family trust which comprised jewellery as the main trust property, then we can see how the facts of *fair-dealing* differ from *self-dealing*.

Family Trust (Trust property = jewellery)

(legal owner of the jewellery = T1+T2+T3)————> PURCHASER (T3)

|

(Equitable owner of the jewellery = beneficiaries)

If the trustee purchases the equitable interest of the beneficiary, it is still liable to be set aside if there is any evidence that the trustee took advantage of his position. Also, any profit made by the trustee through the transaction must be accounted for to the beneficiaries. The main difference from *self-dealing* is that in *fair-dealing* a trustee can defend themselves against an application for it to be set aside by arguing that the transaction is *fair, open and honest*. There is no right available to a trustee where the beneficiaries are seeking to have *self-dealing* set aside.

Consider the following facts:

Mike, the settlor, created a trust in favour of his wife, Winnie, and his three sons Ben, Bill and Bilal. He appoints two trustees, Tara and Tessa. Mike died last year. Bill has decided to sell his equitable interest under the trust, and Tara has offered to buy it.

Tara is a trustee, so she owns the legal interest on behalf of Ben, Bill and Bilal. If she purchases Bill's interest, she is buying something that belongs to him, as the equitable interest is separate from the legal interest, *but it is not at arm's length.*

In the example above, think about what Tara could do if Bill later applied to have the transaction set aside. One of the key ways of proving that the transaction was *fair and honest* is to have an independent valuation of the equitable interests. Tara could seek a valuation or even bid as a buyer at an open auction. Tara could also seek *approval of all the beneficiaries*, having first set out the terms of the transaction.

Exceptions to the fair-dealing rule

- The trustee made *full and frank disclosure to the beneficiaries*;
- The trustee proves that the transaction is *fair, open and honest*; and
- *Authorisation from the court*.

8.4.2 Client advice

If there is no authorisation in the trust instrument or forthcoming from the beneficiaries, then the trustees could seek approval of the court. This is a way to offset any attempt by the beneficiaries to make a sale contravening either the *self-dealing or fair-dealing rules* voidable, but it would always be a last resort because of cost and potential delays.

i) Competition with the trust

A trustee must never put themselves in *competition with the trust*. If a trustee goes into business which is the same as or similar to that of the trust, then the trustee will have to discontinue their business.[2]

2 *Re Thomson* [1930] 1 Ch 203. In this case, the defendant was executor and trustee to a yacht broker. A term in the will directed him to continue with the yacht brokerage business. After the testator died, the trustee set himself up in a similar business in the same town, and the court ordered him to stop trading.

ii) Remuneration as a trustee

The general rule is that no trustee should receive payment in their position as trustee. It is a natural extension of the rule that *no trustee should profit from the trust.* A trustee is entitled to receive *expenses or reimbursements* for costs undertaken on behalf of the trust, but these must cover only actual costs incurred.

Professional trustees have a statutory right to remuneration under the Trustee Act 2000.

Lay trustees also get paid in some situations:

- Payment authorised under the *trust instrument*;
- *Authority of the court*. The courts can order payment and also increase payment that has already been authorised. This is very strictly applied, so only services which are of exceptional benefit to the trust will be authorised by the court;
- Payment can be *authorised by the beneficiaries* if all sui juris and in agreement and also absolutely entitled together to the trust property.

iii) Making unauthorised profits

A trustee cannot *profit from their position as a trustee*. This extends beyond payment for their services. Trustees may receive information through their role as trustee which could be used by the trustee to make a personal profit. If the trustee does make a profit from the trust, then the trustee will hold all unauthorised profits on constructive trust for the beneficiary. This rule is applied very strictly, as shown in the example below which comes from the facts of a decided case.

Consider these facts:

The defendant was a trustee on behalf of a minor. The main trust property was a lease of a market. The lease needed renewal and the trustee applied for renewal on behalf of the beneficiary (the minor) but this was not possible because a minor cannot take a lease. The trustee then asked to take the lease personally and the lessor agreed. The trustee renewed the lease for himself. This was done honestly. This was purely to assist the beneficiaries and the lease renewal was done honestly but it was held that the trustee held the lease for the benefit of the trust.[3]

3 These facts are based on the case of *Keech v Sandford* [1726] Sel Cas Ch 61. It was a very harsh decision as if the trustee had not taken the lease for himself with the intention of helping the beneficiary.

What do these facts tell us? They suggest that whenever a trustee appears to be making a personal profit from their position as trustee, the law will assume that any profits are held on *constructive trust* for the benefit of the beneficiaries and the trust itself. It is irrelevant whether the trustee was in fact taking action as the trustee in the example above for the benefit of the beneficiaries rather than for themself. We will explore this further in relation to other fiduciaries.

8.4.2.1 *Account for profits*

Where a trustee has made a personal profit from their role, the beneficiaries will seek a special remedy in equity: an *account of profits*. This allows the beneficiary to recover from the trustee any unauthorised profits that have been made through the breach.

iv) Retaining fees from a directorship

Where trust assets include company shares, the trustees control the associated voting rights at company meetings. It may be necessary to hold shares in a company in order to qualify as a director. Where a trustee uses the shares held by the trust to take a directorship, the trustee cannot keep the remuneration payable to him as a director for himself.

The position is different if the appointment as director is not associated with the trust and the trustee is entitled to keep the remuneration.

Consider these facts:

(i) Terry has been appointed as a trustee. The main asset of the trust is a large shareholding in a company called Spices from the Far East. The trust has a 25% shareholding. The trust instrument granted the trustees the right to appoint two directors of the company. Terry appointed himself as a director and received a director's salary.

Must Terry account to the trust for the remuneration that he receives?

Compare these facts:

(ii) Terry has been appointed as a trustee. The main asset of the trust is a large shareholding in a company called Spices from the Far East. The trust has a 25% shareholding. Terry is elected as a director by the company. Terry himself has a 30% shareholding in the company.

Must Terry account for the remuneration he receives in these circumstances?

In (i), Terry has only been elected as a director through his position as a trustee; therefore, all remuneration he receives must be accounted to the trust.

In (ii), the position is different as he can argue that his election is outside his position as trustee. He could have been elected as a director without any votes from the trust shares as a 51% vote is needed and if all the trust shares were voted against him he could still have been voted as a director. The position would have been different in (A) if the trust instrument had expressly allowed any trustee appointed through the trust to retain remuneration.

Circumstances when a trustee can retain director's fees:

- If the fees are expressly authorised under the trust instrument;
- If the trustee had been appointed before becoming trustee;[4]
- If the trustee would have been elected to the directorship even if the trust shares the trustee controlled had been voted against him;
- The court authorises the retention of the fees.

8.4.3 Different categories of fiduciaries: those other than trustees

i) **Employees**

The law holds that any profit made by an employee by virtue of his position as employee cannot be retained by him and instead the profit is held on constructive trust and must be handed over to the employer. This is using their contacts or their knowledge to make a personal profit such as taking a bribe.

8.4.3.1 Bribes

If an employee uses his role in his employer's business to make a personal profit, how does the law approach this situation? If someone makes a personal profit through their employment, then that profit would be held on constructive trust. If E is employed to tender for work and is offered a bribe from one contractor, can E keep the bribe?

Surely the bribe arises in E's capacity as an employee?

4 In *re Dover Coalfield Extension Ltd* [1907] 2 Ch 76, a trustee was entitled to keep remuneration received as a director because the appointment was made before he became a trustee and did not use his position as trustee.

Consider this example:

X is employed by a company, A, to purchase supplies. X tenders for supplies from several different companies, but company B offers X a bribe of £5,000 as an incentive to give company B the work.

Suppose X invests the money he receives in land and makes a profit from the land because it increases substantially in value. Can company A recover the land as well as the £5,000?[5]

In other words, is the relationship one of *contract*, in which case company A can only recover the £5,000, or is the relationship one of *constructive trusteeship*, in which case A can recover the land as well? The law today would declare that X holds the £5,000 *and* the land on constructive trust for company A.[6]

The position will be different if an employee exploits an opportunity that is authorised by their employer.

Consider these facts:[7]

Conrad is managing director of D Ltd, a consultancy. Conrad enters into negotiations for a building contract for E Ltd. E Ltd refuses to negotiate with D Ltd because they have a policy not to employ consultants. Instead, they offer the contract to Conrad in his personal capacity. He resigns from his job, but he does not tell D Ltd why he is resigning. He takes a job with E Ltd and receives remuneration.

Is Conrad liable to D Ltd for the profits he receives from his position?

Firstly, is Conrad a *fiduciary*?

Yes. Although not all employees are fiduciaries, Conrad receives *confidential information* in his position as managing director of D Ltd. He therefore becomes a *fiduciary*.

Secondly, is he in breach of his fiduciary duties?

5 These facts are based on the case of *Lister v Stubbs* [1890] 45 Ch D 1. In that case, the employee was not held to be a constructive trustee, so any profit made from the bribe could be kept by the employee. That conclusion has now been reversed, and the case would be decided differently today.

6 The law was changed in the case of *FHR European Ventures LLP v Cedar Capital Partners LLC* [2014] UKSC 45, which declared that money received as bribes or secret commissions should be held on constructive trust, so any additional profit made from that bribe should be held on constructive trusteeship for the claimant.

7 These facts are based on *Industrial Development Consultants Ltd v Cooley* [1972] 1 WLR 443.

Yes. Conrad has used the information received in his position as an employee of D Ltd to get a new job which he would not have heard about without negotiating on their behalf with E Ltd.

Thirdly, does D Ltd have a remedy?

Yes. D Ltd can claim an account for profits received by Conrad. In entering into a contract with E Ltd, Conrad has allowed his duty to D Ltd to conflict with his personal interests.

ii) Solicitors advising a trust

Where someone is advising a trust, such as a solicitor, the law will regard them as a *fiduciary* and will expect the high standards of other fiduciaries in all their dealings with the trust. The solicitor is not a trustee, but in their capacity as adviser to the trust, they will receive a considerable amount of information about the trust which they could use to their own advantage. So, as a *fiduciary*, a solicitor cannot use any information gained in their capacity as trustee to their own personal advantage.

Consider these facts (based on the facts of a well-known case):

A trust created by the settlor in favour of the settlor's wife and children had a 27% shareholding in a particular company. The trustees were the settlor's widow, a daughter of the settlor and an accountant. The solicitor to the trust and one of the settlor's sons were unhappy about the way the trust was being handled and felt that the trust was receiving very poor returns on their investment in the company. They decided to buy some shares themselves in order to have control over the company. The trust was not in a position to buy any more shares because the investment clause in the will would not allow it, and also there was no available cash anyway to buy the shares. As a result of the control acquired by the solicitor and the beneficiary after the purchase of the shares, the company became profitable. All the shareholders profited, including the beneficiaries of the trust.

The claimant who was one of the settlor's other sons brought an action claiming that the solicitor should account to the trust for the *personal profits* made by the solicitor from the shares.[8]

Consider the following:

- Do you think that the solicitor should account to the trust for the profits made?
- If so, in what circumstances do you think he should be allowed to keep them?
- Would it make any difference if the beneficiaries had authorised his purchase of the shares in the company?

8 These facts are based on the case of *Boardman v Phipps* [1967] 2 AC 46.

In this case, the solicitor had to *account for the personal profit* that he had made from the shares. In his capacity as solicitor to the trust, the solicitor was a *fiduciary* and therefore he was accountable to the trust for any profit that he made through the trust. By attending shareholders' meetings, he would acquire knowledge that was only available to him in his capacity as a fiduciary.

The circumstances in which the solicitor should have been allowed to retain the personal profit made were: if he had made full disclosure to the trustees and the beneficiaries of what he was doing and if they had given their consent assuming that they were sui juris. The problem here was that one of the beneficiaries was not sui juris. The settlor's widow suffered from senile dementia and was unable to give consent. The solicitor had sought consent from the other two trustees who had agreed with the sale, but he had not fully explained the position to the beneficiaries, so there was not full disclosure.

It would have made a difference to his defence if the beneficiaries had authorised his purchase of the shares. The problem for the solicitor was that he had not fully explained what he was doing to the beneficiaries.

As he was a solicitor, he should have been aware that he was acting in a *fiduciary capacity* and that he had *breached that duty*, and he had not gained *informed consent* from the beneficiaries to whom he owed a duty.

Did the solicitor in *Boardman v Phipps* receive anything for his services to reflect how he had helped the trust?

Unusually, the court used its powers to award the solicitor an equitable allowance, called a *quantum meruit*. This would not have been awarded in a case where bribes or secret commissions had been received or

iii) Receipt of trust property by a third party from a trustee

Where a third party, albeit innocently, receives trust property from a trustee, the third party cannot enjoy that property for themselves; instead, the law would say they are holding the property as a *constructive trustee*.

The law holds that third parties who receive trust property knowingly or in circumstances where they should realise it might be trust property hold that property on *constructive trust*.

Consider this example:

Frederic is a relative of a trustee, T1. Frederic knows T1 is a trustee. The trust property includes a number of paintings by a well-known modern artist. Frederic is a collector of modern art. T1 tells Frederic, 'I have a special present for your birthday next week'. T1 gives Frederic a painting from the trust over a quiet drink in a local pub. T1 hands over the wrapped picture in a large supermarket carrier bag and says, 'Keep this quiet; I am giving you something special for your birthday because I know you appreciate good art'. Frederic opens the present when he gets home and recognises the artist and the fact that it is very valuable.

Surely, in these circumstances, F would question T1 further and ask him about the present?

Frederic should be aware that these are suspicious circumstances. When Frederic receives the trust property, you could argue that even if he does not ask any questions of T1, the circumstances will make this suspicious, and Frederic will know that his actions are against good conscience.

We will consider this example again in the next chapter when we consider the *liability of strangers to the trust.*

Chapter 8 Revision Points

- Key features of a fiduciary relationship are a duty to be loyal and to be honest;
- A fiduciary must not let their personal interests conflict with their duty as a fiduciary;
- All trustees are fiduciaries;
- Some relationships become fiduciary because of the nature of their role, such as an employee;
- No trustee can keep unauthorised profits; unauthorised director's fees; set up in business in competition with the trust; purchase trust property unless authorised; retain fees from a directorship unless permitted; claim remuneration unless a professional or expressly permitted;
- Where a fiduciary is in breach of their duties, they may be liable to account for any profits that they make through the breach.

8.5 Multiple-Choice Questions

Question One

Francis is one of three trustees to a large trust which comprises a farm with a considerable amount of land and several buildings on the land. The beneficiaries are four children, two of whom are still at school. The trust needs to raise capital because they need money to pay several beneficiaries who have met the conditions set for them in order to benefit. One of the buildings is an old barn, and Francis suggests that it should be sold, thereby raising capital. The other trustees agree. Francis has the barn independently valued and offers to pay the full asking price. The trustees agree that this would save money and also time. Francis approaches all the beneficiaries, and they all agree that Francis should be allowed to purchase the barn.

Last week, the eldest beneficiary read in the paper that the sale of barns attracts a very high price. He is seeking to set aside the sale as he believes that Francis did not pay the full value.

Which of the following statements best reflects the position with regard to the barn?

- **A.** The sale cannot be set aside because Francis paid full price and had it independently valued.
- **B.** The sale cannot be set aside because Francis sought permission from the other trustees and they agreed.
- **C.** The sale cannot be set aside because Francis obtained permission from all the beneficiaries.
- **D.** The sale can be set aside because Francis did not get permission from the beneficiaries as two of the beneficiaries were underage.
- **E.** The sale can be set aside because trustees can never purchase trust property from a trust as they own the legal estate.

Question Two

William is a solicitor to a trust fund. The beneficiaries are four children, one of whom is underage, and their mother, who recently had a stroke and who is currently in hospital unable to care for herself. One of the main trust assets is a large shareholding in a private company, Barlows. There are two trustees who were friends of the settlor. They have little business experience. William recently inspected Barlows' company accounts in his role as trustee and discovered that it was not being run very efficiently, so he decided to buy some shares for himself. He told the trustees what he was doing, and they gave their consent. The combination of his shareholding and that of the trust gave him control over the company. After a year, he turned the company's performance around and managed to make it profitable. Both the trust benefited from this, as well as William. One of the beneficiaries has discovered that William has shares in Barlows as well as the trust, and William has made a profit, and he wants William to account for the profits that he has made on the shares.

Which of the following statements best reflects the position with regard to the shares?

A. William does not have a duty to account for the profit on his shares because the trust has profited from his actions as well as himself.

B. William does not have a duty to account for the profit on the shares because the success of the company was due to his hard work.

C. William does not have to account for the profit on the shares because the purchase was a personal transaction and he used his own money, not the trust money, for the purchase.

D. William does not have to account for the profit he made on the shares because he was not a trustee of the trust.

E. William must account for the profit he made on the shares because he was in breach of his fiduciary duty.

9 Liability of strangers to the trust

9.1 Chapter overview

This chapter follows on from some of the issues raised in Chapter 8. It looks at how third parties who are not appointed expressly as trustees can sometimes themselves be regarded by the law as trustees. The law will then regard the third party as a 'stranger' rather than an innocent third party. This is particularly important where a trustee has disappeared or is now bankrupt as it is a possible way that a beneficiary can recover their property if it has been misappropriated by the trustee. These people are termed *'strangers to the trust'*. Their liability can arise in several different ways. We explore the three main ways that a stranger can become liable to a trust. Firstly, someone who receives trust property can be found liable for *recipient liability*. Secondly, a person who assists in a breach of trust can be liable for *accessory liability*. In these cases, they do not receive trust property into their hands, but they become involved in the breach of trust. Thirdly, someone can be liable when they undertake the duties of a trustee when they have not been expressly appointed as a trustee. They are called *'trustees de son tort'*. In all these cases the third parties may be liable as constructive trustees, and this makes them liable as if they were trustees and the beneficiaries can seek to recover lost trust assets from them. It is usually the last resort for the beneficiaries who are seeking to recover their lost assets. The basis of liability will always be *'knowledge'*, which is sufficient to place liability on them. We will consider the complicated issue of what the law regards as *'knowledge'*. This does not always involve *actual knowledge*. It can be *constructive knowledge* when a third party ought to have known they were in receipt of trust property.

9.2 Different types of remedies against strangers to the trust

The main point of a beneficiary suing the stranger is to recover assets or money to cover the loss of trust property. There are two distinct types of remedy that they can pursue: *proprietary remedies* and *personal remedies*. The beneficiaries may be able to claim both. We will examine both in detail below. We have already considered proprietary rights, which are based on rights in the property itself rather than rights to sue for the value of property. Proprietary rights give priority over other claimants, in particular creditors.

DOI: 10.4324/9781003583660-11

9.2.1 Proprietary remedies

A *proprietary remedy* is important because it allows the claimant the right to recover the property or assets themselves. Items of trust property may carry a special significance, and recovery of the property rather than its monetary value may be especially important to a beneficiary. It also allows the claimant to take priority over other claimants such as creditors.

Consider this example:

Sarah is a trustee of a family trust. She has wrongfully taken some jewellery from the trust for her own enjoyment. She intended to sell the jewellery because her own business is in trouble and she needs the money. Before she can sell it, the beneficiaries discover what she has done and bring an action to recover the property. They have the right to recover the jewellery itself. We will discuss this in more detail in Chapter 14. This is a *proprietary action***.** It would be particularly valuable if Sarah's business fails and she is declared bankrupt, as in those circumstances, a personal claim is unlikely to be satisfied in full. A proprietary remedy will allow the beneficiaries' claim to be placed above those of ordinary creditors.

If Sarah does not sell the jewellery but decides instead to give it as a present to her daughter, Tanya, then her daughter could become a *stranger* herself if she has any suspicions that the jewellery does not belong to her mother.

If Tanya receives it innocently, then the beneficiaries can seek a *proprietary remedy* to recover the property. This will not involve proof of knowledge about the fact that it was from the trust, as it is possible to recover trust assets from innocent third parties who are volunteers through the process of *tracing* discussed in Chapter 14.

9.2.2 Personal remedies

If a stranger participates in the commission of a breach of trust but does not receive trust property or has sold or destroyed the assets, a proprietary remedy will not be available. In these cases, the beneficiaries must rely on a *personal remedy*. The beneficiaries will be seeking restoration of the trust assets. They will be seeking *restitution*, which is an equitable remedy based on the principle of *unjust enrichment*.

In the example above, if Tanya sells the jewellery, then if it is proved that she is a stranger to the trust because she had 'knowledge of the fact that the jewellery came from the trust', then the beneficiaries may have a *personal action* against her even if they have no *proprietary right* and cannot recover the trust property itself. In this case, Tanya would have to make good the value of the jewellery from her own personal assets. She was not expressly appointed as a trustee, but the law will regard her as a *constructive trustee*.

9.3 Recipient liability

The main way that a third party may become involved as a 'stranger' will be where they are in receipt of trust property and the third party is aware of or ought to have been aware that the property has come from a trust or at the very least that there has been a breach of trust or breach of fiduciary duty. The third party may not be aware at the time of receipt but they may become aware at a later date. Both these circumstances can be described as *'recipient liability'*.

An example was briefly mentioned at the end of Chapter 8.

You will recall the following facts:

Frederic receives a present from a relative who is a trustee. The present consists of paintings which are actually trust property. The receipt of a present from a relative would not normally be regarded as suspicious, and so normally, even if the present is actually trust property, Frederic would be regarded as an *innocent volunteer.* An innocent volunteer will have to return trust property if it is still in their possession, but if they have lost it or sold it or given it away, they are no longer liable to the beneficiaries for its value.

In this case, the circumstances are fairly suspicious. Frederic receives the present wrapped in a plastic bag, and T1 asks him to keep quiet about it. Frederic fails to ask questions about the present that you might expect someone to ask, even if it is a generous relative! Therefore, Frederic may be regarded as a *constructive trustee.* If he had asked questions and had got answers that were plausible, then he might escape liability.

9.3.1 Proving recipient liability

In order to successfully claim against a third party for *recipient liability*, the beneficiary needs to prove the following:

- The trust assets must be disposed of by the trustee in *breach of trust* or *breach of their fiduciary duty*;
- The defendant *received assets* from the trustee;
- *Knowledge* of the breach of trust or breach of fiduciary duty.

9.3.2 Disposal of the trust assets

The beneficiaries must prove that the trustee took assets of the trust and disposed of them in breach of trust. The obvious example would be to take an asset and give it to someone other than a named beneficiary.

9.3.3 Receipt of the assets

In the example above, the law is looking at the transfer of title to the third party, Frederic. In receiving a present from a donor, the donee receives title to the property. Frederic believes that he now owns the paintings for himself.

9.3.4 Knowledge

A claimant, usually a beneficiary, must prove that the stranger either had *actual knowledge* or *constructive knowledge* of the *breach of trust* or *breach of fiduciary duty*.

Actual knowledge is easier to prove. There must be proof that the recipient was aware of the breach by the trustee, but this is rare. Most people, if told they are in receipt of trust property, would refuse to take it or question the circumstances.

Constructive knowledge is proof that the stranger had no actual knowledge but instead *wilfully shut their eyes to the obvious or wilfully and recklessly failed to make enquiries that an honest and reasonable person would have made*. This situation is far more likely to arise where someone is naive or unworldly; then they may not find certain circumstances suspicious in the way that a more experienced person might.

Compare the two following situations:

(A) Karen is given a valuable watch by her Aunt Geeta. She knew that Geeta was a trustee of a trust of a family friend who was very rich. Karen also knows that Geeta has never had very much money. Geeta has often spoken about the fact that the trust has a lot of jewellery and watches which are all kept in a bank vault. Karen is very surprised to receive the watch and has her suspicions that the watch may have come from the family trust. Nina is the sole beneficiary of the trust.

(B) Leila is given a diamond brooch by her Aunt Geeta for her 18th birthday. Geeta has always said she is short of money, and Leila knows she does not own her own house and has modest earnings from her job as an English language teacher in a school for foreign students. She does not know that Geeta is a trustee to a large trust. Leila is rather surprised when she gives her the diamond brooch, but she does not ask any questions about where Geeta got the necklace or how she got the money to pay for it. She really likes the necklace and wants to keep it. Mika is the sole beneficiary of the trust.

Consider the advice that you would give to the two beneficiaries of the trust: Nina and Mika.

They have recently discovered that a number of items have been taken from the trust by Geeta the trustee. Geeta has just been declared bankrupt.

Obviously, the best claim would be against Geeta, who is in *breach of trust*. We will be discussing the duties of a trustee in more detail in Chapter 11 but where a trustee takes trust assets for themselves, it is clearly a breach of duty. However, in this case, Geeta is now bankrupt and has disposed of the trust assets, so there is no point in the beneficiaries pursuing her for recovery of the loss.

Nina and Mika would be advised to seek a remedy against Karen and Leila. In order to do so, they must prove the following:

i) Trust assets have been *disposed of by the trustee in breach of trust*;
ii) The assets have been *received by a third party*; and
iii) The third party had *knowledge* of the facts.

If all these can be proved then thay may be successful.

Trust assets have been taken by Geeta and given to Karen and Leila. If it can be proved that they had *actual or constructive knowledge of the trust*, then they would step into the shoes of Geeta and become *constructive trustees*.

As they have both retained the items given to them, Nina and Mika will claim the actual objects back, but pursuing them as constructive trustees has other advantages.

For example, they would be able to claim any losses to the trust because the items have been damaged or perhaps Karen and Leila have sold them, and the beneficiaries could recover the value from Karen and Leila as constructive trustees. If Karen and Leila were innocent volunteers and the items were damaged, they could not recover for damage or their value when sold to a bona fide purchaser.

Consider what Karen knows: She is aware that Geeta is a trustee, and she is aware of the nature of the trust assets. She also knows that Geeta does not have money of her own. On the facts, she actually believes that the necklace may have come from the trust. This could be classed as *actual knowledge*.

Consider what Leila knows: She does not know that Geeta is a trustee, but she knows that Geeta does not have much money and is presented with a valuable present from Geeta, albeit for a special birthday, her 18th. She chooses not to question her further. In a situation like this, the law would expect her to ask further questions in order to protect herself against any liability.

In this situation we could say that Leila has *wilfully and recklessly failed to make enquiries that an honest and reasonable person would have made*.

In both the above cases it may be that their behaviour initially does not make them liable as strangers. Perhaps they could justify their suspicions if Aunt Geeta had given them expensive presents in the past. However, it would be different if they became aware later that the property is trust property and then the law would regard them as constructive trustees as soon as they became aware that the property comes from the trust.

9.4 Test for dishonesty in recipient liability

In determining whether a third party has become a stranger and therefore is liable for dishonest receipt, the courts have set a standard to be applied to them when they receive the trust property.

> The courts will ask *'Was the stranger's knowledge or suspicions such as to make it unconscionable to deny the claim against them...'*?[1]

In the example above, Leila does not pursue her suspicions of Geeta. She does not know that she is a trustee, but nevertheless, she does not ask any questions about the necklace. A court would assess her behaviour as likely to make it unconscionable to deny a claim against her.

9.5 Bona fide purchasers

If the recipient of the trust property gives *valuable consideration*, then claimants against the trustee will *not* be able to claim a proprietary remedy against that property unless the sale is made in suspicious circumstances.

Suppose Geeta sold the watch to Lee. Lee knows nothing about who Geeta is but has responded to an advert about the watch placed in an online marketplace by Geeta. If Lee provides valuable consideration, then the law would protect them as a *bona fide purchaser* and Lee can keep the watch, and the beneficiaries will have to try to pursue their claim against Geeta.

Think about possible scenarios that might make the sale suspicious.

These are some examples:

- The sale could be at gross undervalue;
- It could take place in a far less public way than an online marketplace;

1 The Court of Appeal set this as a standard for assessing what constitutes knowledge in cases of knowing receipt in the case of *BCCI v Akindele* [2001] Ch 437. The test does not require the defendant to take part in any fraud but merely to be aware of facts that should put them on notice so that keeping any property received in these circumstances would be unconscionable.

- Geeta could refuse to answer questions that Lee asks about the source of the watch. Lee could not just stand back but should follow the questions up or make some checks herself before the purchase.

In all these situations, Lee would cease to be regarded as a *bona fide purchaser* and would become a constructive trustee.

Chapter 9 Revision Points – Recipient Liability

- Recipient liability depends on proof of:
  - Receipt of trust property;
  - Knowledge that it is in a third party breach of trust or breach of fiduciary duty;
- The test for knowledge is whether it is unconscionable for the recipient to deny the claim against them;
- Bona fide purchasers are excluded from having recipient liability if they have given valuable consideration;
- Claimants can pursue a proprietary remedy to recover their property or alternatively pursue a personal remedy against the recipient.

9.6 Proving accessory liability

An alternative way that a claimant may be able to recover for loss of trust property is to prove assistance in a breach of trust. This is really a last resort for claimants and is more difficult to prove than recipient liability. So a stranger may not have received the title to trust property but may still be liable to the claimants/beneficiaries if they *have dishonestly assisted* the trustee in a breach of trust.

There are *four* requirements[2] for *dishonest assistance*:

- Proof of the *existence of a trust or a fiduciary relationship*;
- There was a *breach of trust or breach of fiduciary duty*;
- A stranger *assisted in the breach of trust*; and
- The stranger was *dishonest*.

9.6.1 The test for dishonesty

The claimant must prove that the defendant was dishonest in the way that they assisted in the breach. This involves assessing what the defendant knew or ought to have known at the time.

2 These criteria were laid down in the case of *Royal Brunei Airlines v Tan* [1995] 2 AC 378. In this case, the claim was against an agent of a travel agency. The travel agency had not acted dishonestly, but the agent had. Prior to this case, the claim against the stranger depended on proof that the trustee as well as the stranger had been dishonest. The law changed in *Tan*, so it was now only necessary to prove that the stranger was dishonest in order to succeed in proving dishonest assistance.

The test today for *dishonesty* in dishonest assistance can either be *subjective or objective.*

9.6.1.1 Objective and subjective tests of honesty

People vary in what they see as being dishonest behaviour. A young child might take an apple at a supermarket and not differentiate that from taking an apple from a fruit bowl at home.

9.6.1.2 The current test for dishonesty

The law has set the test of honesty today for dishonest assistance as an *objective test.*

A *subjective test* has been rejected as it allows the defendant to argue that they were unaware of the circumstances although others who were as experienced as them might have been aware that a breach of trust had taken place.

Under the current test, there is some flexibility as the standard will vary according to the nature and experience of the defendant.

9.6.2 What does an objective test for dishonesty mean?

It means that people are not free to set their own standards of honesty. It is not possible to simply say 'I did not know that that behaviour was wrong'. The standard would be a general standard of honesty of ordinary honest people.[3]

Note that there is a *subjective* element. The standard will depend in each case on what the defendant actually knew at the time.

However, the defendant cannot set a standard based on whether he thought that ordinary honest people would think that his behaviour was dishonest.

Consider this example:

Supposing a bank clerk has acted in a way that could be termed dishonest because they did not properly question a customer who was taking a large amount of money from an account.

3 The test can be described as '...not acting as an honest person would in the circumstances...' *Barlow Clowes International v Eurotrust International* [2006] 1 All ER 333. In a more recent case, *Ivey v Genting Casinos UK Ltd (t/a Crockford Club)* [2017] UKSC 67, Lord Hughes stated, 'There is no requirement that the defendant must appreciate that what he has done is, by those standards dishonest...'

In order to assess whether the bank clerk was liable as a stranger, the law would consider his behaviour according to the standards of *ordinary honest people*. The standard could take into account their seniority in the bank.

If the bank clerk was very junior and very young, then the law would assess dishonesty in the light of his experience.

Whereas if the bank clerk was very experienced and had been a bank clerk for several years, then the expectations of their behaviour would rise.

Once that test has been considered, it would then consider whether what that bank clerk did *fell below the ordinary standards of honesty*.

The law does not allow the bank clerk to set their own standards and argue that they did not know that what they did was dishonest, perhaps arguing their own inexperience. The test then is an *objective test* rather than a *subjective* test, but there is a subjective element which allows for a level of experience and what the person actually knew at the time.

9.6.3 Remedies for dishonest assistance

A *proprietary remedy* cannot be claimed for dishonest assistance because the stranger has never received trust property for themselves. The stranger never holds any trust property in their own name.

Note that when we considered dishonest receipt, we saw that the claimant can claim a *proprietary remedy* or a *personal remedy* against the stranger.

If dishonest assistance can be proved, then the beneficiaries can claim a *personal remedy*. This means that the stranger must personally compensate the trust for the loss.

Chapter 9 Revision Points – Dishonest Assistance or Accessory Liability

Liability for dishonest assistance depends on proof of:

- The existence of a trust;
- Breach of that trust or breach of fiduciary duty;
- Assistance by a stranger in that breach;
- Proof of dishonesty of the stranger;
- Dishonesty is assessed by an objective rather than a subjective standard.

9.7 Liability as a trustee de son tort; intermeddling with the trust

The third type of third-party liability as a stranger arises when someone acts on behalf of a trust and deals with the trust as if they had the authority of the trustee; then that person could be liable for their actions as if they were a trustee. This is most likely to arise when someone has died and a person close to the deceased deals with their estate. They are called *'trustees de son tort'*, which can be interpreted as a trustee in his own wrong.

9.7.1 Examples of situations of intermeddling

- Selling assets
- Disposing of the deceased's personal possessions
- Paying debts owed by the deceased
- Collecting debts due to the deceased
- Carrying on the deceased's business

In all of the examples above, the third party is acting on behalf of the estate, but there is scope for the third party to take advantage of their situation and enjoy the property for themselves.

In these circumstances, then the *trustee de son tort* becomes a constructive trustee and is treated as an express trustee, and the beneficiaries will have both a *personal* and a *proprietary remedy* against them. A proprietary remedy is available because the *trustee de son tort* holds the property in their own name. This liability differs from recipient liability because here the third party is receiving the property on behalf of the estate. It means that any property taken from the estate must be returned, and any damage to that property or losses incurred must be reimbursed.

Table of the various forms of stranger liability and the remedies available

Different types of stranger liability	Requirement for proof	Available remedy
Recipient liability (knowing receipt of trust property)	A stranger receives trust property for their own use knowing it is in breach of trust or shuts eyes to the obvious or fails to make enquiries.	Proprietary claim/ recovery of trust property Personal claim Tracing
Accessory liability (dishonest assistance in a breach of trust)	A stranger assists a trustee or fiduciary in a breach of trust.	Personal claim

Different types of stranger liability	Requirement for proof	Available remedy
Trustee de son tort (intermeddling in a trust)	A stranger who acts on behalf of the beneficiaries of a trust taking on the role of trustee and causes a loss to the trust.	Proprietary claim/ recovery of trust property Personal claim Tracing

9.8 Preparation for the SQE

There are three types of stranger liability: *recipient liability, accessory liability* and *intermeddling*. If faced with a problem or question about stranger liability, consider the facts in stages.

- Firstly, consider if the third party *receives* any trust property for themselves;
- If the answer is *'no'*, then could the third party have assisted in the breach and would therefore be liable as a stranger for *accessory liability*;
- If the answer is *'yes'*, then consider if the third party takes on any responsibility as if they were a trustee for the trust;
- If *'no'*, then could the third party be liable for *recipient liability*;
- If *'yes'*, then the stranger could be liable for *intermeddling* in the trust. Consider whether they have received trust property for their own benefit or on behalf of the trust;
- Finally consider the remedies available to the claimants: *proprietary or personal*.

9.9 Multiple-Choice Questions – Part 2

Question One

Sevi creates a trust in favour of his wife, Zandra, and on her death, for their four children Alex, Ben, Cam and Debbie. He appointed three trustees: his wife; his daughter, Debbie; and his friend, Evan, who is an accountant. Fergus is solicitor to the trust. He is aware that one of the assets of the trust is a 30% shareholding in a private company, but he is also aware that the company is in a poor financial position. He discusses this with Alex, and together they purchase enough shares each to have a controlling interest in the company. Fergus explains what he intends to do to Zandra and all four children, but he is aware that Zandra is suffering from a degenerative disease which makes it difficult for her to make decisions. The company becomes profitable and the trust makes a profit of £50,000, and both Fergus and Alex make £40,000. Ben and Cam have now found out about the purchase of the shares by Fergus and seek a remedy against him.

Consider the following options and decide which best describes the likely result of any action that they choose to bring.

A. The beneficiaries can recover the £40,000 profit made on the shares from Fergus and he will receive nothing.
B. The beneficiaries cannot recover the £40,000 profit made on the shares from Fergus because he was not a trustee.
C. The beneficiaries cannot recover the £40,000 made on the shares from Fergus because he had gained consent to his actions from two of the trustees.
D. The beneficiaries have no remedy against Fergus because he acted honestly throughout and did not try to hide the purchase.
E. The beneficiaries have no remedy against Fergus because the trust also benefited from his action.

Question Two

Jack is one of two trustees to trust A. The assets of the trust include shares in a company, and Jack is a director of the company receiving a substantial annual fee. Jack also has a shareholding in the company. The beneficiaries of trust A have just found out about the fee and are now claiming that Jack is profiting from his position as a trustee and must pay the fee back.

Which of the following statements best describes the legal position with regard to the director's fee paid to Jack?

A. Jack must account for the fees because the trust assets include shares in the company and there is a conflict of interest.
B. Jack must account for the fees if his appointment was made after he became trustee to Trust A.
C. Jack need not account for the fees as they are paid for time spent on company affairs.
D. Jack need not account for the fees if he was appointed through votes independent of the trust shareholding.
E. Jack need not account for the fees if he had been honest about the receipt of the fees as director to the beneficiaries.

Question Three

Vernon is trustee to a family trust. The assets include a farm and a farmhouse as well as a substantial shareholding. The beneficiaries are the settlor's widow, Dee, and three children: Emmy, Felix and Georgie. There are two other trustees, Tom and Teri. Dee is now in residential care, and the farmhouse is empty. None of the children want to live in the farmhouse, and the trustees agreed unanimously that the farmhouse should be sold as soon as possible to save costs. Vernon tells the trustees that he intends to buy it. The trustees agree and have an independent valuation, and Vernon goes ahead to buy the farmhouse and pays the full price for it. The beneficiaries have just found out about the sale and want it to be set aside.

Which of the following statements best describes the legal position with regard to the sale of the farmhouse?

- **A.** The sale must be set aside because it was not made through a public auction.
- **B.** The sale must be set aside because Vernon did not get full approval of the beneficiaries.
- **C.** The sale can stand as Vernon gained the approval of his co-trustees.
- **D.** The sale can stand as the farmhouse was valued by an independent valuer.
- **E.** The sale can stand as Vernon paid the full market price.

Question Four

Maddie and Max are twins. They are beneficiaries of a trust set up by their uncle who had no children. Irma and Imam are trustees to the trust. The trust property consists of a commercial property which is currently let out to tenants. The beneficiaries receive a very good return on the dividends from the rent from the property. Maddie wants to start her own business and wishes to sell her interest under the trust. Max would also like to sell his interest so he can go travelling. Irma would like to purchase their interest and she tells Imam that this is what she intends to do. An independent valuer is approached and Irma pays Maddie and Max the full price. Two months later Maddie changes her mind and seeks to have the transaction set aside.

Which of the following statements best describes the legal position with regard to the purchase of the property by Irma.

A. The sale to Irma of both Maddie and Max's interests can be set aside because the law presumes against a purchase by a trustee of trust property.
B. The sale to Irma of Maddie's interest can be set aside because the law presumes against a purchase by a trustee of trust property.
C. The sale to Irma will be upheld because Irma made full disclosure to her co-trustee.
D. The sale to Irma of Maddie's interest will be upheld because Irma made full disclosure to the beneficiaries and obtained an independent valuation of the interest.
E. The sale to Irma will be upheld because it is too late for Maddie to object.

Question Five

Carrie is in the process of buying a house. She does not have enough money to pay the deposit. Her mother is a trustee of a large trust and she takes money from the trust fund and gives it to her daughter. Carrie is aware that her mother is a trustee and that the money has come from the trust fund and tells her mother that she does not want her to get into trouble and will pay her back as soon as she has the money. The beneficiaries are now aware that the money was taken and would like to recover the money from Carrie as her mother was declared bankrupt last month.

Which of the following statements best describes the rights of the beneficiaries?

A. The beneficiaries cannot recover the money from Carrie because she is not a trustee.
B. The beneficiaries cannot recover the money from Carrie because she is not a fiduciary.
C. The beneficiaries cannot recover the money from Carrie because she was an innocent volunteer.
D. The beneficiaries can recover the money from Carrie as she became a fiduciary when her mother told her about the source off the money.
E. The beneficiaries can recover the money from Carrie because she is liable for knowing receipt.

Question Six

T1, a trustee, takes money from the trust fund to use for herself. Her husband is aware that she is a trustee. T1 asks her husband to advise her on investing the money. Her husband is suspicious about the source of the money as he knows she has never saved any money and has not worked for the past two years. He gives her advice, and the investments are very successful. The beneficiaries are now aware that T1 has taken the money from the fund and wish to recover the money from T1, but she has now disappeared. The beneficiaries wish to claim the money back from the husband.

Which of the following statements best describes the rights of the beneficiaries?

A. The beneficiaries cannot recover the money from the husband because he did not take the money from the trust.
B. The beneficiaries cannot recover the money from the husband because he was not a trustee.
C. The beneficiaries cannot recover the money from the husband because he was not in a fiduciary relationship with the trust.
D. The beneficiaries can recover the money from the husband because he is liable for knowing assistance.
E. The beneficiaries can recover the money from the husband because he is liable for knowing receipt.

PART

III

Trustees appointment, retirement, removal

The duties and powers of trusties, breach of trust and the liability of trustees

10 Trustees appointment, retirement and removal

10.1 Chapter overview

This chapter concentrates on the way trustees are appointed and the circumstances where they may be replaced either voluntarily or because they are no longer suitable to act as a trustee. We will be concentrating on trustees of express trusts. It examines their initial appointment and considers who can act as a trustee. Every trust must have trustees to carry out the terms of the trust and its day-to-day administration. Both express and implied trusts will have trustees, but the trustees in an express trust will be initially chosen and expressly appointed by the settlor, whereas the trustees in an implied trust are not usually chosen, and in many cases, they are not aware that they are acting as a trustee. The second part of the chapter examines who is responsible for appointing new trustees during the currency of the trust. It will no longer be the settlor as they no longer have any control over the trust. We will consider the possibilities of who this can be. The rules have been set down by statute, and we will consider these and the problems that this can sometimes cause.

10.2 Trustees appointment, retirement and removal

If you are a settlor setting up a trust in your lifetime, the choice of trustee will be very important. You will want people who you trust and who you know will act in the best interests of the beneficiaries and carry out the terms of the trust as you have stated. It will not matter if the people that you choose as trustees are not necessarily people with experience of investments or managing property. It is always possible and sometimes a duty for the trustees to take advice from someone with experience about these issues.

10.3 Appointment of trustees

There are only two occasions when trustees are appointed: the setting up of a trust and later the replacement of a trustee of an existing trust when a trustee is either removed or replaced, or they choose to retire.

DOI: 10.4324/9781003583660-13

10.3.1 Who can act as a trustee?

Settlors have a very wide choice of who can act as a trustee with some provisos.

A person under the *age of 18* cannot act as a trustee. A person cannot act as a trustee if they lack *capacity due to a mental disorder.*

Certain people are prevented from acting as trustees because they are assumed to be unfit.

These include the following:

- Someone *adjudicated bankrupt*
- Someone previously *convicted of an offence involving dishonesty or deception*
- Someone previously *removed from a trust because of mismanagement of the trust*

10.3.2 How many trustees?

The number of trustees depends on the type of property held in the trust. The maximum number of trustees of land is *four*, and the minimum number is *two.*

If the trust property is personalty such as jewellery, cars or paintings, there must be at least *one trustee*, but there is *no maximum* number. Of course, it is sensible to keep the number of trustees to a manageable number, as the administration of the trust could become difficult, especially as trustees have to act unanimously.

10.4 Client advice

Consider these facts:

Herbert comes to you for advice. He wants to set up a trust in favour of his wife and three daughters. The trust property consists of the family home, a sizeable shareholding and a collection of valuable modern pictures. He is unsure of whom to appoint as trustees. He likes the husbands of two of his daughters, who both work in finance, but he is worried as to whether or not they will be impartial. He has a friend, Cindy, who has been a headteacher for many years, and he is very close to her as he was a governor at her school. He believes she would be reliable, but she has no background in handling large sums of money.

You should advise Herbert that he must appoint at least two trustees as the trust property includes land. It will not matter that Cindy does not have experience in making decisions about investments or property, so he should be advised to appoint her. He can also appoint the husbands of his daughters as their advice will be valuable, but Cindy will be there to counteract any possibility of bias.

10.5 Appointment of trustees

If it is an inter vivos or lifetime trust, then the first trustees are appointed by the settlor in the *trust instrument* when the trust is set up.

A testator can also appoint trustees when setting up a trust under their will.

Once appointed, the trustees will have the title to the trust property conveyed to them, so they become owners of that property on behalf of the beneficiaries. A person can *disclaim or refuse to act as trustee* any time up until acceptance. This can be done in a number of ways, including by deed or orally, or simply by conduct, such as ignoring the invitation to become trustee. Once a person has accepted trusteeship, then a trustee can only step down by *retiring from the trust*.

The appointment of *additional or replacement* trustees is governed by statute,[1] and there is a strict order as to who can do this:

- Any person nominated in the trust instrument by the settlor to appoint new trustees (if no person has been nominated);
- The surviving or continuing trustees or the personal representative of the sole surviving trustee (or as a last resort);
- The court has power to appoint new trustees.

The appointment of an *additional* trustee can be by deed or simply in writing, but as discussed below, if a new trustee is appointed by writing, then a deed must be executed in order for the trust property to be vested in them.

The appointment of *replacement* trustees.

Sometimes a person may wish to step down from acting as a trustee. Trusteeship can be an onerous position, and it is usually unpaid. There are also circumstances when, under the law, a trustee must be replaced because they are no longer regarded as fit to act as a trustee or they no longer meet the criteria for a trustee, such as remaining out of the country for over a year. The beneficiaries have power to appoint a trustee where there is no one available with that power and the sole surviving trustee is incapable through ill-health.[2]

NB: The statutory list above will apply to the appointment of replacement trustees as well as additional trustees.

1 Trustee Act 1925 s.36.
2 Power granted to the beneficiaries under ss.19, 20 Trusts of Land and Appointment of Trustees Act 1996. All beneficiaries must be of age, legally competent and together entitled to the trust property and in full agreement.

Consider these facts:

Ivan draws up a trust of land in favour of his two grandchildren Bella and Carl. He appoints his two close friends Deepa and Evan as trustees. He nominates another friend Felix as the person to appoint any replacement or additional trustees. Ivan, Deepa and Evan go out for a meal together. Tragically, Ivan and Deepa are killed in a motor accident on the way home. Evan is seriously injured and dies in hospital three days later.

Who is responsible for appointing the new trustees?

In this case, Ivan has appointed Felix in the trust instrument to appoint any additional or replacement trustees, and so the responsibility falls on his shoulders to appoint a new trustee.

What would be the position if Felix had not been nominated in the trust instrument?

If no one has been nominated in the trust instrument to appoint additional trustees, then as there are no surviving trustees, it is the personal representatives of the last of the trustees who died who must appoint the new trustees. In this case, Evan dies last, so it would be their personal representative.

You may comment that the personal representatives of trustees are very remote from the original settlor and may not have even met them; they may refuse to act, in which case, the court must step in and make the appointment.

10.6 Client advice

It is important when advising a client on drawing up a trust to discuss who should take on the responsibility of the appointment of new trustees to replace those appointed by the settlor themselves. It is often better to ensure that someone is nominated in the trust instrument to appoint new trustees rather than leaving the possibility that the personal representative of the surviving trustee makes the appointment. As suggested above, a personal representative of the last trustee alive is somewhat removed from the original settlor.

In the example above, Evan's personal representatives may not have known Ivan and have no understanding of the sort of person that Ivan would wish to act as trustee, so it is far better that Ivan has appointed Felix to be the person to appoint new trustees.

10.6.1 When should a new trustee be appointed?

The circumstances when a *new trustee* can be appointed are[3] when a trustee:

- Has died
- Remains out of the country for more than 12 months
- Desires to be discharged
- Refuses to act
- Is unfit to act as a trustee
- Is incapable of acting as a trustee
- Is an infant
- Has been removed under a power contained in the trust instrument

Comments on these provisions:

i) Note that a trustee can be removed for being *unfit to act* and also is *incapable of acting*. There is a difference between the two;
ii) A trustee who is *unfit to act* is one who is bankrupt or has been convicted of a crime such as dishonesty. So in this case, it is the behaviour of the trustee that is material;
iii) A trustee who is *incapable of acting* is one who is unable to act due to health reasons such as a mental disorder. This is quite distinct from being unfit to act because a trustee is bankrupt. This circumstance is beyond the control of the trustee;
iv) If a trustee *dies*, their trusteeship will automatically come to an end, and their rights to the trust property will pass to the surviving trustees through *survivorship* (as discussed below). The trust property does not form part of the trustee's personal estate when they die, even though it will be vested in their name;
v) A trustee can be *removed* under the statute namely because they are *refusing to act* or because they have been *out of the country for over 12 months* or because they are *underage*. The removal of a trustee who remains out of the country for over 12 months is a very outdated provision and reflects a time when communication with someone abroad was more difficult, but it remains as law;
vi) Apart from the reasons above, it is also possible for the court to *remove a trustee* if someone, usually one of the beneficiaries, makes an application to the court or alternatively the *beneficiaries of a trust of land* apply to remove a trustee. The beneficiaries can only make this application if they are of age and all in agreement. It is possible for beneficiaries of a trust of personal property to appoint a new trustee if they are of age and in agreement, and together are entitled to the trust property, this power must be exercised in writing by the beneficiaries;

3 Trustee Act 1925 s.36(1).

vii) Where a trustee wants to retire, then the retirement must be *by deed*, and all the remaining trustees must consent, and there must be at least two remaining trustees after their retirement;

viii) Remember the principle under equity *'no trust will fail for want of a trustee'*. This means that the court can always make provision for the appointment of a new trustee.

Consider the following facts:

Ivan draws up a trust of land for his two grandchildren, Bella and Carl. He appoints his close friends, Deepa and Evan, as trustees. He nominates another friend, Felix, as the person to appoint any replacement or additional trustees. Deepa is finding the responsibility of being a trustee very hard and wishes to step down, but Evan has been out of the country for over 12 months and has done nothing to help in the administration of the trust.

i) Can Deepa step down; and
ii) Who will be responsible for the appointment of new trustees?

i) Deepa can step down from the trust. A trustee can step down at any time after appointment. In many cases, the retiring trustee will be responsible for appointing the new trustee, but where the settlor has nominated a person to make the appointment, the retiring trustee has no further duties other than to hand over any documents concerning the trust and ensure that the new trustee is appointed. If the new trustee is appointed by deed, then the trust property will be vested in the new trustee;

ii) Felix will be responsible for appointing new trustees. Evan can be forced to step down and a new trustee appointed in his place. As this is a trust of land, then Felix must appoint two trustees to replace Deepa and Evan. If Felix had not been nominated to appoint the trustees, Deepa would have had to do so as she would be seen as a surviving trustee, even though she wishes to step down herself. If Evan has been out of the country for over 12 months, he would not be seen as a continuing trustee, so his agreement would not be needed for the appointment of a new trustee.

10.7 Appointment of a new trustee by the court

Sometimes the retiring trustees or the person appointed by the settlor to appoint a trustee refuses to make an appointment. In these cases, the appointment must be made by the court.[4]

4 Under s.41 Trustee Act 1925.

When making an appointment, the court will consider the intentions of the settlor and other matters such as whether the appointment will be in the best interests of the trust.

10.8 The right of survivorship

Where there are two or more trustees, then they will all *jointly hold the trust property*, and if one dies, then the legal title to the property will simply *remain with the survivors*. When a new trustee takes over, the title to any property must be transferred to them. This is called *'vesting'*. If the appointment of the new trustee is made by deed, then the property will automatically pass to the new trustee, but if the appointment is made in writing, then a deed must be executed in order for that property to pass to the new trustee. This is important as the new trustees now have ownership over the trust property, so it must pass to them by the appropriate means.

Chapter 10 Revision Points – Appointment and Removal and Retirement of Trustees

- The settlor appoints the first trustees;
- There is no limit to the number of trustees of personal property, but trustees of land are limited to four;
- All trustees must be over the age of 18 and have legal capacity and not be deemed unfit to act as a trustee;
- The settlor may also nominate in the trust instrument a person/s to choose any replacement trustee;
- If no person has been nominated to choose trustees, then the surviving or continuing trustees can choose replacement trustees;
- If no trustees remain, then the personal representative of the last surviving trustee/s must choose the new trustee;
- Trusteeship ends on death or retirement;
- A trustee can be replaced if they remain out of the country for over 12 months, are incapable of acting, are unfit to act or are appointed underage.

11 The duties of trustees

11.1 Chapter overview

This chapter looks at all the various duties of trustees and also their powers under the trust, which can also be quite significant. Two important aspects of this are the general duty of care owed by a trustee and the standard of care that is expected of a trustee. These are both examined at the start of the chapter, looking at the change from a common law duty and standard of care to the duty of care that arises through statute.

The chapter also considers the way the law treats different trustees, especially those who have professional experience.

The chapter shows that the specific duties of trustees in any trust derive from a number of sources: the trust instrument, which lays out the duties of the trustees specific to that trust; the common law; and finally, most of the duties of a trustee are laid down in various statutes, in particular, the Trustee Act 2000. The chapter concludes by comparing the duties of a trustee with the powers of a trustee. It examines how they differ and what rights a beneficiary may have if the trustee does not carry out a duty or decides not to exercise a power.

11.2 The duty of care owed by a trustee

Before discussing the various duties of a trustee, we need to consider the general *duty of care* owed by the trustees to the beneficiaries when acting on behalf of the trust. The duty of care is now a statutory duty laid down in the Trustee Act 2000.

Trustees have a *duty to act with 'such care and skill as is reasonable in the circumstances'.*[1]

This duty can be broken by a trustee simply doing nothing as well as doing something that breaches that basic duty. So a trustee who sits back and lets a fellow trustee actively commit a breach of trust is just as much in breach of trust even though that

1 Trustee Act 2000 s.1.

DOI: 10.4324/9781003583660-14

trustee has not interfered with or taken trust funds for themselves. This is the difference between *omission to act* and the *commission of a breach of trust*. Later in this part of the book we will look in more detail at what constitutes a breach of trust and the distinction between a trustee's *omission to act* and their *commission of a breach* of trust.

11.3 The standard of care expected of a trustee

The duty of care of a trustee is to act with such *'care and skill as is reasonable'* in all the circumstances. When assessing what is *'reasonable'* in all the circumstances, the common law standard of care is used.

A trustee is expected to *'conduct the business of the trust in the same manner that an ordinary prudent man of business would conduct his own'.*[2]

Professional trustees and trustees with relevant experience are expected to act with a *higher standard of care*.

You could not expect an ordinary lay trustee to understand investments in the same way as someone who worked in the city as an investment analyst. Nevertheless, you would expect the trustee to consider the investments and to undertake them with a degree of caution or 'prudence'.

11.4 Duties of trustees when assuming office

There are several things that a trustee must do on appointment:

- Become acquainted with the trust instrument, the trust accounts and any trust documentation;
- Check the names of the beneficiaries and the nature and extent of each of their interests under the trust;
- Check the nature of the trust property.

These are the initial duties of any trustee, but their duties will continue. Some of these duties must be repeated over the whole period of time whilst they are a trustee, such as checking the trust property and ensuring that it is invested properly. A trustee cannot argue that, on becoming a trustee, they checked all the documentation and the property but then did not follow this up at a later date with further checks and so were unaware of a potential breach of trust.

2 See *Bartlett v Barclays Bank Trust Co Ltd* [1980], where Brightman J set down this test as the common law standard of care. This has been adopted in part in the Trustee Act s.1 2000.

Consider these facts and give the appropriate advice:

Graham has just been appointed as a new trustee to an existing trust. He is to replace one of two retiring trustees.

Advise Graham on what he should do on appointment.

- Can we assume that Graham can become a trustee in the first place i.e. is he over 18 and is he disqualified in any way from becoming a trustee?
- Graham should be advised that it is important also to check the trust assets, as if the assets include land, then a second trustee must be appointed. He cannot act as a sole trustee;
- Graham must check all the documentation that has been passed to him to ensure that there have been no breaches of trust in the past by previous trustees, as he will be responsible for those even if he was not a trustee at the time, if he has not first checked that no breaches have occurred;
- Graham should also check the terms of the trust to ensure that he is familiar with the nature of the trust. Is this a fixed or discretionary trust? If it is a fixed trust, are the gifts vested or contingent? If contingent, then have the contingencies been satisfied?
- If it is a discretionary trust, what is the nature of the discretion? Who are within the group of discretionary trustees?
- He must also be made aware of his duty to repeatedly check the trust assets and documentation of the trust: it is a continuing duty.

11.5 Ongoing duties of a trustee

There are a number of key duties that a trustee must carry out while he is trustee, and these are viewed as continuing duties, so they must be reviewed from time to time.

- Investment of the trust funds
- Exercising any discretions laid down in the trust instrument
- Keeping accounts and records

11.5.1 Duty of a trustee to invest the trust funds

Trustees have a duty to *invest the trust funds*. A trustee would be in breach of their duty if they assumed office and did nothing with the trust fund at all. The basic duty is to review the *investment of the funds* and decide whether the return is the best in the circumstances. Even if the fund is small and invested in a bank account, the trustees must at least consider whether the account is making the best return for the trust.

Consider these facts:

A has been appointed as co-trustee to a small family trust. The fund consists mainly of money in a bank account and a house let currently to tenants.

A has a duty to consider whether the return on the bank account is the best that can be obtained. Are there other banks or building societies offering a better rate of interest?

What are the terms of the lease of the property? Is it best to retain the property or consider a sale?

The statute makes it clear that this duty is only discharged if the trustees continue *to review the investments* from time to time at regular intervals.

The duty also varies according to the *size of the fund*. A relatively small fund will limit the possibilities for investment and possible growth, whereas a fund which is much bigger makes investment options more varied.

11.5.2 What is meant by an investment?

An investment is generally assumed to be income producing, but more recently, since the Trustee Act 2000, it also includes any property which will not produce income but will increase in capital value.[3] The trust instrument can increase investment powers for trustees, and they can also be excluded or limited by the settlor.

When investing the funds or just reviewing the investments, the trustees must consider all the beneficiaries, so they must consider those in *receipt of income* from the trust and those in *receipt of capital*. The trustees are also bound by the modern *portfolio policy*, which means that they must look at each investment in the light of the *entire portfolio* rather than looking at just one investment. So, there may be some investments which carry a higher risk than others.

Consider this example:

S has recently died. She was a wealthy woman and she has left a trust fund for her husband for life and then to their three children on his death.

The trust funds comprise a house and money in a savings account and two valuable paintings.

The trustees in this case must consider how to maximise income for the husband.

3 Trustee Act 2000 s.6.

The savings account may yield very little income if the interest rate is quite modest.

Perhaps the trustees could consider different accounts or making investments in the stock market.

11.5.3 Investment duties for trustees

When assuming office trustees must apply what is known as the *'standard investment criteria'*. They must consider:

- The *suitability* of the investments of the fund;
- The need for *diversification* of the funds;
- The need to take *proper advice* before investing. Proper advice is advice from someone who the trustees believe is properly qualified to give advice. Advice can be dispensed with if the trustees believe that it is unnecessary or appropriate to do so; and
- The need to *review the investments* from time to time with reference to the standard investment criteria.

Consider the following facts:

Tom and Tess are appointed as trustees of a large testamentary trust fund which mainly comprises shares in a privately quoted company on the stock exchange. The terms of the trust are to Xanthe for life, remainder to Yolande and Zed. The settlor died last week.

What are the main investment duties of Tom and Tess on assuming office as trustees of the fund?

Look at the *standard investment criteria* above. The trustees must consider whether the current investments are suitable for this trust. A large trust holding may yield income for Xanthe but there may not be capital growth. Tom and Tess need to consider whether the funds are *suitable* and whether they are sufficiently *diverse*. They will need to consider whether they need *advice* from someone who is qualified to give that advice.

Perhaps Tom and Tess have experience themselves in investing funds. It does not matter if this is not their job but only that they have sufficient experience.

Tom and Tess must also be aware that adhering to the criteria when they first take office is not sufficient to avoid a potential action for breach of trust; they must also review the investments regularly and reconsider diversification and whether they need further advice.[4]

11.5.4 Duty to take advice and what constitutes 'proper advice'?

Under the Trustee Act, trustees have a duty to take *proper advice*. It is important to understand what is considered to be *'proper advice'* and also when the duty to take advice can be dispensed with.

Consider these facts:

Seth and Sam have been appointed as trustees by a family friend. The trust funds are relatively small and mainly consist of monies in three different savings accounts at a bank. Both Seth and Sam have jobs but are young and have had limited experience in handling and investing sums of money. They are aware that they need advice on investments. They are thinking of approaching a friend, Vince, who is in his final year at university studying mathematics and accountancy.

Would Vince be appropriate to give the trustees advice about investing the trust assets? Is it necessary for them to seek advice?

11.5.5 What is proper advice?

- The Trustee Act states that *advice* is only needed when it is *appropriate* and *necessary* to do so. In a small trust, even lay trustees may have sufficient expertise themselves in order to deal competently with the trust assets;
- If Seth and Sam do not feel properly qualified to deal with the investment of the trust funds, then they need to seek *'proper advice'*;
- Seth and Sam must believe that Vince is *properly qualified* to give advice. A degree in accountancy would give him proficiency in figures; it would not necessarily cover investment strategies. If they took advice from Vince and the investments lost money, it is unlikely that the courts would regard Vince as qualified to give 'proper advice' to the trust;

4 In *Nestle v National Westminster Bank plc* [1993] 1 WLR, a large fund worth £54,000 in 1922 left by William Nestle fell in value to £270,000 in November 1986. It should have been worth considerably more. The claimant was the settlor's only granddaughter. She argued that had the fund been invested properly it would have been worth £1.8 million. The trustee was a bank which had both exercised undue caution and also had failed to understand the powers of investment under the terms of the trust. In spite of criticism from the Court of Appeal, the claimant failed in her claim as the court did not believe the bank was in breach of trust. The main problem was that the claimant could not prove that had the trustees taken a different approach, the trust fund would have produced a better result. It was a very narrow approach and has been subject to criticism.

- We are not told about the amounts contained in the bank accounts. If it really is a relatively small trust with limited assets, then it may not have been necessary to take advice at all.

11.6 Choice of investments

The trustees have a fairly free hand in choosing the type of investment so long as it is deemed to be an investment. Some trustees may have strong views about the way the funds are invested.

11.6.1 Ethical investments

The duty of the trustees is to invest the funds and an investment is expected to produce income. Trustees must act in the *best interests of the beneficiaries*. Does that mean *financial interests* or *non-financial interests*? *Non-financial interests* could include such matters as ethical considerations such as not investing in certain businesses because of personal views. Examples could be not investing in oil or tobacco companies.[5]

There are some occasions where the trustees are entitled to take ethical views into consideration when making an investment:

- *Authorisation of a specific investment* under the trust instrument;
- *Agreement between all the beneficiaries* (if consent is unanimous and freely given and all are of age); and
- Investment in an ethical investment *would produce the same return* as a non-ethical investment.

11.6.1.1 Revision of duty to invest

- Trustees have a duty to invest trust funds;
- When assuming office trustees have a duty to review the investments;
- Trustees must consider the *suitability and diversification* of trust funds when making investments;
- The trustees need to take proper advice on investments unless qualified to do so or it is not appropriate;
- 'Proper advice' is advice from someone who the trustees feel is qualified to give that advice;

5 In *Cowan v Scargill* [1984] 3 WLR, the defendants were trustees of a pension scheme for mineworkers. They objected to an investment plan because the investments were against the investment policy as they were in companies in direct competition with British coal. The Court of Appeal held it would be a breach of trust to refuse to adopt the plan because the duty of the trustees was to maximise profits for the beneficiaries of the scheme.

- Trustees can take views on whether an investment is ethical in very limited circumstances;

11.7 Duty to exercise a discretion granted under a discretionary trust

Sometimes the settlor leaves the final decision as to who will benefit amongst a group and how much they will receive from the trust to the trustees.

Think about the reasons why a settlor might want to do this:

- It could be that the beneficiaries are very young and the settlor may want the trustees to consider their needs as they grow older;
- Alternatively, the settlor may not want to choose between a group but leave the choice to the trustees so they may not look as if they are favouring one beneficiary above others, particularly if they are close relatives.

You will remember from Chapter 1 that there are two types of *express trust*:

- A *fixed trust* and
- A *discretionary trust*

Under a *fixed trust*, the duty placed on the trustee is to distribute to the beneficiaries named in the trust instrument, the trustees have no choice as to who will benefit.

In a *discretionary trust*, the choice of beneficiary and size of share is left to the trustees.

It is important to remember in this context that, unlike beneficiaries in a *fixed trust*, no beneficiary in a *discretionary trust* has a *right in the trust fund*. They have certain rights against the trustees, such as the right to bring an action if the trustee chooses a beneficiary who is not one of the group named by the settlor.

E.g. if a settlor leaves a discretionary trust for the benefit of their nephews and nieces and the trustees mistakenly go ahead and exercise their discretion to someone outside the group, such as a cousin of the settlor.

In this case, any of the group would have a right to bring an action against the trustee because they believe the trustee has acted in breach of trust. The group can do this even though they cannot claim ownership of an interest in the trust fund. The law regards them as having *locus standi*, which literally means the right to stand in the place.

In law, it means someone who has sufficient interest, giving them a right to be heard in court.

The *discretionary beneficiaries* may also bring an action if they feel that the trustees are not carrying out certain duties such as the duty to invest.

Under a discretionary trust, the trustees are given discretion to decide who will benefit and also the size of each share.

Each beneficiary merely has the hope of a share, and they cannot bring pressure on the trustees to choose them above others.

The exercise of the *discretion is completely private*, and the beneficiaries have no right to challenge a decision unless, as discussed above, the trustees exercise their discretion in favour of someone outside the group.

11.7.1 The group interest under a discretionary trust: the rule in *Saunders v Vautier*

Although no beneficiary under a discretionary trust has a proprietary interest as a group, the discretionary beneficiaries have a right to bring the trust to an end, and then each will be given an equal share of the trust fund.

We looked at the rule in *Saunders v Vautier* and when it might apply earlier in the book (see Chapter 4).

11.7.1.1 Revision of the rule in Saunders v Vautier

The rule only applies if the following *conditions are met*.

- All the objects of the trust are entitled to both income and capital;
- All the objects agree that the trust should be brought to an end;
- All the objects are of age; and
- All the objects are of sound mind.

Consider these facts:

A settlor leaves a trust fund of £800,000 to Angie for life and remainder on her death and to any or all of Angie's children appointed by the trustees at their absolute discretion.

Angie has three children: Benjie, Carly and Don.

Can the four beneficiaries bring the trust to an end?

Under the rule in *Saunders v Vautier*, the four beneficiaries can act together and bring this trust to an end. Each will receive a share of £800,000. However, the rules are very strict, and *all four beneficiaries must agree to terminate the trust.*[6]

The three children may be reluctant to agree because on Angie's death one of the children may be chosen to receive the whole of the fund rather than a share.

Angie may not agree because she may be receiving a very good return on the trust fund during her lifetime.

11.7.2 The duty of a trustee in a discretionary trust

In a discretionary trust, the trustee has a duty to choose a beneficiary or beneficiaries amongst the group and also to decide on the size of share that each will receive. They do not have to consider every potential beneficiary in the group, especially if it is very large. They must not allocate trust funds to someone outside the group.

When trustees exercise their discretion, they must do so in private, and their reasons for their decisions are not part of the trust information. In particular, the beneficiaries have no right to see the reasons for their choice.

There are good reasons why the reasons for a trustee's choice are kept private. Potential challenges from beneficiaries could be time-consuming and costly, using up trust funds if the trustees seek to defend their actions.

11.8 Duty to provide accounts and information

The trustees are under a duty to provide certain information to the beneficiaries. This includes any *accounts and also documentary information about the management of the trust*. If the trustees refuse, then the beneficiaries have the right to go to court and ask for this information.

Nevertheless, the law holds that although the beneficiaries have a right to see this information, they do not have the right to question any decision made by the trustees unless they were in breach of trust.

For example, a beneficiary cannot challenge decisions on investment by the trustees unless they can show that they were in breach of the terms of the trust because an investment in a particular asset is expressly excluded under the trust instrument.

6 In *re Smith* [1928] Ch 915, it was held that discretionary beneficiaries could bring a trust to an end because they were all of age and in agreement and jointly entitled to the entire fund.

11.9 Powers of trustees

In contrast to the *duties* discussed above, trustees also have a number of *powers*. You will recall from Chapter 1 that there is a distinction between a *power* and a *duty*.

Revision Points

- Any *duty* placed on a trustee is *obligatory*, which means the duty has to be carried out. If the duty is not carried out, the trustee is liable for a possible action in *breach of trust*.
- A power is *discretionary*, which means there is no obligation on a trustee to carry out the power. There are a number of powers that trustees can exercise, but it is the *powers of maintenance and advancement of capital* that are the most significant.

11.9.1 Powers of maintenance and advancement

During the currency of the trust the trustees have the power to *apply income for the maintenance of beneficiaries who are under the age of 18 and also apply capital for the advancement of all beneficiaries*. This means that some beneficiaries will be able to enjoy either the income and/or the capital for their benefit earlier than specified in the trust instrument.

Remember this provision only applies to a *fixed trust* because the beneficiaries have a proprietary right. It does not apply to a *discretionary trust* because the beneficiaries have no proprietary right, merely the hope that they will receive a share.

Trustees are under a duty to treat the beneficiaries equally and not to favour any one above the others.

It means that when they are looking at the possibility of applying any income for the benefit of one or more beneficiaries, then the trustees must consider the needs of all the beneficiaries.

11.9.2 Power of maintenance

The power of maintenance will apply to all minors if they have:

- A *vested interest*
- A *contingent interest if it carries the right to intermediate income*

What is intermediate income?

Intermediate income is the *right to income under the trust irrespective of other circumstances.*

It is available in *all vested gifts* and *some contingent gifts* unless the gift is a pecuniary legacy (a sum of money) under a will.

You will recall that we discussed the difference between a vested and a contingent gift, which was in Chapter 4.

A *vested gift* is a gift which has no conditions attached to it.

E.g. £40,000 to be held on trust to be distributed in favour of my four daughters.

This is a gift for all the daughters of a share of £40,000 and does not depend on any condition to be fulfilled other than to prove that they are a daughter of the settlor.

By contrast, a *contingent gift* is a gift which involves satisfying *certain conditions.*

E.g. reaching a certain age or qualifying in a certain profession such as accountancy.

'T1 and T2 hold a fund on trust for my sons A, B, C and D so long as they reach the age of 25'.

The contingency here is reaching a certain age, and once that age has been reached, then each of the beneficiaries will hold a vested interest rather than a contingent interest.

In this example, perhaps at the time of the gift, A is aged 25, B is aged 21, C is aged 18 and D is 16. At the time of the gift, only one of the sons satisfies the contingency, A. As each of the sons reaches the age of 25, they can claim that their gift becomes vested. If any of the group fail to reach the age specified, then their right to the gift is lost.

NB: For the purposes of the SQE, it is important to understand the need for the gift to carry the intermediate income in order to allow the trustees the power to apply income for a beneficiary, but you do not have to understand the full range of circumstances when a contingent gift will carry the intermediate income or not.

11.9.2.1 The exercise of the power of maintenance by the trustees

The power of maintenance is a discretion given to trustees to pay or 'apply' income for the benefit of an infant or child beneficiary. This is a statutory power[7] although it may also be a term of the trust instrument.

The statutory powers allow use of the income for *'the maintenance, education or benefit'* of the beneficiary. This is important for the beneficiaries as they have the possibility of receiving their share much earlier than specified in the trust.

11.9.2.2 Prior interests

Two questions must first be asked: Is there another beneficiary entitled to the income from the trust? Is there a beneficiary with a prior interest?

If a trust fund is held for A for life, remainder to B, then B is unable to claim the income for maintenance because, at the time, A is entitled to the income.

By contrast, if the gift is left for the enjoyment of A and B, who are both under 18 at the time of the gift, then there is no prior interest.

How does the trustee decide whether or not to exercise the power of maintenance?

When deciding whether or not to exercise the power to apply the income, the trustee used to be under a statutory duty to consider certain matters such as the age of a beneficiary and their specific needs. Today the power of maintenance can be exercised by the trustees 'as they think fit'.[8] If income is applied for the beneficiary, then it is paid to the child's parent or guardian rather than directly to the child.

Consider these facts:

Beema is 14. She has just been offered a place at a famous ballet school. The fees are £50,000 per year. She lives with her father and younger sister. Her mother died when she was ten, leaving a trust fund of £500,000 in Beema and her sister's favour. There are no prior interests.

The trustees of the fund wish to know whether they can exercise their power of maintenance in favour of Beema.

7 See s.31 Trustee Act 1925.

8 See Inheritance and Trustees' Powers Act 2014 s.8, which replaced the statutory duty to decide on the basis of age, need and other income tax that could be used for this purpose with the more general test of 'as they think fit'.

Advice to the trustees:

This is an express fixed trust. There are no contingencies to be satisfied. There are no prior interests. The purpose is for education. The trustees can pay a sum from the trust fund towards Beema's fees. Their decision will be guided by the statute which states that they can exercise the discretion 'as they think fit'.

Their decision would be different if there were a prior interest. The income cannot be used for maintenance.

Compare these facts:

Beema has been offered a place at ballet school and the fees are £50,000 per year. She lives with her father, Colin, and younger sister, Dee. She is the beneficiary of a trust fund of £500,000 per year. The terms of the trust are: 'to Colin for life, remainder to Beema and Dee in equal shares'.

Your advice to the trustees would be different because here there is a *prior interest*, namely Colin. The prior interest prevents the income from the trust from being used under s.31 for the maintenance of Beema.

11.9.3 Power of advancement

The Power of advancement gives the trustees the power to pay or apply *capital* for the *advancement of any beneficiary*. It is discretionary, so the trustees do not have to give reasons for any decision made.

11.9.3.1 What constitutes advancement?

The court has given a wide interpretation of what constitutes *advancement*. It is interpreted as anything that will improve the beneficiary's material situation. This can include paying towards the beneficiary's liability to inheritance tax or even paying a sum towards their existing debts. It can also include an indirect benefit, e.g. a sum advanced to allow a partner or spouse to set up in business could be allowed.

11.9.3.2 How much capital can be advanced?

Prior to 2014,[9] only one-half of the presumptive share could be advanced, but since 2014, the trustees can advance the entire share, subject to the following conditions:

- Once the beneficiary becomes *absolutely entitled* to their share, the sum advanced must be taken into account. In practice, it will be deducted from the amount due to be paid out under the trust to them;

9 The Inheritance and Trustees' Powers Act 2014.

- Anyone with a *prior interest* in the trust fund i.e. someone with a life interest must be of age and must also give written consent to the advancement.

Consider these facts:

Connie leaves her entire estate (worth £900,000) to her partner Cleo for life and on her death to Connie's children from her previous relationship, Des, Erin and Felix. Erin has requested an advance of £100,000 to help purchase a flat. The trustees must first ask Cleo if she agrees to the advance, as the income Cleo will receive in the future will be reduced because the fund will be smaller.

Each of the children will eventually be entitled to a share of £300,000, so Erin's share will be reduced by £100,000 on Cleo's death, and she will only be able to claim £200,000. Erin has only asked for part of her eventual share, so that is within the rules.

She is limited to claiming £300,000 or less.

The *power of advancement* is not limited to cash; it can include the advance of any type of property.

Chapter 11 Revision Points

- In a discretionary trust, the choice of beneficiary and size of share is left to the discretion of the trustees;
- Beneficiaries have no right to see the trustees' reasons for the exercise of a discretion;
- Beneficiaries under both fixed and discretionary trusts have the right to bring a trust to an end under the rule in *Saunders v Vautier*;
- The conditions for *Saunders v Vautier* are that all the beneficiaries must be *sui juris* and in agreement and are together entitled to all the trust monies;
- All beneficiaries have a right to see trust information, including the accounts, but they have no right to see minutes of decision-making;
- Beneficiaries under 18 are entitled to ask to have a sum of money for their maintenance advanced if certain conditions are satisfied;
- No money can be advanced to a beneficiary for maintenance if there is a prior interest;
- All beneficiaries can ask for an advance of capital if it is for their benefit; this is discretionary;
- The trustees can advance the whole of a beneficiary's interest, but this must be accounted for later;
- There can only be an advancement of capital if someone with a prior interest gives written consent.

12 Breach of trust

12.1 Chapter overview

In the previous chapter, we looked at the duty of care that a trustee owes to the beneficiaries. Trustees have a duty to act with 'such care and skill as is reasonable in the circumstances'. If they fail to act according to this standard, then they can be sued by the beneficiaries for breach of trust. So, in this chapter, we will examine the circumstances when a trustee might be liable for a breach of trust. There are a number of duties owed by all trustees of express trusts to the beneficiaries, such as the duty to invest. Trustees may also owe specific duties laid down in the trust instrument by the settlor. Breach of any of these duties may lead to an action by the beneficiaries. We will look at the test that must be satisfied in order for a trustee to be found liable for a breach. If that test is satisfied, then there are various remedies available to the beneficiaries. Finally, we consider the various defences that a trustee may raise and the use of exemption clauses within a trust instrument.

12.2 Nature of a breach of trust

The role of trustee is an onerous position and carries a very high level of responsibility. It is important to remember that not all trustees are well qualified for the responsibilities that they carry, and yet the law may still hold them responsible for any mistakes that they might make.

Consider the following situations:

i) A trustee, X, is told by a fellow trustee, Y, that one of the beneficiaries is called Mary Smith and he must transfer a share to her. As X knows the settlor's surname was Smith, he transfers the money to Mary Smith. He should have paid Mary R. Smith the money;
ii) A trustee, B, is told by a friend on the train that investing in a company that makes a certain children's toy is an excellent investment. Trustee B makes a substantial investment of trust monies and the company goes into liquidation a month later;
iii) A trustee, T, wishes to have some of the assets of the trust valued. They are paintings by a modern artist. Trustee T does not know any art valuers, so instead

DOI: 10.4324/9781003583660-15

he takes advice from someone he selects from the internet. They are incorrectly valued, and the trust makes a substantial loss.

In all these situations the trustees X, B and T have all potentially committed a breach of trust. It will depend on the circumstances but each of the trustees has fallen below the standard expected of a trustee which we looked at in the previous chapter. The duty of care owed by a trustee is to exercise such *care and skill as is reasonable in the circumstances.*

This can be varied if the trustee has any *special knowledge or experience*, and also it is important always to check to see if the trustee is acting in the course of a business or a profession. In these circumstances, the law will place a higher duty of care on them.

You should also revisit the various duties of trustees, in particular their duty to invest. Trustees are not expected to have qualifications and experience in making investments, but it is expected that they will take 'proper advice' and also check the terms of the trust instrument personally. They should never just rely on their fellow trustees for information and advice on investments or any other matter. Trustees can always seek advice from an expert on any matter that they do not feel they have the proper qualifications to act.

Trustee X should have checked the terms of the trust instrument before paying out any money to a beneficiary to ensure that the money is being transferred to the correct beneficiary. He should not simply rely on what trustee Y told him.

Trustee B should have taken 'proper advice' before investing trust money. This is a statutory duty under the Trustee Act 2000.

The same would apply to *trustee T*, who should have taken reasonable steps to find an expert to value the paintings and not simply rely on the internet. If each of these steps had been taken, then the trustees would escape liability even if a loss had occurred to the trust.

A breach of trust occurs whenever a trustee fails to discharge their duties in relation to the trust. This could include duties in relation to the trust property or their duties to the beneficiaries. Remember that all beneficiaries are able to bring an action for breach of trust. This includes beneficiaries of a discretionary trust who think the trust is not being properly administered.

12.3 Omissions and commissions

It is important to also note that a breach of trust can occur by *omission or commission*. This means that the trustee who does nothing in relation to a trust can be just as liable for a breach of trust.

12.3.1 Omission

When we discussed the duty to invest, we looked at the duty on the trustees to review the trust investments from time to time and also the duty to consider diversification. Failure to review or consider diversification would in itself constitute a breach of trust because it is an *omission to act*.

It would be the same if one trustee left the administration of the trust to another trustee who committed a breach. Failing to check on a co-trustee is considered a breach of trust.

12.3.2 Commission

The *commission* of a breach of trust is far more obvious. This could include trustees taking trust property for themselves, transferring trust property to the wrong beneficiary or making an investment of trust property recklessly without taking proper advice.

12.4 General principles of breach of trust

- The law places an *absolute duty* on the shoulders of trustees to carry out their duties and to act in the interests of the beneficiaries. It is an absolute duty, and the intention of a trustee plays no part in whether or not they are liable for a breach of trust;
- Trustees are liable for their own *personal breaches of trust*, and so where there are several trustees, a single trustee will not be liable for the breaches of their fellow trustees. A trustee may be liable where the breach has been caused by a fellow trustee because a breach of trust can be caused by *omission* to act as well as *commission* to act. They have a duty to check to see if the trust is being administered properly. They should check the actions taken by any fellow trustee;
- Trustees are not liable for breaches that occurred *before* they took up their duties, but they have a duty to read the trust documents before becoming a trustee, and so they may be liable if they fail to notice that a breach of trust has occurred before they took office,
- Trustees are not liable for breaches that occur *after* they retire from office. They will still be liable if they retire in order to avoid an action for a breach; they will remain liable for any breaches committed whilst they were a trustee. If one or more trustees refuse to act in a certain way that would be regarded as a breach of trust. If the trustee retires so a new trustee can be appointed who is willing to commit that breach then the retiring trustees will be liable as they were aware of the breach of trust to be committed on their retirement;[1]

1 This happened in the case of *Head v Gould* [1898] 2 Ch 250. In this case, existing trustees had paid out sums to the beneficiaries which were within their powers but refused to pay out further sums as

- Beneficiaries have the right to sue any one or more of the trustees where a breach has occurred or all of the trustees as the law regards their liability as *joint and several.* There could be reasons why they choose to sue just one trustee, such as that trustee may have more money than the others. So it is possible, where a breach has occurred, such as one trustee personally profiting from the trust, to sue the other trustees to recover the money because they should have been checking on that trustee to ensure no breach of trust had occurred.

Consider this example:

Francis is a successful businessman, and along with Gurvinder and Hari, who are both students, was a trustee of a trust which had considerable assets, including investments in reputable companies, and was making a good return for the trust. Together, they took the decision to sell all the shares and invest in one start-up company run by Hari's brother, Ira. After a year, Ira's company failed, and the trust lost a considerable amount of money.

All three trustees are liable for the breach, but the beneficiaries may choose to sue only Francis. This is because Gurvinder and Hari may not have any money to compensate for the breach.

12.4.1 The test for causation in a breach of trustee

The beneficiaries will only be able to successfully sue the trustees if they can show a causal connection between the breach and the loss to the trust.

12.4.2 Causal connection between the breach of trust and the loss to the trust

The beneficiary must show that a *breach of trust* by one or more of the trustees led to the direct or indirect *loss to the trust.* The beneficiaries are also entitled to claim any profit arising through the breach even where the trust suffers no loss.

Once a beneficiary can show a *causal connection* between a breach of trust and a loss to the trust fund, the trustee must restore the trust to the position before the breach. This is referred to as *compensation.* This is not the same as damages payable in other cases such as contract and tort.

The duty of the trustee will be to restore to the trust fund the value of the lost assets.

that would exceed their powers. Those trustees retired, and new ones were appointed who paid out sums to the beneficiaries in breach of trust. The retiring trustees were held jointly liable for the breach because they were fully aware that the new trustees intended to make the payments.

Proving a *causal connection* depends on showing that the *omission or commission* by the trustees *caused* the loss to the trust fund.

Consider these facts. (They are based on a real case.[2])

A very successful businessman died, leaving a substantial amount of money on trust for various members of his family. Eventually, the settlor's granddaughter became the solely entitled beneficiary of the fund. Although the fund had increased in value, it was discovered that it was many thousands of pounds short of the value it should have been if the fund had been managed properly (we looked at this case in Chapter 11 under duty to invest).

12.4.3 Breach of trust by the bank

The trustees were a bank (The NatWest Bank) and had been in breach of trust in several different ways.

i) It had misinterpreted the terms of the trust;
ii) It had failed to take legal advice;
iii) The bank had also failed to review the investments.

They were clearly in *breach of trust*. However, the claimant failed in her action because she could not show a *causal connection* between the breach of trust and the loss to the trust fund.

The court concluded that even if the bank had used its wider powers of investment, there may still have been a loss to the fund. The court also concluded that the uncertainties of the stock market make predictions of how investments might fare difficult to predict. For that reason, a conservative approach to investment was welcomed by the court. This ensured that the fund maintained stability rather than growth.

The court took a very restrictive approach to what constitutes a *causal connection* between a breach of trust and a loss to the fund.

Consider this example:

Borrowers had borrowed money using property as security. They had borrowed a sum in excess of the true value of the property. They had been able to do this because there had been an incorrect valuation, and so, although the lenders did have the title to the property which was security against the value of the loan, the lenders could not recover the full amount in the event of the borrowers defaulting. Added to that, the property market was in recession at the time of the loan; this meant the value of

2 See *Nestle v National Westminster Bank plc* [1993] 1 WLR 1260.

the property had fallen even lower. The lenders sued the solicitors for breach of trust. The solicitors had acted and, in fact, committed a breach of trust in the transaction by paying out mortgage funds without authority *but* the claimant lenders could not show that the solicitors had caused the loss to the trust fund.[3]

The loss had occurred for two reasons:

i) The inflated valuation
ii) The recession in the property market

Cases showing a *causal connection* between a trustee's breach and a loss to the trust fund would include payment of trust funds to the wrong beneficiary; investing in unauthorised investments and failing to recover property within the trust.

12.4.4 Liability of each trustee

If a settlor, X, has left a trust fund to be paid equally to Y and Z and the trustees pay half the fund to A, then that clearly is a breach of trust. The trustees will try to recover the sum lost from A, and if for any reason they cannot do so, they will each be *personally liable* to repay the sum.

12.5 Indemnity from fellow trustees

Where it can be proved that a trustee has committed a breach of trust, then that trustee must pay back the value of the loss. This is referred to as *compensation* to the trust fund. We discussed this earlier. Each trustee must pay this out of their own personal funds. In some circumstances, the trustee can recover the amount paid or part of the amount from their fellow trustees. This is called an *indemnity*. There are also circumstances when this can be recovered from beneficiaries as well.

The cases where an *indemnity* from a fellow trustee can be claimed are fairly limited:

- **Fraudulent benefit from a breach of trust**

Where one trustee has fraudulently obtained a benefit from a breach of trust, the other trustees can claim an indemnity against the fraudulent trustee. In this case, proof of fraud by the trustee is necessary.

- **Breach committed on the advice of a solicitor-trustee**

Where it is proved that one of the trustees is a solicitor and the solicitor-trustee gives advice which results in a breach of trust and the co-trustees relied on that advice and

3 See here the case of *Target Holdings v Redferns* [1995] 3 AER 785, on which these facts are based.

did not exercise independent judgement, then an indemnity can be claimed from the solicitor-trustee.[4]

- **Where a trustee is also a beneficiary**

In cases where a trustee is also a beneficiary and benefits from a breach of trust the trustee-beneficiary must indemnify the loss suffered by the trust to the full extent of their share. If the loss then exceeds that share, the rest of the loss will be shared equally between the trustees.

It is also possible to claim an *indemnity against a beneficiary* who consented to or instigated a breach of trust.

12.6 The Civil Liability (Contribution) Act 1978

The right of contribution from a fellow trustee is now governed by *statute* under the *Civil Liability (Contribution) Act 1978*. The court has a discretion concerning how much one trustee can recover from their fellow trustees in respect of a loss suffered by the trust.

The governing rule is *'what is regarded as just and equitable'* looking at the person's responsibility for the damage in question.

The 1978 Act does not apply to the three examples discussed above:

- *Fraud*;
- *A breach caused by the advice of a solicitor-trustee*; and
- *Where a trustee is also a beneficiary.*

12.7 Defences available to trustees for a breach of trust

A trustee may be found to be in breach of trust but they may escape liability in part or wholly for the breach if they can rely on a defence.

They may also escape liability because the trust instrument may contain an *exemption clause.*

4 In the case of *Re Partington* [1887] 57 LT 654, a solicitor trustee had given advice to his co-trustee about an investment in an improper mortgage. This had resulted in a loss largely because the solicitor trustee had failed to check certain facts about the mortgagor. A full indemnity was ordered by the court in favour of the lay trustee.

The following are the main defences that a trustee can rely on in an action for breach of trust:

- *Statutory relief under the Trustee Act 1925 s.61*: This section allows a trustee to escape liability if they can prove that they acted *honestly and reasonably and ought fairly to be excused*. It allows the court to relieve them from liability either wholly or partially for the breach. The reason that this section was introduced was to encourage lay people to agree to act as trustees. The idea that one could be personally liable for the extent of loss that may occur if one makes a mistake or fails to check a document or instructions is likely to put many people off from agreeing to act as a trustee. To act *honestly* under the section means to *act in good faith*; to act *reasonably* means the trustee acted with the standard of care expected for that trustee and *ought fairly to be relieved* means that any trustee who has acted honestly and reasonably must be excused by the court. It does depend on whether the trustee is a lay trustee or a professional trustee and if the trustees have taken advice.[5] The courts are more likely to apply the section to a lay trustee than a professional trustee;
- *The limitation period*: The law lays down time limits within which some legal actions must be brought. The limitation period for breach of trust is *six years (Limitation Act 1980)*. There are exceptions such as *fraud*, where the trustee was party to the fraud; cases where the claimant has a *disability* when the breach occurred (this includes children under 18 and those suffering from a mental disability); and cases where trust property is in the *personal possession of the trustee*. In cases where the trustee deliberately conceals their actions which are in breach, time will not begin to run until the claimant becomes aware of the actual *facts that have been concealed by the trustees or there has been a mistake by the trustees*. Note that in a trust where there is a life tenant and a remainder man, e.g. To X for life, remainder to Y, time does not run against the remainder man (Y) until their interest falls in. This means that after six years, time will have run for X to bring an action for breach of trust, but Y may bring the action within six years of X's death;
- *Laches*: This defence is similar to the defence under the Limitation Act but is a common law defence as opposed to a statutory defence. As the limitation period does not apply to some breaches of trust as discussed above, the court has discretion to refuse an action for breach which is brought by the beneficiaries fully aware that a breach has occurred many years after the event. The court must decide that it is *inequitable* to allow the claim to proceed. The doctrine is usually applied where the delay has resulted in the defendant trustee *changing their position*. This might mean that the trustee has spent a sum of money or sold assets which belonged to the trust assuming that no action is going to be brought for a breach of trust or being led to believe by the beneficiaries that

5 In *Bartlett v Barclays Bank* [1980] Ch 515, a professional trustee was refused relief under s.61 because the court held that it had acted unreasonably as it had failed to check the status of investments.

no action is going to be brought. The trustee will rely on the argument that the beneficiary has acquiesced in their actions;

- *Acquiescence, release or concurrence by the beneficiary*: An action for breach of trust will be brought by the beneficiaries, so if the beneficiaries discover a breach but have at an earlier stage waived their right to sue, then the trustees will escape liability. This can only happen if the trustees can prove that the beneficiaries were in possession of all the facts and were over 18 and not under any disability and all in full agreement. So, if there are three beneficiaries aged 21, 19 and 16, the trustees could not rely on *acquiescence* even if they were all in agreement and aware of the facts. It is also not available where the trustees have brought pressure on the beneficiaries to agree;
- *Impounding the interest of a beneficiary*: If one beneficiary agrees to a breach of trust but not the others and then personally profits from the breach, the trustees have the right to impound the interest of that beneficiary. That beneficiary is required to indemnify the trustees. This means that that beneficiary can be made to pay towards the loss to the trust. The court has a discretion whether or not to enforce this under *s.62 Trustee Act 1925*. It is not a defence to a trustee who has committed a breach of trust, but it is at least a way of limiting the amount to be repaid.

12.8 Exemption clauses

Exemption clauses are used widely in a number of areas of law. They can also be used to protect trustees from an action for breach of trust. They can be inserted into a *trust instrument* and cover a wide range of potential breaches of trust by trustees.

The important thing to remember about *exemption clauses* is that they exempt a trustee from negligence and lack of care. This is quite acceptable.

An exemption clause can never exempt liability for the basic duties that a trustee owes to the beneficiaries, such as *duties of good faith, honesty and acting in the beneficiaries' interests*.

Consider the following clause which was inserted into a settlement: *'the trustees are not liable for any loss or damage to the income or capital unless such loss or damage shall be caused by the trustees' own actual fraud'*.

This was the clause contested in the case of *Armitage v Nurse*.[6] The courts allowed the trustees to rely on the clause because it could not be shown that the trustees had been dishonest, merely negligent.

6 *Armitage v Nurse* [1998] Ch 241

It means that an *exemption clause* in a trust instrument can cover negligence, even gross negligence, but it can never apply to the *irreducible core of trust obligations*.

The result is that trustees can be exempted even where they have deliberately committed a breach of trust so long as their actions were in good faith and also that they were acting in the honest belief that their actions were in the best interests of the beneficiaries.

Exemption clauses are available for lay trustees and also for professional trustees as well. The court will always be stricter in its interpretation of an exemption clause that has been relied on by professional trustees than by a lay trustee, as the professional trustee is relying on a clause protecting them from their own negligence.

12.9 Client advice

In advising a client who wishes to set up a trust, you should explain that an exemption clause can always be inserted into the trust instrument. Explain the context of their use and the way that they operate, especially the limitations placed on them. So, it is important to explain what is meant by the 'irreducible core of trust obligations'. You should also advise that lay trustees may feel more confident about acting if there is an exemption clause in place. Family members or friends of the settlor may be reluctant to act when they become aware of the personal nature of their duties and their potential liability. You should advise that potential trustees may feel more inclined to agree to becoming a trustee if they were exempted from liability for a genuine mistake when administering the trust.

Brief summary of defences and protection for trustees against an action for breach of trust

s.61 Trustee Act 1925	**A trustee can rely on s.61 if they can show that they acted honestly and reasonably and ought fairly to be to be excused.**
Limitation period (Limitation Act 1980)	A claim against a trustee for breach of trust must be brought within six years. The time runs from the discovery of the breach. There are exceptions for fraud; where a trustee holds trust property for himself; if a beneficiary is under a disability; where a breach of trust has been concealed by the trustee or there has been a mistake by the trustee.
Laches	A court may dismiss an action for breach outside the Limitation Act if there has been unnecessary delay by the claimant beneficiary. The sort of action that may fall outside the Limitation Act is where a trustee has committed fraud or has in their possession trust property.

s.61 Trustee Act 1925	**A trustee can rely on s.61 if they can show that they acted honestly and reasonably and ought fairly to be to be excused.**
Acquiescence by the beneficiaries	If the beneficiaries consented or instigated the breach of trust.
Impounding the interest of a beneficiary	The court can take the interest of a beneficiary who consented to or instigated a breach to indemnify the trustees.
Exemption clauses	The trustees can rely on an exemption clause in a trust instrument covering their breach. No exemption clause will be upheld if it attempts to protect a trustee against their dishonesty.

Chapter 12 Revision Points

- A trustee must take such care and skill as is reasonable in the circumstances;
- A trustee commits a breach of trust where they fail to meet this standard either in carrying out their general duties or duties laid down in the trust instrument;
- A breach of trust can be committed by omission as well as commission;
- Trustees are only liable for a breach of trust if the beneficiaries can prove a causal connection between the breach of trust and the loss to the trust fund;
- Trustees are jointly and severally liable for each breach of trustee;
- Trustees can rely on a number of defences where they have committed a breach: s.61 Trustees Act 1925; The Limitation Act 1980; the doctrine of laches; acquiescence by the beneficiaries;
- Trustees can rely on an exemption clause which can be used where they are in breach of trust through negligence but never where their breach of trust is dishonest.

12.10 Multiple-Choice Questions

Question One

Caspar and Donny were appointed trustees last year. The settlor, Emil, was their cousin. On their appointment, he had included a clause in the trust instrument as follows: 'the trustees shall be exempted from liability for loss or damage which may happen from any cause whatsoever unless such damage shall be caused by his own actual fraud'. Caspar and Donny were aware of the exemption clause.

The trust property includes a substantial sum of money in a bank account to which the trustees have unlimited access. Caspar and Donny run a business together, and earlier this year, Caspar needed a substantial sum of money to pay their employees, and he took the money from the trust intending to pay it back as he believed the business would soon be profitable. Donny was aware of what Caspar had done.

Which of the following statements best describe the legal position as to whether the trustees can claim protection from the exemption clause?

A. Both trustees are liable for breach of trust, and the exemption clause cannot protect them against an action by the beneficiaries.
B. Only Caspar is liable for the breach of trust as he took the money from the trust. Donny can rely on the clause.
C. Neither trustee is liable for breach of trust as the exemption clause is wide enough to protect them.
D. Neither trustee is liable for breach of trust as they always intended to return the money to the trust.
E. Neither trustee is liable as their actions were not fraudulent.

Question Two

Tess and Tex are trustees appointed for a family trust on the following terms: 'to Annie for life, and on her death, to Bilal'. The settlor, Chaz, died nine years ago. The terms of the trust included a clause that forbids any investment in property let as a tenancy. Eight years ago, Tess and Tex decided to invest in a property which they let to tenants, believing it to be a good investment. Annie agreed with this course of action. At the time, Bilal was 16. The lease came to an end last year, and the trustees have discovered that the property has fallen in value because the tenants did not properly maintain it, and there are considerable arrears in rent owing. Annie died this month, and Bilal now wishes to recover the losses suffered by the trust.

Which of the following statements best describe the legal position as to whether Bilal can recover the losses suffered by the trustee?

A. Bilal cannot recover the losses from the trustees because Annie had agreed with the course of action.
B. Bilal cannot recover the losses from the trustees because the breach was eight years ago.

C. Bilal cannot recover the losses from the trustees because they thought it was a good investment.

D. Bilal can recover from the trustees because he did not agree to the investment at the time.

E. Bilal can recover from the trustees because his interest accrued to him under six years ago.

Question Three

Easy Loans Ltd was a finance company which entered into an agreement to advance a loan secured on a commercial property. The borrower was a developer who had employed a firm of valuers who had overvalued the property. Easy Loans had employed a firm of solicitors called White & Co. White & Co had forwarded the title of the property in breach of trust before the mortgage was complete. The transaction had been dealt with by a junior member of the firm who was unaware that they were in breach. The mortgage was eventually completed but some months later the developers went into liquidation and when Easy Loans tried to sell the property, they made a considerable loss because it had been overvalued, and the property market was in recession. Easy Loans want to recover the outstanding amount from White & Co.

Which of the following statements best describe the legal position as to whether Easy Loans can recover the losses they have suffered from the solicitors?

A. Easy Loans can recover the whole of the outstanding amount from the solicitors.

B. Easy Loans can recover some of the amount outstanding from the solicitors.

C. Easy Loans cannot recover any of the amount outstanding from the solicitors because there is no causal link between the loss and the breach.

D. Easy Loans cannot recover any of the outstanding amount because they should have double-checked the valuation of the property themselves.

E. Easy Loans cannot recover any of the outstanding amount from the solicitors because they were unaware that they were in breach of trust.

12.11 Multiple-Choice Questions – Part 3

Question One

Gerry died last year. During his life, he had set up a trust in favour of his wife and two children who are both currently at school. It comprises a sum of money in a savings bank account and two terraced houses which are currently let to tenants. He appointed his two sisters, Sal and Shadia, and a friend, Finn, as trustees. Sal wishes to stand down as a trustee because she has a new job and has very little spare time. Shadia and Finn both think a new trustee should be appointed.

Which of the following statements best describe the legal position as to whether it is necessary to appoint a new trustee to replace Sal?

A. A replacement trustee must be appointed because the trust had three trustees when the trust was created.
B. A replacement trustee must be appointed because the trust fund has land as well as money.
C. A replacement trustee must be appointed because the children are still minors.
D. A replacement trustee need not be appointed because there are still two remaining trustees.
E. A replacement trustee need not be appointed because the trustee is retiring voluntarily and not being replaced because they are either unfit or unable to act.

Question Two

Hal and Hari are two trustees of a discretionary trust. The beneficiaries of the trust are a number of relatives of the settlor, who was a very rich businessman. Recently, the trustees have exercised their discretion in favour of two beneficiaries who are both relatives of the settlor. One of the other beneficiaries, Isaac, thinks the discretion was exercised wrongly and wants the trustees to give reasons for their decision. The other beneficiaries disagree.

Which of the following statements best describe the legal position as to whether the beneficiaries have a cause of action against the trustees?

A. Trustees do not have to give reasons to the beneficiaries for the exercise of their discretion.
B. Trustees must always give reasons for the exercise of their discretion.

C. Trustees can choose whether or not to give reasons for the exercise of their discretion.

D. Trustees only need to give reasons for the exercise of their discretion if all the beneficiaries are of age and in agreement.

E. Trustees have complete freedom in the exercise of their discretion under a discretionary trust.

Question Three

Aaron created a trust worth £1 million ten years ago in favour of his three children and his three nephews. He appointed Tristan and Taylor as trustees. They were close friends of Aaron, but neither had any financial expertise. They have never taken advice with regard to investments. They annually review the trust funds but have not changed the investments since the creation of the trust. Bilal is one of the beneficiaries of the trust. He thinks the investments of the trust have fared badly and that the value of the trust has fallen. He asks for advice as to whether the trustees have discharged their duties with regard to investments.

Which of the following statements best describe the legal position as to whether the trustees have discharged their duties with regard to their duty to invest the trust fund?

A. Tristan and Taylor have discharged their investment duties because they have reviewed the trust funds every year.

B. Tristan and Taylor have discharged their investment duties because trustees do not always have to seek advice about investments.

C. Tristan and Taylor have not discharged their investment duties because they have never changed the investments since the creation of the trust.

D. Tristan and Taylor have not discharged their investment duties because they have not discussed the investments with the beneficiaries.

E. Tristan and Taylor have not discharged their investment duties because they have never sought proper advice.

Question Four

Vernon is a stockbroker and also a committed vegan. He was appointed sole trustee of a small trust fund of his brother's two years ago, replacing his sister, who had acted as a trustee for several years. The beneficiaries of the fund are the two nieces of the settlor, Han and Ira. Since becoming a trustee, Vernon has reinvested the funds. He sold the shares in a meat processing company, which had been bringing in a very good return for the trust, and instead bought shares in a company specialising in vegan products. Ira believes the fund has dropped dramatically in value because of the choice of investments and intends to bring an action against Vernon for breach of trust.

Which of the following statements best describe the legal position as to whether Vernon has discharged his duty with regard to the trust fund?

A. Vernon has the right to choose an investment based on his personal beliefs.
B. Vernon should have sought advice before changing the investments of the trust.
C. Vernon cannot make an investment based on his moral and ethical beliefs unless the return is equally or more profitable.
D. Vernon should have explained his beliefs to the beneficiaries before making the investment.
E. Vernon should have appointed a second trustee to help him make the decision.

Question Five

Ross and Serena are 16-year-old twins; they live with their mother, Teri. They are beneficiaries under a trust set up by their father, Quentin, four years ago on the following terms: 'to Teri for life, and on her death, to Ross and Serena'. Quentin died last year.

Serena has been offered a place at drama school, but the fees are very high, and she would like to use her share in the trust fund to pay for her place at drama school. Teri does not want Serena to go to drama school and would like her to stay on at her current school and study for her A levels.

Which of the following statements best describe the legal position with regard to the use of the fund to pay for the fees for Serena?

A. Trustees can always apply part of the fund towards the education of a beneficiary.
B. The money cannot be used to pay the fees of Serena because there is a prior interest.
C. The money cannot be used to pay the fees of the drama school because her mother does not give her consent for her to go.
D. The money cannot be used to pay the fees for one of a group of beneficiaries as it would not be fair on the rest of the group.
E. Trustees can always apply part of the fund towards the maintenance of a single beneficiary if they think it is fit to do so.

Question Six

Gavin, Kevin and Mikey were appointed trustees to a large trust fund by the settlor ten years ago. The beneficiaries were the settlor's twin granddaughters, Nora and Orla. They were both 13 when the trust was set up. The settlor had stipulated in the trust instrument that the trustees were only to invest in companies situated in the UK. The trust property consists of various shareholdings; some commercial properties and a sum of money deposited in a building society savings account. Seven years ago, the trustees decided to invest some of the money in the building society account in an American company, which provided an excellent return for the trust. Kevin did not scrutinise the purchase of the new shares but simply signed all the documentation. Recently, the shares have fallen in value and Orla has discovered that the investment in the American company was in breach of trust.

Orla wishes to bring an action for breach of trust against all the trustees.

Which of the following statements best describe the legal position with regard to the liability of all the trustees?

- **A.** None of the trustees are liable for the loss to the fund because the investment was made because it would produce a good return for the trust.
- **B.** None of the trustees are liable for the loss to the fund because it is over six years since the investment was made.
- **C.** Only Gavin and Mikey are liable for the loss to the fund because Kevin did not take the investment decision.
- **D.** Kevin is solely liable because he omitted to check the actions of the other trustees.
- **E.** All the trustees are liable because they were all in breach and time is still running against them.

PART IV

Equitable tracing

Equitable remedies

13 Equitable tracing

13.1 Chapter overview

This chapter examines a process called tracing. Tracing is not regarded as a remedy but a process that allows beneficiaries to recover trust property or even its equivalent. This process may allow recovery of actual trust property such as a particular painting or a piece of jewellery from third parties. They may be innocent volunteers, or they may be strangers to the trust who have received trust property wrongly. Tracing is of particular value when a trustee is either bankrupt or may have disappeared and the beneficiaries must then rely on other means to recover losses to the trust fund. The chapter will examine the requirements to be satisfied before tracing can take place. It will also explore some of the rules of tracing in particular tracing into bank accounts. These can pose particular problems. The final part of the chapter looks at defences that may be raised to tracing.

13.2 Tracing in equity and at common law

Earlier in the book, we have discussed the personal liability of trustees to *compensate the trust fund* for any loss that has been caused by their breach. Sometimes trustees have no money to restore the trust fund or they cannot be found, so an action against them will be pointless. Equity allows the beneficiaries the right to take action against others who may have innocently received trust property and can be used even where the trust property has been sold and replaced by other property. We have already discussed what happens when property falls into the hands of a third-party *stranger* (see Chapter 9), but the beneficiaries need to rely on a right to recover the property back from the stranger, especially in circumstances where an action for breach of trust against the trustees is unlikely to ensure recovery of property. This process of recovering the trust property is called *tracing*.

There are two forms of tracing: *common law tracing* and *tracing in equity*, but this chapter concentrates almost exclusively on the rules of equitable tracing because the SQE only requires knowledge of tracing in equity. Just be aware that there is this second type of tracing.

DOI: 10.4324/9781003583660-17

13.2.1 How does a tracing action work?

Consider these facts:

Faisal is a sole trustee of a trust fund held for the settlor's wife and three children. Faisal wanted to purchase a car for his father, but he had no surplus funds. He withdraws £50,000 from the trust fund, which he gives to his father, who was unaware that it came from the trust. The father purchases a car. The beneficiaries are now aware of what the trustee, Faisal, has done. They are also aware that Faisal is on the brink of bankruptcy.

Under the rules of tracing, the beneficiaries can pursue an action against Faisal's father to recover the car. Faisal's father had no idea that the money had come from the trust, so he cannot be liable for *knowing receipt*, but the beneficiaries can still take action to recover the car through *tracing*. This would be available even if he had replaced the first car with a second one a few months later. In order to recover the car or its value, certain conditions must first be satisfied. We will discuss these in more detail below, but most important of all, they must show that they have proprietary rights in the property i.e. they own property rather than a mere personal right to sue the trustee, Faisal. In this case, they can show that they have equitable rights in the trust fund because they are beneficiaries.

13.3 Advantages of a tracing claim

Before we examine the requirements of tracing, we can first consider the advantages of using the process. It has a number of advantages over a personal claim against a trustee who has committed a breach of trust:

- It is irrelevant whether or not the defendant is bankrupt as the claim is for a piece of property and will therefore always rank higher than a creditor;
- The claimant may be able to take advantage of any increases in value of the property;
- Interest is payable from the date the defendant acquired the property rather than on the date of judgement;
- The limitation periods do not apply for claimants tracing their property in the possession of the third party or the trustee.

13.4 Tracing in equity

The *right to trace* in equity is available against the following:

- *A trustee*
- *An innocent volunteer*

- *A constructive trustee*

In the example above, Faisal is a *trustee* and the beneficiaries can take action to recover the £50,000 from Faisal when he first withdraws the funds. When the money is given to his father, his father is an *innocent volunteer*. He is unaware of the source of the money. If he becomes aware that it has come from the trust because either Faisal tells him, or he is told by someone else, or he has a strong suspicion that it came from the trust, then he would be liable for knowing receipt and he could become a *constructive trustee*.

13.5 Requirements of tracing

Tracing is not always available. The beneficiaries must be able to prove the following:

- There must be a *fiduciary relationship* between the claimant and the trustee;
- The claimant must prove an *equitable proprietary interest* in the property;
- The property must be *traceable/must not be dissipated*; and
- It must not be *inequitable to trace*.

13.5.1 Fiduciary relationship

Tracing in equity relies on proof that there was a *fiduciary relationship* between the claimant and the trustee. It is not necessary to prove a fiduciary relationship between the claimant and the innocent volunteer who holds the property. In the example above, once the trust has been created, the beneficiaries will have a *fiduciary relationship* with Faisal because he is a trustee of the trust.

13.5.2 Proof of an equitable proprietary interest in the property

The right to trace is reserved for anyone who can show that they have rights over the property which are known as *proprietary rights*. A beneficiary of a fixed trust has a *proprietary interest* in the property as soon as the trust is fully constituted.

13.5.3 The property must be traceable

If Faisal in the example above took £50,000 from the fund and instead of giving all of it to his father to buy a car he kept back £10,000 for himself and used it for a luxury holiday, the trust property no longer exists. The beneficiaries still have the right to sue Faisal personally for the £10,000, but they can no longer rely on the right to trace for that money as it has been dissipated. It is no longer traceable. Trust monies spent on such things as holidays, theatre tickets or meals can never be recovered.

If Faisal gave his father £50,000 and he spent part of it on a holiday, then there is an even greater problem for the beneficiaries because the father is an innocent volunteer and not a constructive trustee, so there is no further right of action against the father.

13.5.3.1 Mixed funds

Sometimes the funds become *mixed* with the personal money of the trustee or the innocent volunteer, and it is no longer possible to trace directly into an asset.

Suppose Faisal's father purchased a car worth £60,000. In this case, he has had to use some of his own money (£10,000), so the two funds are mixed.

We need to ask if the beneficiaries still have the right to trace into an asset which has been partly purchased using trust money and partly using money from the innocent third party?

In this case, the rights in the car would be apportioned between the beneficiaries and the innocent volunteer, Faisal. Neither party would take priority.

The law would look at this differently if Faisal's father had become a *constructive trustee* himself because he was aware that the money came from the trust fund or he thought that it might have come from it.

Consider these facts (based on a decided case):

Money was entrusted by a number of investors to a property developer who said he intended to use it to purchase property abroad. The property developer did not use the money from the investors to purchase property. In fact, he used part of it to pay premiums on a life assurance policy in favour of his children. The policy was worth £1 million. There were five premiums to pay on the policy, and the property developer used his own money to pay the first three; he then used the clients' money to pay for the last two (£40,000). He later committed suicide and the clients sued for the return of their money. Could they recover the actual value of the premiums **or** a share of the actual proceeds of the policy proportionate to the size of the contribution (£400,000)? The policy had paid out the full £1 million.

In *Foskett v McKeown* [2001] 1 AC 102, on which these facts are based, the House of Lords held that the clients were entitled to £400,000, which was a proportionate share of the total proceeds. Their claim was a claim in tracing, and they had established both a *fiduciary relationship* and an *equitable proprietary interest* in the fund.

The property developer was regarded as a trustee in this case. A *fiduciary relationship* had arisen as soon as the investors had transferred their money to him to invest in the development project.

The case illustrates how a *trustee relationship* can be established where money is transferred to another for a purpose to be carried out. Although the words trust and trustee are not used, the relationship can become one of a trustee and beneficiary.

13.5.4 It must not be inequitable to trace

Tracing in equity is governed by equitable principles and so tracing will be refused where it could result in any *undue hardship to the defendant*. This could be because of a *change of position*. Supposing Faisal's father had very little money of his own and when he received the £50,000 he used some of the sum to carry out essential repairs to his house rather than spend it all on a car?

Would it be fair for the beneficiaries to argue that they now have an interest in his house?

A volunteer who has used the trust's funds in this way can rely on the defence of *change of position* i.e. doing something that they would not have done, such as improvements to their house but for the receipt of the money.[1] They would be arguing that the money was an unexpected surprise.

The defence would not be available for a *trustee* or a *constructive trustee*. In this case, if Faisal's father knew it was trust money or had a strong suspicion it was trust money, he would have become a *constructive trustee*.

Consider the following two situations and decide whether the defence of *change of position* can be used:

i) Carrie receives £25,000 from a relative who was a trustee of a trust fund. She is surprised but also delighted. She uses the money to make improvements to her house. She had in fact saved £25,000 for this purpose. The trustee has made a mistake, and the correct beneficiary wants to recover the money or the car from Carrie through *tracing*.
ii) Debbie was given £15,000 by her uncle, who tells her he has just won a large sum of money from a premium bond and wants to share his winnings with her. Debbie has no savings and uses the money to replace her boiler in her house

1 In *re Diplock* [1948] Ch 465, beneficiaries of an estate from which trust monies had been wrongly transferred to a number of charitable institutions were unable to recover monies from those charities which could plead the defence of 'change of position'. If the charities had put the monies into bank accounts or purchased assets with it, then it could be recovered through tracing.

and also a number of windows which needed replacing. Her uncle has taken the money from a trust fund which has made a large profit through careful investment. Can the beneficiaries recover the £15,000 from Debbie through tracing?

Debbie is able to rely on the defence of *change of position* because she has carried out work which she would not have done if she had not received the money from her uncle.

Carrie's position is different because she has already saved the money to carry out the improvements and so has not done something new because she received the money. She cannot rely on the defence of *change of position*. She cannot be said to suffer *undue hardship*.

13.6 The rules of tracing into various funds

The rules of tracing depend on whether the funds become mixed with other money or whether the recipient purchases an asset using partly their own funds and partly trust monies.

There are also special rules for tracing into bank accounts where the recipient mixes the trust monies with their own personal money.

13.6.1 Unmixed funds

If the recipient receives a trust asset and keeps it separate from their own property, then tracing is very straightforward. There has been no mixing here of funds or of assets.

Consider the following facts:

- Artie receives a valuable painting from his aunt. It has in fact come from a trust fund. He is told by his aunt, who is also a trustee, that she is moving house and wants more room on her walls. Artie is unaware that his aunt is a trustee and is delighted with the gift. The painting can be recovered. In this situation, recovery of the actual painting will be through a process called *following*;
- If Artie sells the painting, then the result will depend on what he does with the proceeds of sale. If he puts the money he receives for the painting into a *separate bank account* because he wants to save some money, then there is no mixing and that *money can be traced*. If, instead of saving the money, Artie uses it to buy another painting because he did not like the painting his aunt gave him, the second painting can be *traced* because it has still not been mixed;
- If Artie receives the painting and immediately sells it but puts the proceeds into a bank account which has his own money, then there has been mixing and different rules which are specific to bank accounts will apply. Different rules

would also apply if he sells the painting and then uses the proceeds as well as his own funds to purchase another painting.

13.6.2 Mixed funds

It is possible to trace into *mixed funds* but different rules apply as to whether or not the trustee has mixed trust money with their own money or whether the trust monies have been mixed with that of an innocent volunteer.

13.7 Tracing against a trustee

In the case of *Foskett* discussed above, a trustee mixed trust money with his own and used it to purchase a life assurance policy. In that case, the funds of the trust used to purchase the asset could be distinguished from the trustee's own funds, and so it was possible to divide the asset between the trustee and the beneficiaries.

The rule is that the assets should be divided between the two claimants on a proportionate basis. This is called dividing the assets *pro rata*.

If the trustee used the funds to *purchase an asset* that could not be clearly separated, then the beneficiaries will always have the first claim on the asset.

Consider these examples:

- Suppose a trustee uses £40,000 of trust money and £10,000 of their own money to purchase a painting worth £50,000, then the trust will have the first claim on the asset. If the painting has fallen in value and is now only worth £40,000, the trustee cannot claim any of the proceeds of sale of the painting as there is no money left over after the trust has had the full value of the funds taken by the trustee replaced;
- If a trustee takes money £40,000 from a trust and pays that money into their account which has a balance of £10,000, it is now a mixed account. It is impossible to distinguish between the money of the trust and his money in the account. However, if the trustee then takes out £10,000 to pay for a holiday abroad, the presumption is that he uses his own money first. This is a long-established rule called the rule in *Hallett's case*.[2] It means that the beneficiaries can claim all the remaining money in the account.

The rule can be reversed in the beneficiaries' favour as shown in the example below:

2 *Re Hallett's Case* [1880] 13 Ch D 696. In this case, Mr Hallett was a solicitor and trustee. He paid in money from the trust as well as money that he held on behalf of an innocent volunteer into his own bank account and withdrew certain amounts. At his death, there were sufficient funds to repay the beneficiaries of the trust and the innocent volunteer but not all the creditors. The court held that the trust and the innocent volunteer should be repaid in full.

- A trustee, Hari, takes trust money (£20,000) and puts it into his bank account, which has £20,000 already in it (£40,000). Hari spends £20,000 on buying an expensive picture and then he spends a further £20,000 on a lavish holiday in South America. On his return from his holiday, Hari is declared bankrupt. If we apply the rule in *Hallett's case*, the trustee's creditors will be able to claim the value of the painting. This would mean that the beneficiaries would not be able to recover their loss. In these circumstances, the *rule is reversed* and the beneficiaries can first claim against the asset that has been purchased from the mixed fund.

The rule here can be explained as follows:

In a mixed fund (i.e. trust money and money of the trustee), if part of that fund is used to buy an asset which can be identified and the remainder of the fund has been dissipated or there is simply not enough to satisfy the claim of the beneficiaries, then the beneficiaries can claim against the asset purchased by the trustee.

13.8 Tracing against a third party or against another trust

Where the trustee has mixed funds, the rules of tracing always presume against the trustee. The position is going to be more complicated where there are *two or more innocent parties*, and the funds are insufficient to satisfy all the claims.

13.8.1 Bank accounts

If funds are mixed by a trustee which belong to two or more trusts and/or an innocent volunteer and there is insufficient money left in the account to satisfy both, then there is a real problem because both parties have an equal claim to what is left in the account. Some rules have been developed over the years to try to bring about as fair a solution as possible.

13.8.1.1 The Rule in Clayton's Case [1816] 1 Mer 572

This rule established in the nineteenth century applies to money of two or more innocent parties in a current account in the name of the trustee. The rule is very simple: the first money in is assumed to be the first money taken out by the trustee.

So it is generally known as the rule of *'first in, first out'*.

The rule works as follows:

T (the trustee) has a current account in his name. The following transactions take place.

May 2026 T deposits £30,000 from Trust A
June 2026 T deposits £30,000 from Trust B
July 2026 T **withdraws** £20,000 for building work on his house
August 2026 T **withdraws** £10,000 for a holiday.
September 2026 **balance in the account £30,000**

In September, T is declared bankrupt.

Trust A and Trust B both claim the remaining £30,000 in the bank account.

Try applying the rule in *Clayton's Case*.
Can Trust A claim the £30,000?
Can Trust B claim the £30,000
Or is the money to be shared equally between the two trusts?
Or finally, can T's trustee in bankruptcy claim the remaining £30,000 for T's creditors?

The rule says that *'the first money in is the first money out'*, so the first money deposited into the account is assumed to be the first money taken out.
The reasoning for this is that it is based on a time when money was physical coinage, and so the money put in first would be the money taken out first.

In this case, the first money put into the account was from Trust A, and so when there are withdrawals in May and in June, they are both assumed to be from the money of Trust A.

The result would be that Trust B can claim the remaining £30,000, and Trust A and T's creditors will get nothing.

Compare this scenario:

T (the trustee) has a current bank account in his name. The following transactions take place:
May 2025 T deposits £10,000 from Trust A
June 2025 T deposits £10,000 from Trust B
July 2025 T deposits £10,000 from Trust A
August 2025 T withdraws £15,000 for a holiday
September 2025 **balance in the account £15,000**
September T is declared bankrupt

Who can claim the £15,000 remaining in the bank account?
Trust A;
Trust B;
Or both trusts;
Or T's creditors?

Applying the rule *'first in, first out'*, the money is to be shared between Trust B (£5,000) and Trust A (£10,000). The creditors do not have a claim, as the beneficiaries have first claim on any money in the account. The reason why Trust A is satisfied in full is that, although the May deposit is taken to be spent on the holiday, the second deposit is made in July after the deposit from Trust B.

13.8.1.2 Pari passu *or proportionate sharing of the funds*

It can be seen how the rule in *Clayton's Case* can result in an unfair outcome. There is no logical explanation why the first money deposited should be assumed to be withdrawn first by the trustee.

In recent years, the court will not apply the rule where it is either impractical or where it results in an unjust outcome. The court will then consider if there is an alternative and fairer method available to deal with the shortfall.

A preferred option derives from *Barlow Clowes International Ltd v Vaughan* [1992] 4 AER 22.[3] This is to apportion any remaining monies between the parties *proportionately*. This is seen as a much fairer and more practical approach.

Consider these facts:

T (the Trustee) opens a current account. The following transactions take place:

May 2025 T deposits £10,000 from Trust A

June 2025 T deposits £20,000 from Trust B.

July 2025 T withdraws £15,000 for a holiday.

September T is declared bankrupt.

There is £15,000 left in the account. Under *pari passu*, that will be shared proportionately between them according to how much of their money was deposited.

3 In *Barlow Clowes International Ltd*, an investment company had gone into liquidation and there were not sufficient funds to satisfy all the claims of the investors. At first instance, the court had applied *Clayton's Case* but the Court of Appeal applied a different rule i.e. the rule apportioning funds between the claimants. It found that *Clayton's Case* usually produced unjust results and proportionate sharing of the funds was a much fairer solution.

Here it will be shared 2:1 in favour of B; Trust A will receive £5,000, and Trust B will receive £10,000. This approach is generally adopted today.

13.8.1.3 Tracing into the lowest intermediate balance

This rule limits tracing into a bank account to the account's lowest balance after the money from the trust fund has been paid in. The rule is very practical and assumes that money taken out must have come from the trust funds. If more money is paid in at a later date, then that could not be from the trust funds. In practice, this rule means that it will never be possible to trace into an overdrawn account.

Consider these facts:

May 2025 Trustee T takes £5,000 from Trust A and deposits it into his bank account.

June 2025 T withdraws £3,000 and spends it, leaving £2,000 in the bank account.

July 2025 T deposits £4,000 in the account.

Trust A is limited to claiming £2,000 under the *lowest intermediate balance* banking rule. It cannot argue that the money £4,000 deposited in July belongs to it because it was deposited after the balance in the account fell to £2,000.

The trust can make a personal claim against the trustee for the remaining £3,000, but it cannot claim it through tracing. The success of the personal claim will depend on whether T is solvent.

13.9 Backwards tracing

Although the law does not allow *tracing into an overdrawn account*, a rule has developed which can allow tracing into an *asset purchased with monies from an overdrawn account* if trust money has been deposited in it.

The claimants must prove that there is a *connection between the trust money that has been taken and the purchase of the asset.*

In other words, what is needed is to show that the trust money was used to make up a shortfall after the asset was purchased.

Consider these facts:

In April, T (a trustee) buys an expensive sports car for £90,000, and as a result, his current bank account, which only had £5,000 in it, becomes overdrawn. He becomes very worried about his financial position, and in May, T takes £90,000 from Trust A and deposits it into his current account to put it back into credit.

T suddenly dies, and he is found to be insolvent on his death.

The beneficiaries of the trust claim that they have rights in the car.

The claim is based on the argument that *the purchase of the car and the taking of the £90,000 from the trust fund are connected.*

In this case, the beneficiaries of Trust A are likely to be able to assert rights in the sports car. This is because the events leading up to the purchase of the car are very closely connected.

The position would be different if T bought the sports car in April and his bank account becomes overdrawn. He also settles an outstanding account with the Inland Revenue for unpaid tax. T struggles financially for several months and then takes out a loan in June.

Much later in the year, in October, T takes money from Trust A and pays it into his account. Although the taking of the money does put his account back into credit, it is not directly connected with the purchase of the car, which was several months earlier.

It cannot be described as one coordinated scheme.[4]

13.10 Defences to a tracing action

A defendant has a limited number of defences that can be raised against a tracing action. Most of these defences have been briefly mentioned earlier in the chapter.

- Tracing is not possible where the trust monies have been *dissipated*. Any monies spent on holidays or meals cannot be traced as there is no asset for the beneficiary to claim;
- Tracing is not possible if the defendant can claim *'change of position'* making it inequitable to trace. Tracing into something like home improvements made to the defendant's property that would never have taken place without the receipt of the trust money is not possible. You will recall that this defence is not available to the trustee, only an innocent volunteer;

4 In *Federal Republic of Brazil v Durant* [2015] UKPC 35, it was held that 'backwards tracing' may be allowed if there is evidence of a clear transactional link between a debit to an account i.e. to purchase an asset and a credit to the account with the intention of making up a shortfall in the account such as an overdraft. The facts of the case concerned money received as bribes by the mayor of São Paulo. The claimant was the local municipality who claimed that it should receive the whole of the bribes received for road building contracts that had been received by the mayor rather than the sum representing the lowest intermediate balance. This was successfully argued.

- Tracing is not available where the trust property passes into hands of a *'bona fide purchaser for value'*. This means someone who has paid consideration for the property. There must be proof that the money was paid in good faith, meaning that the purchaser was not aware that the property was trust property. If T sells a piece of jewellery from a trust fund to a purchaser under conditions that would not arouse suspicions of the purchaser, then that purchaser is protected against an action for breach of trust;
- Tracing relies on proof of a proprietary right and is therefore not subject to the limitation period, but it is subject to the doctrine of *'laches' or delay*. If the claimant, who is sui juris and fully aware of the original breach of trust and is fully aware of all the facts, then takes excessive time to bring an action to recover their property, a court may refuse to hear the claim. Even an innocent volunteer may be able to retain property received from a trust.

13.11 Summary of key issues on equitable tracing

- Equitable tracing depends on proof of a fiduciary relationship and an equitable proprietary interest;
- It is not possible to trace where the property has been dissipated or if it will produce an inequitable result or where there has been excessive delay by the claimant in bringing the action;
- Tracing is not possible against a bona fide purchaser who has no notice that the asset is trust property;
- Tracing can still be possible into a substituted asset;
- Tracing is possible into a mixed fund;
- A claimant relying on tracing can claim any increase in value in the fund.

13.12 Summary of the rules of tracing into mixed funds in a bank account

- Where a trustee has mixed their own money with that of a beneficiary or innocent third party, the trustee is presumed to have withdrawn their own money first;
- Where a trustee purchases an asset using mixed funds and the account is in deficit, the beneficiaries have first claim over that asset;
- In a mixed fund comprising trust monies of two or more trusts and/or an innocent volunteer, either the 'first in, first out' rule applies, or the fund is split proportionately between the two claims;
- Any claim by a beneficiary against a trustee's bank account is restricted to the 'lowest intermediate balance' after the trust money has been deposited;
- 'Backwards tracing' may be allowed where the purchase of an asset and the use of trust monies by the trustee can be seen as a coordinated scheme.

14 Equitable remedies

14.1 Chapter overview

This chapter examines some of the equitable remedies that can be awarded to a claimant. It will show that, unlike common law remedies, a court has *discretion* as to whether to grant a remedy, and if a court chooses to do so, it has a choice as to which remedy to grant. We will consider the issues that might influence a court when making its decision. The chapter also briefly examines the main principles or *maxims of equity* which can influence the court's decision. Finally, the chapter looks at four of the most important equitable remedies: *specific performance, rectification, injunctions* and *rescission*. These remedies are used in many areas of law, and you may have encountered them already in contract and tort and also land law.

14.2 The award of equitable remedies

Under common law, a claimant is entitled to damages if successful in a claim. So, if P brings a successful action for negligence against a neighbour, N, for an injury caused on their land, the court will award damages. The size of the award will depend on a number of factors, but damages will be awarded to P as of right. Equitable remedies are different because they are *discretionary*. A court has the choice as to whether or not the remedy will be given. It will look at a range of factors, including the defendant's defence, and decide if it is equitable in all the circumstances to award a remedy and, if so, which remedy will be appropriate.

Sometimes an equitable remedy will be more appropriate than the award of a sum of money in the form of damages.

Consider the following situations and think about the most suitable remedy in each case:

i) A purchaser has agreed to purchase your house and contracts have been exchanged. You are about to buy another house, Greenacres, but your purchaser wants to withdraw from the sale;

DOI: 10.4324/9781003583660-18

ii) You have set up a trust in favour of your children and grandchildren, but your solicitor made a mistake and failed to include your children in the trust deed;
iii) Your neighbour has started a building project and you know from your own plans that they are trespassing on your land;
iv) You are buying a new car and have signed a contract agreeing to pay £30,000, which you paid yesterday. You found out this morning that the seller has lied to you about the true state of the car. You tried to start it today, and you found there was a serious defect with the engine, and it would not start. The seller told you it was in good condition.

In (i), if your purchaser withdraws, then your loss will not only be of your sale but also possibly of the purchase of your new house, Greenacres. Once a purchaser has exchanged contracts, then you have the right to take action to enforce the contract, asking the court for an order for *specific performance*. That order will compensate you far better than an award of damages.

In (ii), as discussed in Chapter 1, once the trust deed has been drawn up and the trust fully constituted by the transfer of assets to the trustees, the settlor cannot revoke the trust. The legal title to the property lies with the trustees. However, where there has been a mistake in the terms of a legal document, such as in a trust or in a will, the court will allow a document to be changed or *rectified* where a genuine mistake has been made in some of the details.

In (iii), your main worry is that once your neighbour has built on your land, you will not be able to get the building removed. You do not want a sum of money in compensation, but instead, you want an order from the court to stop the work. The court can award an *injunction* which will force your neighbour to stop the work. He may dispute your contention that he is building on your land but the injunction will stop any further building until the issue of ownership of the land has been decided.

In (iv), you have signed a contract to buy the car from the seller. Once you have signed the contract and paid the money, you are bound by contract law, but if you discover that there is a fundamental mistake, namely the description of the state of the car you will no longer want the car, so you would now like the contract to be set aside. In these circumstances the appropriate remedy is rescission, which puts the parties back in the position they were in before entering into the agreement.

In each of these situations, the court will consider such matters as whether the award of damages would in itself be insufficient to remedy the wrong complained of by the claimant. The court also looks at the defendant's position to decide whether it is fair to the defendant to award the remedy rather than award damages. In (i), the court may consider whether it is equitable to make an *award of specific performance* against the defendant. The defendant may not wish to pursue the sale because they have suffered a serious illness or accident, and the court may take that into account.[1]

14.3 Factors relevant to the decision to award an equitable remedy

The court considers the following factors in deciding whether or not to grant an equitable remedy:

- Is the remedy at common law (i.e. damages) *inadequate*?
- Has the conduct of the claimant been *inequitable*?
- Will the award of the remedy cause *hardship* to the defendant?
- Whether there has been a *delay* in bringing the claim to court?

The court weighs all these factors before deciding on an award. It is also possible to award an equitable remedy as well as damages.

14.4 The maxims of equity

Equity is influenced by certain principles referred to as *'maxims'*. These are general principles which can be referred to, but unlike a statute or a precedent from case law, they will never be binding on the court. The following maxims are relevant to the award of remedies, but it is important to realise that there are many more.

- *Those who come to equity must come with clean hands.* This means that anyone claiming an equitable remedy must show that they have acted properly; this is limited to the claim itself. Improper behaviour in another action will not prevent a claim from arising;
- *Delay defeats equity.* In considering whether to grant an order, the court will look at whether the claimant delayed in bringing an action. The court will consider whether the delay was unreasonable in the circumstances; in particular, did the claimant have the full facts of the case?
- *Equity looks at substance rather than form.* This remedy is similar to the one below. Equity looks at the intent or effect of an agreement rather than the words used;

1 In *Patel v Ali* [1984] 1 AER 978, the claimant sought an order for specific performance against the defendant who refused to proceed with a purchase of a house owned by the claimant after contracts had been exchanged. The defendant wanted to remain in the property after a series of life-changing events. She was reliant on nearby family and neighbours to give her help and support. The court did not make the order, believing it would inflict undue hardship on the defendant.

- *Equity will not allow a statute to be used as an instrument of fraud*. This means that where a document has not complied with the formalities of statute and one of the parties uses this to their advantage, equity will still enforce even if a formality has not been met;
- *Equity will not assist a volunteer*. This maxim was discussed in Chapter 2. A trust which has not been fully constituted cannot be enforced by beneficiaries because they are volunteers. This is a principle that runs through law, in particular the law of contract.

14.5 Equitable remedies

14.5.1 Specific performance

What is an order for specific performance?

An order for *specific performance* is an order of the court that a party to a contract or agreement will perform whatever was agreed under the terms of the agreement. The party must carry out their part of the bargain, and if they fail to do so, they will be found to be in contempt of court.

Like all equitable remedies, the grant of the remedy is discretionary, so the court may refuse to grant it and order damages instead.

When can specific performance be ordered?

Specific performance is only available when damages are inadequate. Typically, it will be awarded where the property involved is unique and cannot easily be replaced e.g. a specific painting by an artist. *Land* is always considered to be unique, so specific performance will usually be granted after contracts have been exchanged for the sale of land.

Specific performance is not available in certain types of contract e.g. contracts for personal services. The courts have been reluctant to order a person to work for another. The main problem is one of supervision.

14.5.2 Rectification

Rectification allows the parties to rectify a document that does not reflect the true intentions of the parties. Formal documents are usually strictly enforced and cannot be changed because above all we need certainty in law. We need to be sure that there is no chance for the parties to go back on an agreement because they have simply changed their mind about something and no longer want to be bound. Where someone has made a mistake in the drawing up of the document, then equity allows a document to be rectified. If a trust document has been drawn up but the terms do not reflect what the settlor intended, then the trust deed can be rectified. It is the fact that the document does not reflect what the parties intended to agree that is important.

14.5.3 Injunctions

14.5.3.1 Definition of an injunction

An injunction is an order from the court which will stop the defendant from behaving in a particular way (*a prohibitory injunction*) or force a defendant to do something (*mandatory injunction*).

Consider these examples:

Francis believes that a magazine article is going to be published next week, which is untrue. He wants to prevent it from being published. He can go to the court and request a *prohibitory injunction* which will stop it from being published.

Garry is having an extension built onto his house. He signed an agreement with a local firm of builders, and they started work last month. The builders have suddenly stopped work. He believes they have started working on another better-paid project.

He can go to court and request a *mandatory injunction* which will force them to resume work on his extension.

14.5.3.2 Types of injunctions

Apart from *prohibitory and mandatory injunctions*, it is also possible to request an *interim injunction* as opposed to a final injunction. An *interim injunction* is a temporary injunction which is imposed to prevent damage to the applicant before there can be a full hearing of an issue. It could be granted in the case of Francis above. It would prevent publication until the full hearing of whether the magazine article is libellous or not. An *interim injunction* might also be awarded in a case where a beneficiary believes the trustee was acting fraudulently and disposing of trust assets. This would prevent the dissipation of the trust assets.

Consider this example:

Xavier set up a trust three years in favour of his wife Xanthe and three adult children. He appointed his sisters, Yvonne and Terri, as trustees. The trust property consists of a shareholding and a quantity of jewellery that was left to Xavier by his great-aunt. Xanthe has heard a rumour that Yvonne has always believed that the jewellery should have been given to them all equally and is intending to sell a diamond necklace at an auction next week. Xanthe has asked you for your advice.

In this situation, once the necklace has been sold for valuable consideration, it will be difficult to recover from a bona fide purchaser, so Xanthe should apply for an *interim injunction* to prevent the sale, ensuring that the trust property is not sold.

14.5.3.3 The terms of an injunction

Injunctions are also awarded at the discretion of the court and will usually be subject to certain conditions. The main condition is that the applicant agrees to give an *undertaking in damages* if the defendant suffers any loss as a result of the injunction.

An *undertaking in damages* is a promise by an applicant where an injunction is sought and there is no time to decide the underlying issue. The court will not know if the application for an *interim injunction* can be justified by the applicant. The defendant to the action may suffer a loss themselves. In the example of Francis above, he may be asked to give an undertaking in damages to compensate the magazine for any financial loss arising from the withdrawal of the magazine.

Sometimes the requirement to give an undertaking in damages is just not possible. The applicant may have modest means, and this is a good reason for delaying an application for an *interim injunction*.

If an injunction is awarded, then anyone who breaches the terms of the injunction will be in contempt of court and may be subject to a penalty such as a fine or imprisonment.

14.5.3.4 Damages in lieu of an injunction

Sometimes an injunction is simply not appropriate. In these cases, the applicant must accept damages as the only remedy.

14.5.3.5 Search orders[2] and freezing orders[3]

There are two specific forms of injunctions: *search orders* and *freezing orders*, which can be useful for an applicant who needs either to ensure that property, such as documents, are not removed from premises; and secondly, to ensure that assets are not disposed of or sent out of the jurisdiction.

2 Search orders were first granted in the case of *Anton Piller KG v Manufacturing Processes Ltd* [1976] Ch 55 and used to be known as Anton Piller orders. These orders now have a statutory basis under s.7 of the Civil Procedure Act 1997. It forces someone to agree to a person mentioned in the order to enter their premises and search for documentation and to either take it away or make a copy.

3 Freezing orders were first granted in the case of *Mareva Compania Naviera SA v International Bulkcarriers SA* [1975] 2 Lloyd's Report 509. Like search orders, these now have statutory force in the Civil Procedure Rules 1999.

Search orders allow a claimant to go to the defendant's premises and seize documentation. It is not generally granted as it is a very extreme order to make. There has to be some proof that the defendant is likely to remove or destroy documentation, and they are only granted under the supervision of a solicitor. Strict rules are applied, such as supervision of the search, and only itemised items should be removed. The claimant must give an undertaking in damages in order to compensate for any loss or damage from the search or subsequently.

Freezing orders, as the name suggests, allow the applicant to request that assets of the defendant are frozen. This will only be granted if the claimant has a good arguable case, has assets within the jurisdiction and there is a real risk that any judgement will go unsatisfied, and it would be just and convenient in all the circumstances to grant the order.

14.6 Rescission

14.6.1 Definition of rescission

This is a remedy that reverses a transaction that has complied with all formal requirements. It makes the formal document no longer enforceable in law. It is clearly a remedy based in equity because it prevents *unconscionable* or *fraudulent conduct*. It is the opposite of a decree of specific performance because rather than enforce an agreement, it reverses an agreement.

14.6.2 When can rescission be granted?

Rescission can be granted where the court believes that a document does not reflect the true intentions of the parties. The order is usually awarded where one of the parties is seeking to profit from the error. One of the main circumstances is a *mistake* where someone may benefit from the mistake in a document. Rescission may also be granted where there is evidence of *undue influence*.

Types of *undue influence*:

- Acts of pressure or coercion;
- A relationship where one party holding a position of strength has taken an unfair advantage over another.

It is possible that a settlor can have been subject to *undue influence* when drawing up a trust or alternatively a testator when making their will. Undue influence must be improper pressure or force rather than a simple act of persuasion. Courts are reluctant to make an order of rescission unless there is adequate proof of undue influence. Where a person receives legal advice, then it is presumed that there has been no undue pressure.

14.7 Client advice

If a client intends to create a trust which is controversial e.g. does not benefit all or any of their children, then it is important that balanced advice is given to ensure that the client has thought about the possible repercussions of such a step. It is also useful to include a written note with the documentation reflecting that the issues have been discussed.

14.8 Wills

An important principle of the Law of England and Wales is *testamentary freedom*. This allows someone the right to leave their property to whoever they wish. It is perfectly possible for anyone with an extensive family to leave them all out of the terms of the will or to choose one or two members of the family and exclude the others. It is rare for the terms of a valid will to be set aside, but where there is clear evidence of undue influence, a court may set it aside.

14.9 Summary of equitable remedies

- Equitable remedies are awarded on a discretionary basis, whereas the common law remedy of damages is as of right;
- Specific performance is an order compelling someone to carry out an action;
- Specific performance can be ordered where the property has unique qualities e.g. land or certain jewellery;
- A court will consider certain matters before making the award e.g. the effect on the defendant; whether damages are adequate;
- Rectification will be ordered where a document does not reflect the true intentions of the parties;
- An injunction is an order directing a party to proceedings to carry out or to stop doing an act;
- An injunction will be granted where damages would not be an adequate remedy;
- There are several different forms of injunctions including: a prohibitory injunction, a mandatory injunction, an interim injunction;
- The court has the power to grant search orders and freezing orders;
- Rescission results in a legal document or transaction becoming unenforceable in law;
- Rescission may be granted on a number of grounds including mistake and undue influence.

14.10 Multiple-Choice Questions – Part 4

Question One

Francis is a trustee of two trusts: Trust ALPHA and Trust BETA. He runs his own business, which has recently run into financial difficulties. He wants to replace his car, and rather than buy a modest second-hand car, he decides to buy an expensive sports car, which he thinks will enhance his image as a businessman. He takes £20,000 from Trust ALPHA in March and puts it into a new bank account. He intends to repay it as soon as his business becomes profitable again. He takes £80,000 from Trust BETA in May and deposits that in the new bank account. He purchases his car for £100,000 in June with the money in the account. His business collapses in September, and Francis is declared bankrupt. The beneficiaries from Trust ALPHA and Trust BETA both claim the value of the car, which is now valued at £50,000.

Which of the following best describes the outcome of a tracing action?

A. The two trusts will share the proceeds equally.
B. Trust ALPHA will receive nothing.
C. Trust BETA will receive £50,000.
D. The trustee in bankruptcy can successfully claim the car.
E. The two trusts will share the value of the car proportionately.

Question Two

A sole trustee, Trixie, withdrew £25,000 from a trust fund intending to repay the money. She deposited it in her own personal bank account, which had a balance of £25,000. She spent £25,000 on a sculpture from a local artist. She spent the remaining money on a holiday. Trixie has recently been declared bankrupt. The sculpture is now worth £40,000.

Which of the following best describes the outcome of a tracing action?

A. Trixie can claim the sculpture because the law presumes that a trustee always spends his or her own money first.
B. The beneficiaries have a charge over the sculpture.
C. The beneficiaries have no right to trace as their money has been dissipated.
D. Trixie and the beneficiaries can share the value of the sculpture between them.
E. The beneficiaries have only one course of action, which is a personal claim against Trixie.

Question Three

Hari is the sole trustee of a family trust, he had very little personal savings and his earnings were low. He was appointed because he was a relative of the family. Hari's widowed mother urgently needed to replace the central heating system in her house. The cheapest system would cost £8,000. His mother relies on her state pension and the small amount that she has saved for her living expenses, and she could not afford the new central heating system. The family trust has liquid assets of £250,000, and Hari takes £8,000 from the trust. He tells his mother that the money comes from a win on the lottery. His mother has the work done. Hari has recently been made redundant and can no longer pay his expenses and so has been declared bankrupt.

Which of the following would best describe the rights of the beneficiaries of the trust?

- **A.** The beneficiaries should take a tracing action against his mother as she should have known that he did not have the money to lend her.
- **B.** The beneficiaries can claim a charge over the house to the value of the new central heating system.
- **C.** The beneficiaries will not be successful in a tracing action against the mother.
- **D.** The mother is personally liable to the beneficiaries to compensate the trust fund for the loss.
- **E.** The beneficiaries can bring a tracing action against Hari to compensate the trust fund for the loss.

Question Four

Sally and Susie are beneficiaries of a family trust set up in their favour by their father several years ago. They have recently discovered that the sole trustee, Tariq, withdrew £30,000 from the trust fund and deposited it in his personal account. The account was already overdrawn by £20,000. He immediately withdrew £10,000 to pay for a facelift for his wife. He told her that he was paying for the facelift because he had received a bonus from his job. The following week, he received a cheque for £10,000 from the sale of his car, which he deposited in the bank.

Which of the following courses of action best describe the rights of the beneficiaries Sally and Susie?

A. The beneficiaries have lost their right to trace.
B. The beneficiaries have the right to trace into the account for the full £30,000.
C. The beneficiaries have the right to trace into the account for £10,000 only.
D. The beneficiaries have the right to make a proprietary claim against the bank.
E. The beneficiaries can make a personal claim against Tariq's wife.

Question Five

A trustee of a large trust fund (Ted) is in serious financial difficulties. His business has run into problems and is operating at a loss. In October, he has the opportunity to purchase a new car for £60,000; he knows it is a real bargain and he does not want to lose this chance. He decides to take money from the trust to pay for it. In early November, he takes £50,000 from the trust and deposits it in his account, which is £10,000 in credit. He then pays for the car. The account is now overdrawn by £10,000. In December, after some very profitable sales from his business, he deposits £70,000 in his current account. The beneficiaries have recently discovered that trust money has been taken from the account. Ted disappeared on New Year's Day and cannot be found. The car that Ted purchased has recently broken down and is now worth only £40,000.

Which of the following courses of action best describe the rights of the beneficiaries?

A. The beneficiaries have lost their right to trace into the trustee's bank account.
B. The beneficiaries have the right to trace into £60,000 from the trustee's bank account.
C. The beneficiaries have the right to trace into £50,000 from the trustee's bank account.
D. The beneficiaries have the right to trace into the car but not the trustee's bank account.
E. The beneficiaries have the right to trace into the trustee's bank account but are restricted to £10,000.

Question Six

Geri wanted to make provision for her children, Anna and Bimbi, after her death. She asked her cousins, Oki and Fran, to come to her house and asked them to act as trustees. She set out the terms of the trust as follows: 'my house to be held on trust for my children, Anna and Bimbi, in equal shares; my diamond necklace to be held on trust for Anna when she reaches the age of 21 and my pearl and sapphire brooch to be held on trust for Bimbi when she reaches the age of 25'. The brooch is much more valuable than the necklace. In fact, the terms were wrongly written down by Oki and Fran, giving the necklace to Bimbi and the brooch to Anna. Bimbi has just discovered that the brooch is to be given to Anna as she has just turned 21.

Bimbi would like to be able to recover the brooch for herself.

Which of the following statements represent Bimbi's best course of action?

A. Apply for an order of rescission.
B. Apply for an order for rectification, changing the wording of the trust deed.
C. Apply for a mandatory injunction ordering the brooch to be transferred to her.
D. Bimbi should accept that he has no rights to compel the transfer of the brooch.
E. Bimbi should wait until the brooch is given to Anna and then take action against Anna.

15 Selected key cases in equity and trusts

15.1 Chapter overview

This chapter sets out a small selection of cases that illustrate some of the principles of the law of equity and trusts that have been discussed throughout the book. Some of these cases will already be familiar.

It is set out in the following way. Each case has a summary of the essential facts and is followed by focused questions on the case. This should enable a reader to identify the key principles in each case using a variety of skills. Each case will conclude with a summary of the outcome, showing how the principles were applied to the facts.

The cases are set out in the same order as the topics appear throughout the book.

15.2 The three certainties

15.2.1 Certainty of intention

Jones v Lock (1865) LR 1 Ch App 25

The facts were:

Robert Jones gave his child a gift; his wife had been criticising him for not giving the child a present. He placed a cheque for £900 in the hand of the baby who was aged nine months and said, 'I give it to baby, and I am going to put this away for him...'

He took the cheque away and put it into his safe. A few days later he died.

The dispute to be decided by the court:

Was the cheque held on trust for the son?

Consider this point in analysing the legal issues:

how does the law determine certainty of intention?

DOI: 10.4324/9781003583660-19

The principle of law applied:

The settlor must show an intention to create a trust. This must be distinguished from a 'loose conversation'. The use of the words 'I give it to baby' does not show an intention to create a trust.

The outcome of the case:

There was no declaration of trust in the child's favour.

Notes:

There could be no gift to the child of the cheque because it cannot outlast a donee. Had the father given the child a watch or a sum of money, the outcome would have been different. There would have been a valid gift.

Paul v Constance [1977] 1 WLR 527

The facts were:

Mr Constance and Miss Paul lived together as man and wife. Mr C received a sum of money in compensation for an industrial injury and he put the money in a deposit account in his own name. He told Ms P on a number of occasions that the money in the account was 'as much hers as it was his'. Later, further money was paid into the account and a withdrawal was regarded as a withdrawal of joint money. Mr C died and Ms P claimed the money in the account from the administratrix of the estate, Mrs Constance, Mr C's surviving wife.

The dispute to be decided by the court:

The courts had to decide if the money in the bank account was held on trust for Ms P or alternatively did it pass to Mrs C as the surviving spouse of Mr C.

Consider these points in analysing the legal issues:

- How does the law determine certainty of intention?
- Does the word 'trust' have to be used?

The principle of law applied:

The settlor must show an intention to create a trust. The words used showed this intention. The word trust does not have to be used so long as there is a clear intention that the property is to be held separately from the rest of the settlor's estate. In this case, was the bank account to be trust property held for the joint enjoyment of Mr C and Ms P?

The outcome of the case:

When Mr C said that the money was to be 'as much hers as it was his', he showed an intention to create a trust

Barclays Bank v Quistclose Investments Ltd [1970] AC 567

The facts were:

Quistclose Investments lent a sum of money to Rolls Razor, a firm experiencing severe financial difficulties. The money was to be used to pay out dividends which had been declared on its shares. Before the money had been paid, Rolls Razor went into liquidation. The liquidators, Barclays Bank, claimed the money was part of the assets of the firm and could be used to pay creditors of Rolls Razor.

The dispute to be decided by the court:

Quistclose claimed that the money that they had lent was held *on trust* for them. Since the express purpose, i.e. paying the dividends, had not been carried out, the money should be returned to them in full.

Consider this point in analysing the legal issue:

How does the law determine intention when a sum of money is transferred as a loan?

The principle of law applied:

The loan of the money from Quistclose was for a specific purpose and it was not for Rolls Razor to use for general purposes. The fact that a purpose was specified showed an *intention* that it was to be held on express trust for the lender. When that trust failed, it had to be returned to the settlor on *resulting trust*.

The outcome of the case:

The money was held on resulting trust for Quistclose. The creditors of Rolls Razor had no claim to the money because it was trust money and was never owned beneficially by Rolls Razor. There was sufficient certainty of intention because Quistclose lent the money for the sole purpose of paying dividends.

Notes:

This case is also relevant for Chapter 7. The money was transferred on express trust. The express trust failed and so the money will be held by the transferee on *resulting trust* for the transferor.

Comiskey and Others and Bowring-Hanbury and Another [1905] AC 84

The facts were:

A testator gave his wife 'the whole of my real and personal estate... in full confidence that... at her death she will devise it to such one or more of my nieces as she may think fit...'. He also added a gift over in default of appointment.

The dispute to be decided by the court:

Was the money to be held on trust by the wife for the nieces or was it an absolute gift for the wife?

Consider this point in analysing the legal issue:

If the testator uses words such as 'full confidence', can that show an intention to create a trust?

The principle of law applied:

What words should be used by a testator when creating a trust? Is it possible to create a trust without using the word trust itself?

The outcome of the case:

The testator had intended to make an absolute gift to his wife rather than a trust in favour of her nieces.

Notes:

The words 'full confidence' do not show certainty of intention and are not sufficient to show that a trust was intended.

Certainty of subject matter

Boyce v Boyce [1949] 16 Sim 476

The facts were:

The settlor left two houses on trust for his two daughters. One of the daughters was required to make a selection from the two houses, and the remaining house would pass to the other daughter. When the first daughter failed to make a decision before she died, the second daughter claimed one of the houses for herself.

The dispute to be decided by the court:

Was the gift dependent on the first daughter making a selection? Could the second daughter claim a house even if the first daughter had failed to make a selection?

Consider this point in analysing the legal issue:

What are the rules for certainty of subject matter where a gift is dependent on a choice by another beneficiary?

The principle of law applied:

A trust will fail if there is no means of ascertaining which part of the subject matter is to go to which of the beneficiaries.

The outcome of the case:

The trust failed; the second daughter could not claim one of the houses for herself as her gift was dependent on the first daughter making her selection.

Notes:

In this case, the trust fails for uncertainty of subject matter. The property itself is certain, but the shares are uncertain. The houses will be held on resulting trust for the settlor's estate.

Re Golay and others [1965] 2 All ER 660

The facts were:

A testator instructed his trustees to allow the beneficiary to enjoy one of his flats during her lifetime and also to receive a 'reasonable income' from other properties.

The dispute to be decided by the court:

Was the subject matter of the trust certain? Was 'reasonable income' sufficiently certain?

Consider this point in analysing the legal issue:

The word 'reasonable' is used in many circumstances in law. Is it sufficiently certain in ascertaining the share of a beneficiary?

The principle of law applied:

It is possible to objectively ascertain what is meant by a 'reasonable income'. This word has an objective meaning. It is not what the settlor subjectively considers to be reasonable.

The outcome of the case:

The word 'reasonable income' was sufficiently certain and the trust was upheld by the court.

Certainty of objects

McPhail v Doulton [1971] AC 424

The facts were:

A trust was created by the settlor Mr Baden on the following terms: 'the trustees shall apply the net income... in making at their absolute discretion grants to or for the benefit of any officers and employees or ex-officers or ex-employees of the company or to any relatives or dependants of such persons in such amounts at such times... as they think fit...'.

The dispute to be decided by the court:

Were the objects of this discretionary trust sufficiently certain? Or would the trust fail for uncertainty of objects?

Consider this point in analysing the legal issue:

In a discretionary trust, the potential beneficiaries do not have an interest; merely a chance to be chosen. The trustees have no obligation to consider all the potential beneficiaries. This contrasts with a fixed trust, where all the beneficiaries have a share under the terms of the trust.

The principle of law applied:

The test for certainty in a discretionary trust is the 'given postulant' test. Under this test it must be possible to say of any given individual that he 'is or is not' within the class. The trustees do not have to draw up a complete list of all the beneficiaries.

The outcome of the case:

The trust was valid and did not fail for uncertainty of objects.

Notes:

The case reset the test for certainty of objects in discretionary trusts.

Re Barlow's Wills Trust [1979] 1 All ER 296

The facts were:

The testatrix left a number of paintings with instructions that '.any member of my family and any friends of mine...' could, when she died, buy any of the paintings at the prices contained in the catalogue of valuations made five years before her death. The prices were below the market value for the paintings.

The dispute to be decided by the court:

Could this gift be valid as it used a term 'friends' which was conceptually uncertain?

Consider this point in analysing the legal issue:

What kind of gift was this? It was neither a fixed trust nor a discretionary trust. Could it be a different type of gift altogether?

The principle of law applied:

There must be conceptual certainty for fixed and discretionary trusts. In both these types of trust, the word 'friend' will fail for conceptual uncertainty. If this were a different type of gift, then could a different test be applied allowing this to be upheld?

The outcome of the case:

The gift was valid because it was held to be a gift subject to a condition precedent. It was not a gift to a class, but instead, it was a series of gifts to the testatrix's friends.

Notes:

Where a gift is made conditional on fulfilling certain criteria e.g. being a friend of the testatrix, then the test for certainty is that at least one person qualifies within the class. It does not matter that there is residual uncertainty about others. This will not defeat the gift. It was held by the court that even the word 'friend' can be certain where you are looking to see if one person fulfils the criteria.

15.3 Constitution of trusts

Milroy v Lord (1862) 4 De GF & 264

The facts were:

An attempt was made to create a trust of 50 shares in the Bank of Louisiana in favour of the claimant by transferring them on trust for Lord. The bank stipulated that the shares be registered in the name of the transferee at the Bank for title to pass. This was never done although a deed of assignment had been executed and the share certificates had been delivered.

The dispute to be decided by the court:

Was this a fully constituted trust?

Consider this point in analysing the legal issue:

What is necessary for a trust to be fully constituted?

The principle of law applied:

The key point is whether the settlor has divested himself of the property and can no longer call it his own.

The outcome of the case:

The trust was not fully constituted and could not be enforced.

Notes:

This is a key case in the development of law on what is a fully constituted trust.

Pennington v Waine [2002] 1 WLR 2075

The facts were:

Ada Crampton owned a large shareholding in a private company of which she was one of the directors. She told her nephew that she was giving him 400 shares and she wanted him to become a director. She repeated this to a company auditor. She signed the stock transfer form, but instead of transferring it to her nephew, she transferred it to one of the auditors. When she died, the form was still with the auditors and she had not made any provision for the 400 shares in her will.

The dispute to be decided by the court:

Could the nephew claim the shares even though the stock transfer form had not been transferred to the nephew?

Consider this point in analysing the legal issue:

The aunt could have withdrawn the gift at any time before she died because the nephew did not have the stock transfer form which would have constituted the transfer.

The principle of law applied:

A court can still uphold a transfer even where there are further steps to be carried out by the transferee, where it would be unconscionable for the transferee to revoke the transfer.

The outcome of the case:

The court held that the nephew could claim the shares.

Notes:

This case is an exception to the rules about fully constituted trust as it allows an incompletely constituted trust to be enforced if it would be unconscionable not to do so.

String v Bird (1874) LR 18 315

The facts were:

The defendant's stepmother lived in his house and paid him for her board and lodging. The stepson owed her £1,100 (a large sum at the time), and they agreed that she would pay a reduced sum to cover the loan. After two quarters, she resumed paying the full amount, and she told him she did not want the debt repaid. In order for this to be enforceable, she should have put this into writing. She died some years later, appointing her stepson as executor.

The dispute to be decided by the court:

Could the stepson argue that he was released from the debt?

Consider this point in analysing the legal issue:

Did it make a difference that her stepson had been appointed executor of his stepmother's estate?

The principle of law applied:

A debt can be released if the debtor has been appointed as an executor. This principle can only apply if certain conditions apply: the donor must have intended to make an inter vivos gift; the intention must continue until the date of death; the donee must have been appointed an executor.

The outcome of the case:

It was held that the stepson could be released from his debt.

Notes:

The debt can also be released where someone is appointed as an administrator.

Wilkes v Allington [1931] 2 Ch 104

The facts were:

The donor had been diagnosed with cancer and as a consequence he made a number of incomplete gifts. He later caught pneumonia and died.

The dispute to be decided by the court:

Could the donor plead *donatio mortis causa* in these circumstances?

Consider this point in analysing the legal issue:

In this case, the donor had contemplated death from a different cause from the reason for his death. Could that influence the court's decision?

The principle of law applied:

The key feature of *donatio mortis causa* is that the donor is contemplating death and therefore makes a gift which he delivers to the donee.

The outcome of the case:

The gift was upheld. It did not make any difference that the actual reason for death was not the same as the one that the donor had been contemplating.

15.4 Formalities of transfer

Vandervell v IRC [1967] 2 AC 291

The facts were:

Mr Vandervell wanted to found a Chair in Pharmacology at the Royal College of Surgeons. He decided to do so by transferring some shares in his company, Vandervell Products (which were held by nominee trustees) to the College. He retained an option to repurchase the shares for £5,000 when the College had sufficient capital to found the Chair. The College received dividends worth over £250,000.

The dispute to be decided by the court:

The Inland Revenue wanted to tax Vandervell on the amount. They argued that at all times Mr Vandervell retained an equitable interest in the shares because he did not comply with s.53(1)(c) Law of Property Act 1925. This section required the disposition of an equitable interest to be evidenced in writing. If it was not evidenced in writing, then the disposition would be void.

Consider this point in analysing the legal issue:

In some limited circumstances the settlor can transfer an equitable interest without having to comply with s.53(1)(c) because it would not be regarded as a disposition.

The principle of law applied:

If both the legal interest and the equitable interest are transferred at the same time, then s.53(1)(c) does not apply. This is because the transferor is no longer transferring the equitable interest separately. It would not be regarded as a disposition.

The outcome of the case:

This was not a disposition under s.53(1)(c) because Vandervell was transferring both the legal and equitable interest at the same time.

Notes:

The transferor Vandervell did not want the transfer to be regarded as a disposition as it would attract stamp duty.

15.5 Purpose trusts

Re Astor's Settlement Trusts [1952] Ch 534

The facts were:

A trust was created with a provision that the trustees were to apply the income from a fund for a number of non-charitable purposes, which included the following 'the maintenance... of good understanding between nations' and 'the preservation of the independence and integrity of newspapers...'.

The dispute to be decided by the court:

Could this trust be upheld as a private purpose trust?

Consider this point in analysing the legal issue:

The trust could not be a charitable trust as it failed to come within the charitable purposes at the time.

The principle of law applied:

A trust will only be upheld if there are human beneficiaries to enforce the trust. A trust for a 'purpose' cannot be upheld.

The outcome of the case:

The trust failed as the trust offended against the beneficiary principle and the objects of the trust were uncertain.

15.6 Resulting trusts

The facts were:

Re Gillingham Bus Disaster Fund [1958] Ch 300

A number of marine cadets were killed or seriously injured in an accident, and a large sum of money was collected for the care of the survivors and also for 'worthy causes'.

The dispute to be decided by the court:

There was a surplus after the injured had been cared for. The court had to decide how to deal with the surplus fund.

Consider this point in analysing the legal issue:

The secondary cause was not charitable, so the surplus could not be applied as if it were for a charitable purpose.

The principle of law applied:

Where funds have been transferred for a specific purpose which later fails, each donor will retain an interest, and it will be held for them on resulting trust.

The outcome of the case:

The fund was held on resulting trust, and it was transferred back to the donors.

Notes:

In this case, many of the original donors could not be found, so some of the surplus had to be applied to a public cause.

Fowkes v Pascoe (1875) 10 Ch App 343

The facts were:

A woman purchased a number of annuities in the joint names of herself and a man called John Pascoe, which raised a presumption of a resulting trust. At the time, she had purchased further annuities in her joint names with another person and annuities in her sole name.

The dispute to be decided by the court:

Was the presumption of a resulting trust rebutted?

Consider this point in analysing the legal issue:

Evidence that the donor had deliberately made a separate purchase for herself alone could be evidence that the joint purchase was a gift to the donee.

The principle of law applied:

Evidence of a gift will rebut the presumption of a resulting trust.

The outcome of the case:

This was evidence that a gift to John Pascoe was intended. This rebutted the presumption of a resulting trust.

15.7 Constructive trusts of the family home

The facts were:

Lloyds Bank v Rosset [1991] 1 AC 107

A married couple purchased a house together. It was registered in the sole name of the husband and he had provided the purchase money. The wife made no contributions towards the purchase monies but she had made contributions towards the renovation of the house. The husband got into financial difficulties and the bank sought to repossess the house. The wife claimed a share in the house in equity based on her contributions.

The dispute to be decided by the court:

Could the wife claim a share in the property based on her non-financial contributions?

Consider this point in analysing the legal issue:

How does the law decide ownership of the family home when the title is registered in one name?

The principle of law applied:

In sole ownership cases, the claimant must prove a common intention to share ownership. A common intention to share must either be expressly agreed or it can be inferred by evidence of contributions to the purchase price. There must also be evidence of detrimental reliance. Where common intention to share is expressly agreed, contributions in kind can qualify as detriment.

The outcome of the case:

There was no evidence of an express agreement of a common intention to share. The wife could not claim a share in equity in the property.

Notes:

Indirect contributions towards the improvements in the house are still not regarded as sufficient to establish an interest in property. Evidence of an express agreement to share can be informal and need not be in writing.

Grant v Edwards [1986] Ch 638

The facts were:

A man and a woman set up home together. A house was purchased by Edwards in his sole name. He told his partner that he had registered it in his name alone because she was currently going through divorce proceedings and ownership of a house might have prejudiced her entitlement to property on her divorce.

The dispute to be decided by the court:

Was Ms Grant entitled to a share in equity in the property based on the conversation that she had had with Mr Grant when the house was purchased?

Consider this point in analysing the legal issue:

Will a conversation about ownership be sufficient even if the outcome was that the claimant was not registered as owner?

The principle of law applied:

An informal discussion about ownership of property can be enough to prove common intention to share.

The outcome of the case:

Ms Grant was awarded a share in the house. It was granted on the basis of the informal discussion of the parties about ownership. She was told she would have been registered as an owner, but her ongoing divorce was the reason why not.

Notes:

Any discussion about ownership of the property would be enough to establish evidence of a common intention to share. The discussion must be based on ownership of the title and not about issues such as care for someone financially or sharing resources; it must be about ownership of the property.

Stack v Dowden [2007] UKHL 17

The facts were:

A couple, Mr Stack and Ms Dowden, had jointly purchased a property. Ms Dowden had previously owned a house that they had shared together, and she had contributed the proceeds of sale as well as her savings towards the purchase of the new house. Their relationship broke down, and Mr Stack moved out. He claimed a 50% share in the family home, which was disputed by Ms Dowden, who argued that she had made the larger contribution towards the purchase price. They had lived together for 19 years and had 4 children.

The dispute to be decided by the court:

Did the couple own equal shares in the property or could Ms Dowden claim a larger share based on her contributions towards the purchase price?

Consider this point in analysing the legal issue:

Where a couple jointly own property at law, the courts apply the principle 'equity follows the law'. This means that the law presumes that if the title is owned jointly at law as a joint tenancy, the equitable title will also be owned jointly. This case considered the circumstances when that principle can be rebutted.

The principle of law applied:

In the absence of common intention, a court will always presume a joint tenancy at law and a joint tenancy in equity. This presumption is rebuttable with evidence that the common intention has changed over the course of time.

The outcome of the case:

Ms Dowden had rebutted the presumption of equality and the courts awarded her a 65% share in the property.

Notes:

The courts will look at a range of factors in order to find evidence that the presumption of equality is rebutted. In this case, there was evidence that the parties had kept their finances separate throughout their long relationship. This was sufficient to rebut the presumption.

Jones v Kernott [2011] UKSC 53

The facts were:

Ms Jones and Mr Kernott purchased a house together in 1985 in their joint names. They made no declaration about ownership of the property. They shared expenses including mortgage payments. Together they had two children. Their relationship later deteriorated and Mr Kernott moved out in 1993. Ms Jones continued to live in the property with the children, paying all the expenses herself. Mr Kernott purchased his own property in 1996. Ten years later, in 2006, Mr Kernott made a claim for a 50% share in the property, which had increased considerably in value. Ms Jones disputed the claim, arguing that she had been solely responsible for mortgage payments and outgoings over the past 13 years.

The dispute to be decided by the court:

Could Mr Kernott claim a share in the property and if so, what was the size of his share?

Consider this point in analysing the legal issue:

Is it possible to displace the initial intentions with regard to ownership of property by later behaviour of the parties?

The principle of law applied:

The court accepted that it was possible to infer or impute a change in the common intention with regard to the ownership of property and this can be reflected in the shares that the parties can claim.

The outcome of the case:

Mr Kernott was awarded a 10% share in the property and Ms Jones a 90% share. This reflected their revised intentions with regard to the property after Mr Kernott had moved out of their jointly owned property.

Notes:

This case introduces the principle that allows a court to infer or impute the intention of the parties. Imputation gives the courts a much wider discretion as it allows it to consider what the parties might have intended if they had taken time to consider ownership at a later date.

15.8 Fiduciaries

Attorney-General for Hong-Kong v Reid [1994] 1 AC 324

The facts were:

The defendant was employed as a public prosecutor for the Hong Kong government. He received substantial bribes in the course of his job. Part of the money was used to purchase three properties in New Zealand.

The dispute to be decided by the court:

Was the defendant liable to hand back the bribe, or was he liable to account for the profit that he had received, namely the profit that he made on the houses he purchased in New Zealand?

Consider this point in analysing the legal issue:

The issue to decide was whether the Government official, who was a fiduciary, held the profit that he had made through his position as a constructive trustee or as a debtor under the law of contract.

The principle of law applied:

A fiduciary who receives a bribe or secret profit through their position holds the bribe as a constructive trustee, and any profit that they make on that money must be accounted to their principal.

The outcome of the case:

The government official held the bribe as constructive trustee and had to account for the profit that they had made to the Hong Kong Government.

Notes:

This decision was later upheld in *FHR European Ventures LLP v Cedar Capital Partners LLC* [2014] UKSC 45. A fiduciary who receives a bribe through their position holds the money as constructive trustee, and the principal has a proprietary right in the money received.

Att-Gen v Blake [1998] 1 AER 833

The facts were:

Blake was a former secret agent, and he wrote an autobiography of his life as an agent. The book was highly successful, and he made a profit from the sales.

The dispute to be decided by the court:

The Crown claimed that publication of the book was in breach of his fiduciary duty and he should account for the profits that he had to the Crown as his principal.

Consider this point in analysing the legal issue:

Is it possible to argue that the relationship of fiduciary and principal lapses after a time, and in the case of a fiduciary in employment, will the relationship lapse when the fiduciary ceases to be employed by the principal?

The principle of law applied:

A fiduciary relationship will cease when the fiduciary leaves the employment of their principal.

The outcome of the case:

Blake did not have to account for the profit that he had made on the sales of his book.

Notes:

Although a fiduciary can argue that he no longer needs to account for any profit once he has ceased to work for the principal, the position is different if the fiduciary deliberately leaves their position in order to breach their fiduciary duty.

15.9 Strangers

Royal Brunei Airlines Sdn Bhd v Tan[1995] 2 AC 378

The facts were:

The claimants were an airline that used a firm to act as agents in ticket sales. In breach of trust, the firm used money from the ticket sales for its own business. The firm became insolvent, and Tan, who was the director of the firm and principal shareholder, was sued for the proceeds of sales.

The dispute to be decided by the court:

The claimants argued that he was an accessory to the breach of trust committed by the now insolvent firm. Tan argued that he should not be liable because although the firm had misused the money, it had not acted fraudulently nor dishonestly and so could not be held liable as a *stranger* to the trust.

Consider this point in analysing the legal issue:

How can a third party become liable for dishonest assistance in a breach of trust? Is it necessary for the breach of trust to be fraudulent, or can the third party be liable where the breach of trust is innocent?

The principle of law applied:

A stranger can be held liable for dishonest assistance in a breach of trust where the breach of trust was neither fraudulent nor dishonest. A stranger can be held liable even where the breach of trust by the trustee is innocent or negligent. The liability of the stranger depends on his personal fault.

The outcome of the case:

Tan was held personally liable for dishonestly assisting in the firm's breach of trust.

Twinsectra v Yardley [2002] 2 All ER 377

The facts were:

Twinsectra agreed to lend money on certain terms to Mr Yardley, who was a businessman. They advanced money to a firm of solicitors who agreed that it would not be advanced to Mr Yardley until it was used for the purchase of property by him. Mr Leach was a solicitor who acted for Mr Yardley. He received the money from the solicitors acting for Twinsectra and immediately advanced it to Yardley without first ensuring that the money was used for the purchase of property. Yardley used the money for other purposes, and the loan was not repaid.

The dispute to be decided by the court:

It was claimed by Twinsectra that the money had been held on trust by the first set of solicitors and Mr Leach had dishonestly assisted them in its application in breach of trust. They claimed that Mr Leach was personally liable for their loss.

Consider this point in analysing the legal issue:

This case turned on the test for dishonesty. Could Mr Leach be said to be dishonest in the way that he had behaved?

The principle of law applied:

The test for dishonesty in dishonest assistance was a combined test. This test combines an objective and a subjective test for dishonesty. Under this test, it must be established that the defendant's conduct was dishonest by the standards of reasonable and honest people and that he himself realised that, by those standards, his conduct was dishonest.

The outcome of the case:

The House of Lords held that there was a trust but by a majority they held that Mr Leach had not acted dishonestly.

Notes:

The test for dishonesty in dishonest assistance is now a combined test. The courts do not judge a defendant by their own moral standards but by an objective standard. The courts will look at an individual and ask the question whether the defendant acted as an honest person would have acted in the defendant's circumstances. So the test does allow the court to take into account the defendant's personal characteristics.

Re Montagu's Settlement Trusts [1987] Ch 264

The facts were:

The 10th Duke of Manchester received a large number of chattels from a family trust. He sold a number of them believing them to be his own. On his death, it was found that he had sold items that should have passed to the 11th Duke of Manchester, who claimed that the 10th Duke held them as constructive trustee. It was argued on behalf of the 10th Duke (now deceased) that the situation had resulted from an honest muddle, which included a failure on behalf of the trust solicitor to make a clear inventory distinguishing trust property from property to which the 10th Duke was absolutely entitled.

The dispute to be decided by the court:

Was the 10th Duke of Manchester liable for dishonest receipt of property in breach of trust, or had he made an honest mistake about the property?

Consider this point in analysing the legal issue:

What is the standard of proof for dishonesty in dishonest receipt of property?

The principle of law applied:

The claimant is not required to prove that the defendant was positively dishonest but merely to establish that the defendant's actions were not consistent with how an honest person would have acted in the same situation.

The outcome of the case:

It was held that the 10th Duke had made an honest mistake about his ownership of the property. He might have known in the past that he was not entitled to the property he received, but he could not be held liable for 'knowing receipt' because, over time and by the time he received the property, he had forgotten which property did belong to him.

15.10 The duties and powers of trustees

The facts were:

Re Beloved Wilkes Charity (1851) 3 Mac & G 440

A group of trustees had the power to select a boy to be educated as a priest in the Church of England with a preference within a certain area. They chose a boy outside the area.

The dispute to be decided by the court:

Could the trustees be forced to give reasons for the exercise of their discretion? Or was the decision-making of the trustees a private matter?

Consider this point in analysing the legal issue:

Consider the advantages and disadvantages of keeping the reasons for the exercise of a discretion by trustees private. There is always the potential for litigation by disappointed beneficiaries in a group of discretionary beneficiaries.

The principle of law applied:

The exercise of a discretion by trustees should never be questioned unless there was evidence of improper use of the discretion.

The outcome of the case:

The trustees had acted properly, and they did not have to give the reasons for their decision.

Cowan v Scargill [1985] Ch 270

The facts were:

Union trustees of the pension fund for the National Union of Mineworkers challenged the investment policy of the pension fund, which included investments in overseas industries in direct competition with the UK coal industry. The investments made a profitable return for the pension fund.

The dispute to be decided by the court:

In exercising their duty to invest, were trustees entitled to make investments based on their social and political views? An argument was put forward on behalf of the beneficiaries of the pension fund that their duty was to make the best return possible on their investments for the beneficiaries.

Consider this point in analysing the legal issue:

Are there any circumstances when trustees can allow their social, political and moral views to affect their decisions on the investment of the trust fund?

The principle of law applied:

The duty of a trustee is to maximise the trust fund on behalf of the beneficiaries; their own personal moral views should not influence their decision unless the return on the investments was as good as that of the investments in companies against which they had personal objections on moral grounds.

The outcome of the case:

The trustees were not allowed to base their investment decisions on their own social and political beliefs unless it made no difference to the return from the investments.

15.11 Breach of trust

The facts were:

Target Holdings v Redferns [1995] 3 All E R 785

£1.525 million was lent by the claimant mortgagees, Target Holdings, to a company to be secured on property which had been fraudulently made to appear to be worth £2 million but in reality was worth £775,000. The defendants, Redferns, were a firm of solicitors and were not party to the fraud but had acted for both the purchasers and the mortgagees. They were instructed by the mortgagees not to forward the mortgage monies until they had secured the title to the property. In breach of trust, they had forwarded the monies but they then did secure the title. The purchasers became insolvent and the property was repossessed by the mortgagees.

The dispute to be decided by the court:

Could the mortgagees claim the shortfall from the sale of the property from the solicitors who were in breach of trust although the breach had not caused the loss to the trust fund?

Consider this point in analysing the legal issue:

Can the law make a distinction between a traditional trust and those trusts which arise in a commercial setting?

The principle of law applied:

In order to be successful in an action for breach of trust, the claimant must show that the loss would not have occurred but for the breach. If there is a causal link, then the trustee would be liable for the whole loss irrespective of the fact that the immediate cause of the loss was connected with a third party.

The outcome of the case:

The solicitors, Redferns, were not responsible for the loss to the trust fund because the claimants could not establish a causal link between the loss and the breach by the solicitors.

Notes:

The basic rule is that a trustee in breach of trust must restore or pay to the trust estate the assets which have been lost or compensation for such loss.

15.12 Liability of innocent volunteers who had disposed of assets wrongly paid to them

Re Diplock [1948] Ch 465

The facts were:

Money from a large trust fund had been paid out to various charities. It was later held that the trust was not charitable and so the next of kin of the deceased could recover the property.

The dispute to be decided by the court:

Were the charities liable to account for the monies they had received from the estate? Were the beneficiaries able to pursue the charities, who were all innocent volunteers, where they had spent the money they had received on improvements to premises? Were the next of kin able to rely on tracing in order to recover their money?

Consider this point in analysing the legal issue:

How does tracing operate against an innocent volunteer?

The principle of law applied:

Tracing is available against an innocent volunteer, but they are able to raise the defence of change of position if the money has been spent on improvements to property, and the right to trace will cease if the money has been dissipated.

The outcome of the case:

It was possible to trace against those charities which still retained the money, but where it had been spent or dissipated, the right to trace ceased.

Answers to multiple-choice questions

Answers to multiple-choice questions – Chapter 1

Question One

The correct answer was **C**. Using words such as 'confident', 'hope', or 'desire' does not show an intention to create a trust, so without a clear intention to create a trust the whole gift fails. A and B are not correct because although it is true that he has clearly identified the beneficiaries, without intention to create a trust, it cannot succeed. D is incorrect because a trust can still arise even where the word trust is not used. E is incorrect because it would not matter if the shares had not been clearly identified as this is a discretionary trust and the choice of the size of shares is left to the trustees.

Question Two

The correct answer is **A**. T1 has set up a discretionary trust. The group of beneficiaries has conceptual certainty. As this is a discretionary trust, evidential certainty is not required as the trustees do not have to draw up a complete list of beneficiaries. They merely have to 'survey the range of beneficiaries'. B and C are incorrect because T1 has made his intentions clear and the beneficiaries have been clearly identified. D is incorrect because a complete list of beneficiaries is not required in a discretionary trust. E is incorrect because evidential certainty is only required for fixed trusts and not for discretionary trusts.

Answers to multiple choice questions – Chapter 2

Question One

E is the correct answer. As Konrad believes that he is going to die from the operation, this would be a valid gift made in contemplation of death. The main problem with the gift is that there is no delivery of the jewellery, but there is symbolic delivery, which is justified because Konrad is in hospital; therefore, C is also incorrect. A is incorrect because although the charity can claim the estate of Konrad, the jewellery will be considered as a lifetime gift and will therefore take effect outside the will. B is incorrect because although Konrad may recover from the operation, he has been told it is a risk and he himself believes he is going to die. D is incorrect because a gift of personalty does not need to be put into writing.

Question Two

The correct answer is **D**. According to the rule in *Strong v Bird*, an imperfect gift from a donor to a donee can be perfected where the donee has been appointed executor of the deceased donor's will. Nina has been appointed executor of Maddie's will, so she is entitled to claim that the flat passed to her on Maddie's death. A is incorrect because although it is true that Oz inherits all of Maddie's estate on her death, she has already transferred the flat to Nina. B is incorrect because Maddie has made a valid will and so this will govern how her property passes on her death. C is incorrect because although it is true that the formalities of transfer were not followed, in particular the need for a deed of transfer to Nina, Nina can claim the flat as executor of Maddie's estate. E is incorrect as, in spite of a clear intention shown that Nina was to have the flat, she could not claim it unless she was executor of the estate.

Answers to multiple-choice questions – Chapter 5

Question One

The correct answer is **E**. The terms of the trust are for the impoverished members of the family of the testator. The law would regard this as a trust for the relief of poverty, which is one of the recognised heads of charity. An impoverished person will be regarded as poor. The fact that it provides housing for family members does not prevent it from being a charitable trust. The perpetuity period does not affect charitable trusts, so it does not matter that this may last beyond 21 years. A is incorrect because although it is a purpose trust, it will be viewed as charitable and therefore a public trust. The rules with regard to beneficiaries are relaxed for public trusts. B is incorrect because although usually where the beneficiaries of a charitable trust have a personal nexus it will fail the public benefit test, it is relaxed for a trust for the relief of poverty and the law allows any trust for the relief of poverty even where the potential group of beneficiaries is small and they have a personal nexus to the settlor. C is incorrect because providing housing for poor members of the settlor's family is regarded as coming within the definition of the relief of poverty. D is incorrect because although a personal nexus with the settlor usually means a charitable trust will fail the public benefit test, in this case, it is relaxed because the trust is for the relief of poverty.

Question Two

C is the correct answer. This will be regarded as a valid purpose trust. The maintenance of the statue infringes the perpetuity period, but this can be severed from the rest of the gift, and so the gift for the erection of the statue can be upheld. A is incorrect because only part of the gift infringes the perpetuity period. B is incorrect because the erection of a memorial statue is an exception allowing for the upholding of a purpose trust. D is incorrect because although it is correct that this is within the named exceptions for a valid purpose trust, the gift as a whole infringes the perpetuity period, so without severance, it will fail. E is incorrect as the gift will be looked at as a whole, and the law in relation to a statute does not apply a wait and see approach as it might for the gift for the maintenance of a single named animal.

Answers to multiple-choice questions – Chapter 6

Question One

The correct answer is **D**. Basil transferred the money to Winston for an express purpose, namely to modernise his showroom. This indicates that he transferred the money on trust. The purpose has been partially carried out; therefore, any surplus must result back to Basil as the purpose of the trust has partially failed. The money would be held on a 'Quistclose' trust. A is incorrect as the money was not transferred for the purpose of purchasing property, so it was not held on a presumed resulting trust. B is incorrect because the wording of the gift is such that it does not indicate an outright gift to Winston. There is a clear direction that the money is to be used for a purpose. C is incorrect because the transfer to Winston was expressed in such a way that a trust arose. It was not a loan on terms, such as 'pay me back in three months', but a transfer with a purpose attached. E is incorrect. The original transfer to Winston was not for the purchase of property, so it was not a presumed resulting trust. The transfer from Basil was for a specific purpose.

Question Two

The correct answer is **B**. This will be regarded as a presumed resulting trust in Timmy's favour. He provided all the purchase money at the time of purchase, and there is nothing to indicate that he intended a gift to Suzi. Suzi will be regarded as a resulting trustee for Timmy. A is incorrect because although she is the legal owner of the flat, she will be regarded as a resulting trustee of the flat because the purchase money was provided by Timmy. C is incorrect because the law does not regard a cohabiting couple as giving rise to rights in the family home. This situation will be resolved by looking at an implied trust. D is incorrect because there is nothing to indicate that Suzi should have a share. She did not contribute to the purchase, and Timmy did not indicate that she should receive a share in the flat. E is incorrect because the presumption of advancement only applies to married couples and Timmy and Suzi are cohabiting.

Answers to multiple-choice questions – Chapter 7

Question One

E is the correct answer. Dee said to Cassie, 'This house belongs to us both'. This is a promise of property rights. The law recognises an informal agreement so long as rights in the property are promised and supported by detriment. The law accepts indirect financial contributions as evidence of detrimental reliance. Cassie has made substantial payments towards outgoings. A is incorrect. It is true that Cassie did not contribute towards the purchase of the property, but as there is evidence of a common agreement, she is able to claim a share in spite of this. B is incorrect. It is true that the law does not recognise cohabitation as a relationship that gives rise to rights, but in this case, Cassie can rely on the evidence of an informal agreement under the law of trusts to give her rights in the property. C is incorrect as Cassie can use the evidence of the contributions that she made to the outgoings as evidence of detrimental reliance. D is incorrect. The law does not recognise indirect contributions as giving rise to rights in property even where the relationship has been long. Only direct financial contributions will count.

Question Two

C is the correct answer. At no time did Tex promise the house to either daughter. He has left a valid will, and under the will, the RSPCA now has rights over the house. A and B are both incorrect because no property rights arise automatically for children or relatives. Ownership of the property depends on whether or not Tex informally transferred rights during his lifetime. D is incorrect because it is up to the transferor to promise rights in the property. Una cannot claim rights based on her own statement which was not acknowledged by Tex. Any rights accruing under proprietary estoppel are based on property rights promised by a promisor which are then acted on by the promisee. E is also incorrect because detriment alone cannot give rise to property rights. Only detriment which arises in reliance on a promise of property rights will give rise to property rights in the Brambles. Una does not get rights based on her care of Tex.

Answers to multiple-choice questions – Part I

Question One

The correct answer was **D**. This is a discretionary trust and the trustees do not have to draw up a complete list of beneficiaries. A is not correct because the objects or beneficiaries are clear. An employee or ex-employee is clear in law. B is not correct because the settlor uses an imperative instruction 'to be divided'. C is not correct because although it is true that the trustees cannot draw up a complete list of employees, it is not necessary, and E is not correct because the instructions given are clear.

Question Two

The correct answer is **D**. Tessa is an executor of Sami's will, and under the rule in *Strong v Bird*, an imperfect gift will be perfected even where the formalities of transfer have not been complied with prior to the death of the transferor. A is incorrect because Sami intended to make an immediate gift, and B is incorrect because the lifetime gift to Tessa is perfected on death and takes effect before the terms of the will. C is not correct because although Sami telephoned his solicitors, the gift is only perfected because Tessa was appointed as an executor. D is incorrect because the failure to draw up the formalities of transfer can be remedied because Tessa has been appointed as executor.

Question Three

The correct answer is **A** because if Jane holds a beneficial interest under a trust and if she wishes to transfer her interest to Katie, she must comply with s.53(1)(c), which requires a written instruction to the trustees. For this reason, the oral instruction in B is not binding, and under s.53(1)(c), it is irrelevant whether or not the beneficiary tells the intended recipient about the gift. D is incorrect because although the creation of a trust of personalty does not need written evidence, the transfer of an equitable interest, whether it is land or personalty, always requires written evidence. E is incorrect because an equitable interest can be freely transferred by a beneficiary at any time.

Question Four

E is the correct answer because Liam has not specified whether the mass in his memory is to be said in public or private and only masses said in public will be upheld. A is incorrect because gifts to single named animals can be upheld and a gift to erect a gravestone will comply with the perpetuity period. B is also incorrect because both the gift to the cat and the gift to erect the gravestone do comply with the perpetuity period. C and D are incorrect because the gift for the saying of the mass will not be upheld as the mass must be held in private.

Question Five

The correct answer is **E**. Janice provided all the purchase money, and there is no evidence that she intended to make a gift of the property to Kev, so he will hold the equitable interest on resulting trust for Janice. A is incorrect because the law will look at both ownership of the legal estate as well as ownership of the equitable estate and the equitable estate lies solely with Janice. B is incorrect because the presumption of advancement does not apply to mother and son. C and D are both incorrect because ownership of the equitable estate lies solely with Janice and Kev does not have an interest.

Question Six

E is the correct answer. When Anise says that they are to share the house, she is declaring a common intention to share the property, which will give rise to a common intention constructive trust. Jofra also needs to prove detrimental reliance, which he can do by pointing to the work he has done on the house. A is incorrect because rights in property are not derived from cohabiting as a couple. B is incorrect because the improvements are not regarded as capital contributions to the purchase price. C is also incorrect because improvements to the property on their own are not regarded as a capital contribution. D is incorrect because unless there is proof of a constructive trust Jofra cannot claim any share at all from the value unless it has been agreed between them.

Answers to multiple-choice questions – Chapter 8

Question One

The correct answer is **D**. If the beneficiaries are of full age and in agreement and have given consent to a sale to the trustee even if it is self-dealing, then they cannot come back later and ask for the sale to be set aside. The problem for Francis is that two of the beneficiaries are not of full age and so they cannot give consent. A is incorrect because this is self-dealing and it can always be set aside unless it comes within one of the exceptions such as permission from the beneficiaries or from the court. B is incorrect because it is not for the trustees to give consent in these circumstances. Only the beneficiaries can give consent to a trustee who wishes to purchase trust property. C is incorrect because although he did obtain permission from the beneficiaries, as two were underage, the law does not regard this as consent, and so one of the beneficiaries is still entitled to challenge the purchase. E is not correct because self-dealing is allowed where the beneficiaries give permission or there is permission given in the trust instrument or the trustee seeks permission from the court.

Question Two

E is the correct answer. As solicitor to the trust, William is a fiduciary, and so he owes fiduciary duties which include not making a profit for himself and not allowing his duty to the trust to conflict with his own interests. William must account for the profit he made on the shares. A is incorrect because it is irrelevant if the trust makes a profit as well as the fiduciary, because any profit made in breach of one's fiduciary duties must be accounted for to the beneficiaries. B is also incorrect because it is irrelevant that the profit was made through the hard work of the fiduciary. C is incorrect because William has used his position as trustee to gain information about the company and therefore he is using trust property as the information belongs to the trust. He must account for the profit made through the information. D is incorrect because although he is not a trustee, he becomes a fiduciary in his capacity as solicitor to the trust.

Answers to multiple-choice questions – Part II

Question One

The correct answer is **A**. The beneficiaries can bring an action against Fergus and recover the profit he made on the shares. B is incorrect because although Fergus is not a trustee, he is a fiduciary and that allows the beneficiaries to bring an action. Although he acted honestly and in the best interests of all the beneficiaries, he cannot keep any profit that he makes through his role as fiduciary for himself. This means that neither D nor E is correct. C is incorrect because although Fergus had sought consent from the trustees, one was not sui juris, and in order to be protected against an action from the beneficiaries to recover the profit from his shares, he should have sought consent from all the beneficiaries. As a solicitor, he should also know that their consent depended on them being sui juris, and in this case, Zandra was not sui juris.

Question Two

The correct answer is **D**. We do not know whether Jack was appointed through the trust shareholding or his own shareholding. The law makes it clear that a trustee must account for a director's fee if it was obtained through shares held by the trust. A is incorrect because there is no automatic conflict of interest if Jack is acting on his own behalf and not that of the trust. B is also incorrect because the timing of his appointment as trustee is irrelevant to the question whether or not he must account for his fee. C is incorrect as the issue is not the time spent on company affairs but how Jack became a director. E is incorrect as in this case it is not a question of full disclosure but instead a question of how he became a director.

Question Three

The correct answer is **B**. Vernon has a conflict of interest as trustee. The purchase is regarded as 'self-dealing' under the law, and so the beneficiaries can have the sale set aside unless they expressly give their consent, assuming all are sui juris. The facts do not tell us the ages of the beneficiaries or whether they are all sui juris and able to give consent. We know that Dee is living in a residential home, so she may not be sui juris. It is irrelevant if the sale was made at public auction, and it is irrelevant if there has been an independent valuation and the trustee pays full market price. A, D and E are all incorrect because the only way Vernon can make a purchase that cannot be challenged is by gaining approval of the beneficiaries. C is incorrect because in self-dealing, the trustee must gain approval of the beneficiaries, not the trustees, in order for the sale to stand.

Question Four

The correct answer is **D**. This is a sale of a beneficial interest under the trust, and so the fair-dealing rule applies rather than the self-dealing rule. Irma must ensure that she behaves in a way that is fair and honest, and the trustee makes full disclosure to the beneficiaries. Irma has had the interests independently valued and has made full disclosure to Maddie and Max. A is incorrect because Max is not seeking to have the sale from him set aside. B is incorrect because Irma can defend any challenge by a beneficiary by arguing that she has behaved in a fair and honest way. C is incorrect because the law requires full disclosure to the beneficiaries rather than a co-trustee. E is incorrect because there is no time delay on challenging a purchase of trust property by a trustee by a beneficiary.

Question Five

The correct answer is **E**. Carrie is liable for knowing receipt as she receives trust money with actual knowledge of its source and knowing it was in breach of trust. She becomes a constructive trustee. Carrie is not liable as a trustee or a fiduciary because she has no direct relationship in law with the trust, so A and B are incorrect. D is also incorrect because Carrie does not become a fiduciary when she is told of the source of the money. She is never a fiduciary; instead, she is a constructive trustee when she is in receipt of the trust money C is incorrect because Carrie is not an innocent volunteer. She has full knowledge of the source of the money given to her by her mother.

Question Six

The correct answer is **D**. The husband is asked for his advice in investing the money, and he is suspicious of the source of the money. He should have asked questions of T1. In order to be found liable for dishonest assistance, it must be shown that there is a trust and a breach of trust and the stranger (the husband) dishonestly assists in the breach. By failing to ask the questions, the law would say that he has acted unconscionably. A is incorrect because it is irrelevant that the husband did not take the money. B and C are incorrect because it is not necessary to show that the husband was either a trustee or a fiduciary in order for him to be liable for dishonest assistance. E is incorrect because the husband was never in receipt of the money for his own benefit, so the husband cannot be found liable for knowing receipt.

Answers to multiple-choice questions – Chapter 12

Question One

A is the correct answer. The exemption clause does not exempt them from actual fraud, and taking the trust money for themselves would be regarded as fraudulent even if they suggested that they were going to give it back. B is incorrect as Donny cannot argue that he is protected by the exemption clause as he was fully aware that Caspar was taking money from the trust. He is just as much in breach even if he did not physically take the money for himself. C is incorrect because this exemption clause does not exempt the trustees from fraud; even if it had included an exemption for fraud, the law has made it clear that an exemption clause can never exempt a trustee from actual fraud. D is incorrect. If a trustee takes money from a trust fund for themselves, there is no defence if they say that they intended to pay it back. They are still liable for breach of trust. E is incorrect because both Donny and Caspar were fraudulent. They took money from the trust, and they knew they had no right to do so.

Question Two

The correct answer is **E**. The trustees are in breach of trust as they have invested in property which is in breach of the terms of the trust instrument. Bilal can sue because his interest did not fall in until his mother Annie died. He then has six years in which to bring an action against the trustees. A is incorrect because Annie could not consent on behalf of Bilal as he was underage. B is incorrect because although the breach was eight years ago, Bilal, who is the remainder man, retains the rights to sue for six years after their interest falls in. C is incorrect because although the trustees thought they were making a good investment, they are in breach of trust and this is not a valid defence. D is incorrect because it is irrelevant what Bilal thought about the investment; he could not give consent because he was underage at the time.

Question Three

C is the correct answer. The solicitors were in breach of trust because they had a duty to only transfer the title when the title was secure and they had forwarded the title before it was transferred, but the claimants cannot prove a causal link between their loss and the breach of trust. A and B are both incorrect because without a causal link, the claimants cannot claim any of the outstanding amount in spite of the breach of trust. D is incorrect because Easy Loans were entitled to rely on the valuation made, and had the causal link been established, they could have recovered the outstanding amount from White and Co. E is incorrect because it is irrelevant whether or not a trustee is aware that they are in breach of trust; liability is strict, and if causation can be established, they would be personally liable for the loss suffered.

Answers to multiple-choice questions – Part III

Question One

D is the correct answer. This is a trust of land, so there must be at least two trustees. Sal is standing down and is leaving two trustees, so it is not necessary to appoint a third trustee. A is incorrect as the trust only needs two trustees; it is irrelevant that there were three trustees at the start. B is incorrect for the same reasons as A. C is incorrect as a trust with minors does not require any more trustees than a trust with adults as beneficiaries. E is incorrect as the reasons for the retirement of a trustee are irrelevant to whether a new trustee needs to be appointed.

Question Two

The correct answer is **A**. The law protects trustees in a discretionary trust from giving reasons for the exercise of their discretion. This is to prevent unnecessary litigation. Isaac could challenge if the trustees had appointed a person outside the group of discretionary beneficiaries named by the settlor. B is incorrect; trustees do not have to give reasons for the exercise of their discretion. C is incorrect; the law does not make this optional in order to protect trustees of all trusts; some may prefer not to share the reasons with the beneficiaries. D is incorrect; the beneficiaries cannot force the trustees to give their reasons, whether they are of age or not. E is incorrect because the trustees have not got complete discretion; they must exercise their discretion within the group of discretionary beneficiaries. If the trustees had chosen someone who was a friend of the settlor, then Isaac may have had an action for breach of trust.

Question Three

The correct answer is **E**. This is a very large fund, and without financial expertise, the trustees should seek advice to guide them. They are in breach of the investment duties and therefore in breach of trust. A is incorrect because the duties of trustees are far wider than reviewing the investments, which includes taking proper advice. B is incorrect because although it is true that trustees do not always have to take advice, they should do so where the fund is large and they do not have sufficient expertise themselves. C is incorrect. Trustees would not be in breach of trust simply by failing to change the investments if they had taken advice and considered whether the investments were suitable and appropriate. D is incorrect because the trustees have no obligation to discuss investments with the beneficiaries.

Question Four

C is the correct answer. Vernon cannot make an investment purely based on his moral and ethical views if the return is lower than other investments to which he is opposed on moral grounds. A is incorrect because the decision in *Cowan v Scargill* states that a trustee cannot base investment decisions on moral and ethical grounds. Their duty is to maximise the return on their investments. B is incorrect as this is a small fund and Vernon is a stockbroker, so he is not obliged to seek advice. D is incorrect because Vernon has no obligation to explain his investment decisions to the beneficiaries. They do not have to be consulted. E is incorrect. The assets of this trust do not appear to include any money, so there is no need to appoint a second trustee. A sole trustee is sufficient.

Question Five

The correct answer is **B**. The trustees have the power to advance income to a beneficiary for the purpose of maintenance which would include education, but this power is subject to some limitations. In this case, there is a prior interest (Teri), so there is no power to do so. A is incorrect because the power to advance income for maintenance is subject to certain limitations, in particular whether or not there is a prior interest. C is incorrect because the decision as to whether or not the income is used for the maintenance of one of the beneficiaries is one purely for the trustees, and they do not have to consult the beneficiaries. D is incorrect as the trustees have an absolute power to advance income to the beneficiaries for their maintenance under a trust but subject always to the existence of a prior interest. E is incorrect because although the exercise of the power is subject to whether the trustees think it is fit to do so, they cannot exercise the power if there is a prior interest.

Question Six

The correct answer is **E**. All the trustees were in breach: Kevin by omission and Gavin and Mikey by commission. The trust instrument prevents any investment in non-UK companies, and they are in breach of this by investing in an American company. Time is still running against them because Nora and Orla were both underage when the investment was first made, and so time did not run against the trustees until they were 18, which was 5 years ago. They still have a year in which to bring an action against the trustees. A is incorrect because investing in the American company was in breach of trust; the return on the investment is irrelevant. B is incorrect because the limitation period did not start to run until the beneficiaries were 18. C is incorrect because Kevin has no defence to an action for breach of trust by arguing that he did not take part in the decision. D is incorrect because Gavin and Mikey are also liable for the commission of a breach of trust. All three trustees are liable.

Answers to multiple-choice questions – Part IV

Question One

The correct answer is **E**. The trustee took money from two trusts and deposited it in a mixed fund. He took a larger amount from Trust BETA, so A will be incorrect because the proceeds will not be shared equally. If the rule in *Clayton's Case*, 'first in, first out', was applied, all of Trust ALPHA's money would be deemed to be used, but it will not apply as it would produce an unjust result so answers B and C are incorrect. The two trusts have a proprietary claim to the car, so D is incorrect; the trustee in bankruptcy cannot claim the car. The value will be shared proportionately between the two trusts. E is the correct answer.

Question Two

The correct answer is **B**. Trixie cannot claim the sculpture because although the usual rule is that a trustee is presumed to spend his own money first under Hallett's Case, this is displaced where there is no money left in the bank account to satisfy the claim of the beneficiaries, and they can instead claim a charge over any asset purchased by the trustee; thus, A is incorrect. C is incorrect because there is an asset over which the beneficiaries can claim proprietary rights. D is incorrect because it is assumed that Trixie spent her own money on the holiday, and therefore her money has been dissipated. E is incorrect because the beneficiaries have a proprietary right over the sculpture which they should pursue first.

Question Three

The correct answer is **C**. The mother has received the money in good faith. She has used it to carry out essential repairs on her house, which she would not have carried out without the money given to her by her son. The beneficiaries cannot trace against her or the house because it would be inequitable to trace in these circumstances. Therefore, B is incorrect as it would be unjust if the beneficiaries had the right to enter a charge against her house, and A is incorrect because tracing is not available where it would be inequitable to trace. D is incorrect because the mother is not a constructive trustee and therefore not liable in a personal action against her brought by the beneficiaries. E is incorrect as Hari has no proprietary rights over any trust assets. He transferred the money from the trust fund to his mother, so there is no right to trace against Hari.

Question Four

The correct answer is **A**. The trustee, Tariq, has withdrawn £30,000 from the trust and deposited it into his personal account, which is already overdrawn by £20,000, so only £10,000 remained in credit. He then withdrew £10,000 for a procedure for his wife, and that is deemed to be dissipated, so the balance fell to £0. According to the rule of the 'lowest intermediate balance', the beneficiaries can only trace into the lowest credit in the account, which is £0. The money paid into the account for the car is not traceable, so C and also B are incorrect. The bank does not owe the beneficiaries any rights in equity as it has no fiduciary relationship with them, so D is incorrect. Tariq's wife cannot be considered to be a constructive trustee as she believed the money for her procedure came from the sale of the trustee Tariq's car, so E is incorrect.

Question Five

The correct answer is **C**. The purchase of the car by Ted and the taking of trust money are two interlinked matters, and in these circumstances, 'backwards tracing' can be applied. This allows the beneficiaries to trace into an overdrawn bank account but only if it can be proved that there has been a coordinated scheme by the trustee to use trust money to defeat a tracing action. So in this case, A is incorrect as there is proof of a coordinated scheme by the trustee, allowing tracing into an overdrawn account. The beneficiaries are limited by the amount in the account so can only trace into £50,000, not £60,000, so B is incorrect. The beneficiaries retain the right to trace into the bank account and not just the car, so they have the right to claim the full amount of the loss to the trust fund rather than just £10,000, so both D and E are incorrect.

Question Six

The correct answer is **B**. The trust instrument does not reflect the wishes of the settlor, Geri, and in these circumstances, the courts will order rectification of a document, allowing it to be changed to reflect the correct terms. A is incorrect. The order would not be appropriate where the rest of the terms should stand. The trust has simply been recorded incorrectly and can be rectified. C is incorrect because Bimbi has no cause of action to apply for an injunction until the trust has been rectified in her favour. Under the terms of the trust instrument, Anna has rights over the brooch. D is incorrect. Bimbi does have a course of action. She can apply for an order of rectification. There is clear evidence that Geri intended the brooch to go to Bimbi. E is incorrect because Bimbi would not have a cause of action against Anna unless the trust is rectified.

Index

Note: Page numbers in **bold** indicate tables

Abrahams v Trustee in Bankruptcy of Abrahams (2000) WTLR 593 61n1
accessory liability 115, 117, **118,** 119
Adams v Kensington Vestry 27 Ch D 9n2, 62n2
advancement 148–149
agency **6**
animals/pets 50–52, 55
Anton Piller KG v Manufacturing Processes Ltd (1976) Ch 55 190n2
Armitage v Nurse (1998) Ch 241 159
Att-Gen v Blake (1998) 1 AER 833 214–215
Attorney-General for Hong-Kong v Reid (1994) 1 AC 324 213–214
awards of specific performance 186–187

bailments **5**
bankruptcy law 65, 69
Barclays Bank v Quistclose (1970) A.C. 567 64–65, 199
Barlow Clowes International Ltd v Vaughan (1992) 4 AER 22 180
Barlow Clowes International v Eurotrust International (2006) 1 All ER 333 116n3
Bartlett v Barclays Bank Trust Co Ltd (1980) Ch 515 136n2, 158n5
BCCI v Akindele (2001) Ch 437 114n1
beneficiaries 3–4, 7–10
  and breaches of trust 152, 154, 159
  and the certainty of objects 13–15
  and conceptual certainty 15–16
  and constructive trustees 113–114
  and contingent interests 41
  and discretionary trusts 142–144, 152
  and equitable estates 35
  and equitable interest transfers 38–39
  estates of 42
  and express trust constitution 21
  and the 'first in first out' rule 180
  and indemnities 157
  and personal remedies 109–111
  pets/animals as 50–52
  and prior interests 147–149
  and proprietary remedies 109–110
  proving accessory liability 115
  requirements for 49–50
  rights of 41–42, 154
  and Saunders v Vautier 44–45, 47
  and solicitors 104–105
  and strangers to the trust 109, 215–217
  and tracing 172, 174, 180–181, 183
  and trust property recovery 171
  and trustee property purchases 98–99
  as trustees 39–40
  and trustees 7–8, 93–95, 100, 111–112, 129–131, 142
  trustees as 157
  and vested interests 41–42, 47, 146
Binions v Evans (1972) Ch 359 75n1
Boardman v Phipps (1967) 2 AC 46 104n8, 105
Boyce v Boyce (1949) 16 *Sim* 476 200–201
breach of contract 69n7
breaches of fiduciary duty 95–98, 103–106
breaches of trust 109, 112–113, 135–136, 141n5, 144–145, 151–152, 215–216, 219–220
  by banks 155
  and beneficiaries 152, 154, 159
  borrowing against property 155–156
  and causal connections 154–156, 219–220
  commissions of 153
  defences for 157–159, **160–61,** 183
  exemption clauses 159–160
  and indemnities 156–157, 159
  limitation periods 158
  omissions 135–136, 152–153
  and profits 154, 213–214
  and tracing 172
bribes 102–103, 182n4, 213–214
Burns v Burns (1984) Ch 317 80n10

change of position defence 175–176, 182–183
charitable trusts 25, 49, 52–57, 60, 208, 220–221
Charities Act 2011 53–54

cheques 197–198
Civil Liability (Contribution) Act 1978 157
Civil Partnership Act 76
Civil Procedure Act 1997 190n2
Clayton's Case (1816) 1 Mer 572 178–180
cohabitation 76–77, 80n10
Comiskey and Others v Bowring-Hanbury and Another (1905) AC 84 200
companies and property rights **6**
constructive trusts 7, 73, 93, 105–106
  common intention constructive trusts 78–79, 81, 93
  and employees 102–104
  and family homes 75–76, 210
  and property rights 74–75
  trustee profits as 100
Cowan v Scargill (1984) 3 WLR 501; (1984) Ch 270 141n5, 218–219
cy-pres doctrine 53

debts **5,** 31–32, 205–206
detrimental reliance 79, 81, 210
discretionary trusts 7–8, 142, 202–203
  and beneficiaries 142–144, 152
  and certainty of object 14–16
  and evidential certainty 16–18
  and trustees 14, 17, 142–144, 218
dishonest assistance 117, 216–217
dishonesty 115–117, 216–217
donatio mortis causa 30–31, 206
duty of care and trustees 135–136, 151

employees 102–104
equitable estates 35, 40
equitable interests 13–14, 37–39, 207
equitable remedies 185–187, 192
equity maxims 22, 26, 185, 187–188, 212
Eves v Eves (1975) 1 WLR 1338 79
express trusts 7, 59, 81, 142, 148
  constitution of 21, 23, 30–33
  and contingent interests 41–43, 47
  creation of 35–36
  failure of 59, 62
  and formalities 35–40, 59
  and surplus monies 62–64
  three certainties 8–18, 59, 61–62
  and trustees 127
  and vested interests 41–42, 47, 146; *see also* charitable trusts
  purpose trusts
  resulting trusts
  three certainties

fair dealing rule 96–99
familial relationships 66–68, 75–77, 81, 210–211
family homes 75–84, 210–211
Federal Republic of Brazil v Durant (2015) UKPC 35 182n4
FHR European Ventures LLP v Cedar Capital Partners LLC (2014) UKSC 45 103n6, 214
fiduciary relationships 93–95, 102, 111, 213–215
  development project 174–175
  and employees 94–95, 102–104
  and solicitors 104–105
  and tracing 173, 183
'first in first out' rule 178–180
fixed trusts 7–8, 142, 148
  and certainty of object 14–15
  and evidential certainty 16–18
  and trustee powers 145
  and trustees 14
Foskett v McKeown (2001) 1 *AC* 102 174–175, 177
Fowkes v Pascoe (1875) 10 Ch App 343 209
future/remainder interests 42, 44

gifts **5,** 209
  and automatic resulting trusts 61, 66
  conditions on 41–44, 145, 203
  and constituted trusts 30–33
  in contemplation of death 30–31, 206
  gifts over in default 43–44, 47, 61, 200
  and intermediate income 145–146
  and perpetuity periods 45–47
  and surplus monies 62–64
  transfers of 25–28n6, 29
'given postulant' test 202
Grant v Edwards (1986) Ch 638 79, 211
gravestones/tombs 50, 52
Grey v IRC (1960) *AC* 1 39n1
Grondona v Stoffel and Co (2020) UKSC AC 540 71

Head v Gould (1898) 2 Ch 250 153–154n1
honesty test for 116–117
Hunter v Moss (1994) 1 WLR 452 12n5

illegal property transfers 69–71
implied trusts 7, 59, 73, 81, 127; *see also constructive trusts*
Incorporated Council of Law Reporting for England and Wales v Att-Gen (1972) Ch 73 55
'individual ascertainability test' 16
Industrial Development Consultants Ltd v Cooley (1972) 1 WLR 443 103n7
informal agreements and property 78–79
Inheritance and Trustees' Powers Act 2014 *s.*8 147n8, 148n9
injunctions 185–186, 189, 192
  freezing orders 190–191
  interim 189–190

mandatory 189
prohibitory 189
search orders 190–191
undertaking in damages 190
intermediate income 145–146
investing: and breaches of trust 155
and ethics 141–142
as trustee duty 137–141, 151–152, 218–219
IRC v Oldham Training and Enterprise Council (1996) STC 1218 55n7
Ivey v Genting Casinos UK Ltd (t/a Crockford Club) (2017) UKSC 67 116n3

James v Thomas (2007) EWCA 1212 79n9
jewelry (family trust) 97–98, 110
Jones v Kernott (2011) UKSC 53 212–213
Jones v Lock (1865) LR 1 Ch App 25 197–198

Keech v Sandford (1726) Sel Cas Ch 61 100n3
knowledge 109, 112–113, 114n1, 172, 217

laches 158–159, 183
land 30–32, 96–98
land-related trusts 26–28, 37, 75, 83, 128, 133; *see also property*
Law of Property Act 1925 26n4, 37–38, 207
leases 100
legal estates 35, 40, 84, 96
life in being 46–47
life interests 42
Lister v Stubbs (1890) 45 Ch D 1 103n5
Lloyds Bank v Rosset (1991) 1 AC 107 77n5, 210

McGrath v Wallis (1995) 2 FLR 114 68n6
McPhail v Doulton (also known as Re Baden) (1971) AC 424 16n7, 202–203
Mareva Compania Naviera SA v International Bulkcarriers SA (1975) 2 Lloyd's Report 509 190n3
Mascall v Mascall (1984) 50 P & CR 42 27–28n6
Matrimonial Causes Acts 76
maxims of equity 185, 187–188
mental capacity and trusts 6–7
Milroy v Lord (1862) 45 E.R. 1185 24, 204
minors: and trustee powers 145–147
and trusts 7
Musset v Bingle (1876) WN 170 52n4

Nestle v National Westminster Bank plc (1993) 1 WLR 1260 140n4, 155n2

pari passu 180–181
Patel v Ali (1984) 1 AER 978 187n1
Patel v Mirza (2016) UKSC 42 69–70
Paul v Constance (1977) 1 WLR 527 11n3, 29n7, 198–199
Pennington v Waine (2002) 1 WLR 2075 29n7, 204–205
perpetuity periods 45–47, 49–53
personal administrators 31
personal remedies 109–111, 117
power of advancement 148–149
power of maintenance 145–148
presumption of advancement 66–68
presumption of equality 211–212
profits: accounting for 74, 94–95, 101–102, 214–215
and breaches of trust 154, 213–214
post-employment relationships 214–215
property 112
and bankruptcy 69
borrowing against 155–156
chattel 29–30
deeds for 26–27
homogenous groups of 11–12
illegal transfers of 69–71
inalienable 45
and informal agreements 78–79
and numbers of trustees 128
perpetuity periods for 45–47
presumed resulting trusts/purchase money resulting trusts 60–61
and presumption of advancement 66–68
and recipient consciences 73–75
recovering 171
and strangers to the trust 109, 114, 215–217
symbolic transfers 30
tangible vs. intangible 12
traceability of 173–174, 181–182
transfer rules 25–27, 29–30
trustees purchasing 95–99, 177–178, 181–182
valuable consideration 114–115; *see also* land-related trusts
property rights: and constructive trusts 74–75
and property purchase 80
and tracing 183
and trustees **5–6,** 8, 94
and trusts **5–6,** 23–24; *see also specific types of rights*
proprietary estoppel 82–84
proprietary remedies 109–110, 114–115, 117–118
proprietary rights **6,** 109–110, 173
purpose trusts 49–51, 57, 208

quantum meruit 105
Quistclose trusts 64–65

Re Astor's Settlement Trusts (1952) Ch 534 208
Re Barlow's Wills Trust (1979) 1 All ER 296 203

Re Beloved Wilkes Charity (1851) 3 Mac & G 440 218
re Bowden (1936) Ch 71 18n8
re Dean (1889) *L.R.* 41 Ch. *D* 51n3
re Diplock (1948) Ch 465 175n1, 220–221
re Dover Coalfield Extension Ltd (1907) 2 Ch 76 102n4
Re Gillingham Bus Disaster Fund (1958) Ch 300 208–209
Re Golay and others (1965) 2 All ER 660 201–202
Re Haines (1952) The Times 7 November 51n2
Re Hallett's Case (1880) 13 Ch D 696 177–178
Re London Wine Co (Shippers) Ltd (1975) PCC 121 12n4
Re Montagu's Settlement Trusts (1987) Ch 264 217
Re Osaba (1979) 2 AER 393 63n4
Re Partington (1887) 57 LT 654 157n4
re Rose (1952) Ch 499 25n3, 27
Re Shaw (1957) 1 WLR 729 54n6
re Smith (1928) Ch 915 144n6
Re Thomson (1930) 1 Ch 203 99n2
Re Trusts of the Abbott Fund (1900) 2 Ch 326 63n3
reasonable 201–202
recipient liability 109, 111–113, 118, **118,** 119
rectification 185–186, 188–189, 192
rescission 185–186, 191–192
resulting trusts 7, 59, 199–201, 208–209
  automatic resulting trusts 60–61
  and land purchases 60
  presumed resulting trusts/purchase money resulting trusts 60–61, 65–66, 75
  Quistclose trusts 64–65
  rebuttals of 66
  vs. constructive trusts 73
Royal Brunei Airlines v Tan (1995) 2 AC 378 115n2 215–216

Saunders v Vautier (1841) 49 E.R. 282 41, 44–45, 47, 143–144
self-dealing rule 96–99
settlors (donors) 3, 6–7
  and certainties of objects 13–17, 61
  and certainty of intention 9–10
  and certainty of subject matter 11–13
  choosing trustees 127–128
  and conceptual certainty 15–16
  identifying beneficiaries 13–14
  and precatory words 10
  and property transfers 24–26
  and resulting trusts 59, 61
  and trust types 7–8
  as trustees 21–24, 26–27
  and undue influence 191
shares **6,** 12, 27
  and bankruptcy 69
  transfers of 24–25, 28–29, 39, 204–205, 207
  and trustees 101–102, 104–105; *see also* *stock transfer forms*
solicitors 104–105, 156–157
Solicitors Qualifying Examination (SQE) assessment specifications vii viii
specific performance 185, 188, 192
Stack v Dowden (2007) UKHL 17 77, 211–212
stock transfer forms 28–29; *see also* shares
stranger liability **118–19,** 215–217
Strong v Bird (1874) L.R. 18 Eq 31–32, 205–206
sub-trusts 39–40
surplus monies 62–64, 208–209

T Choithram International SA v Pagarani (2000) UKPC 46 25n3
Target Holdings v Redferns (1995) 3 AER 785 156n3, 219–220
testators 129
three certainties 17–18, 29, 36, 59, 61, 197–203
  certainties of objects 13–17, 61–62, 202–203, 208
  certainty of intention 9–10, 62, 197–199
  certainty of subject matter 11–13, 200–201
  and express trusts 8–18
tracing 110, 171, 220–221
  against trustees 177–178
  backwards 181–182
  common law tracing 171
  defences against 182–183
  and fiduciary relationships 173, 183
  and mixed funds 174, 176–178, 183
  property traceability 173–174
  and proprietary rights 173
  and proportionate sharing 180–181
  rules for 176–177
  and third parties/multiple trusts 178–179
  tracing in equity 171–173, 175–176, 183
  vs. personal claims 172
Trustee Act 1925 *s.*61 158
Trustee Act 1925 *s.*62 159
Trustee Act 2000 100, 135, 138, 140, 152
trustees 3–4, 36, 99, 127
  appointment of 127–133, 137
  and bankruptcies 110, 112–113, 171, 178–180
  banks as 155
  and beneficiaries 7–8, 93–95, 100, 111–112, 129–131, 142
  as beneficiaries 157

competing with trusts 99
constructive trustees 105–106, 109–111, 113–114, 118, 175, 214
and discretionary trusts 14, 17, 142–144
duties of 136–140, 144–145, 151, 153–154, 159–160, 218–219
and the duty of care 135–136, 151
and exemption clauses 159–160, **161**
and express trusts 127
as fiduciaries 95–99
and fixed trusts 14
and good consciences 74–75, 106
and indemnities 156–157
investing trust funds 137–141 151–152
and legal estates 35
liabilities of 153, 156, 158, 171
omission to act 135–136, 152–153
paying 101
personal representatives of 130
powers of 145–149, 218–219
and property rights **5–6,** 8, 94
purchasing property 95–100
retirement of 129, 132, 153
right of survivorship 133
and the self-dealing rule 96–99
settlors as 21–24, 26–27
and shares 101–102, 104–105
strangers to the trust 109, 114–115, 171, 215–217
tracing against 177–178
'trustees de son tort' 109, **118–19**
unfit 128
unspoken trusts 174–175; *see also* breaches of trust
trusts 3–4
beneficiaries 3–4, 7–10, 13
and commercial cases 9
conditions on 41
creation *of* 6–7 9–10 17–18 23 26 35–36 200
declared void 43
and formalities 35–40, 59, 75
fully constituted 22–25, 32–33, 204–206
homogenous groups of property items 11–12
intermeddling with 118–119
investing 137–141, 151–152
and minors 7, 145–147
and property rights **5–6,** 23–24
rectification of 186
trustees competing with 100
vesting 21
written declarations for 26–27, 37; *see also* charitable trusts
constructive trusts
discretionary trusts
express trusts
fixed trusts
implied trusts
purpose trusts
Quistclose trusts
resulting trusts
settlors (donors)
sub-trusts
three certainties
trusts of personality
Trusts of Land and Appointment of Trustees Act 1996 129n2, 131n4
trusts of personality 26
Twinsectra v Yardley (2002) 2 All ER 377 216–217

unconscionable behaviour 74
and property rights 74–75
undue influence 191–192

Vandervell v IRC (1967) 2 AC 291 207
volunteers 24
defences for 175–176
and equity 188
'equity will not assist a volunteer' 22, 24, 26
innocent volunteers 111, 173–174, 178–179, 182–183, 220–221
and mixed funds 175–177

Wilkes v Allington (1931) 2 Ch 104 206
wills 192
executors 31–32
and fully constituted trusts 23, 36
and land 31–32
and property rights **6**
rectification of 186
and residue 52
and trustees 129
wine 11–12
written declarations: and familial homes 77–78
transfers of equitable interest 38–39
for trusts 26–27, 37

For Product Safety Concerns and Information please contact our EU representative GPSR@taylorandfrancis.com Taylor & Francis Verlag GmbH, Kaufingerstraße 24, 80331 München, Germany